Arctic

Independent to North Russia

Harry C. Hutson

MILITARY MONOGRAPH 219
BENNINGTON, VERMONT
2012

First Edition published in 1997 by the Merriam Press

Sixth Edition

Copyright © 1997 by Harry C. Hutson
Book design by Ray Merriam
Additional material copyright of named contributors.

All rights reserved.
No part of this book may be used or reproduced in any manner whatsoever without written permission, except in the case of brief quotations embodied in critical articles or reviews.

WARNING
The unauthorized reproduction or distribution of this copyrighted work is illegal. Criminal copyright infringement, including infringement without monetary gain, is investigated by the FBI and is punishable by up to five years in federal prison and a fine of $250,000.

The views expressed are solely those of the author.

ISBN 978-1481006682
Merriam Press #MM219-P

This work was designed, produced, and published in
the United States of America by the

Merriam Press
133 Elm Street Suite 3R
Bennington VT 05201

E-mail: ray@merriam-press.com
Web site: merriam-press.com

The Merriam Press publishes new manuscripts on historical subjects, especially military history and with an emphasis on World War II, as well as reprinting previously published works, including reports, documents, manuals, articles and other materials on historical topics.

ALSO BY HARRY C. HUTSON
Grimsby's Fighting Fleet: Trawlers and U-boats During World War Two

Contents

Dedication 5
Acknowledgments 7
Glossary 11
Introduction 13

Chapter 1: The Ships, the Men and Their Adversaries 19
Chapter 2: The First and the Last of the Few 35
Chapter 3: The Loss of SS William Clark 87
Chapter 4: Ordeal and Rescue 105
Chapter 5: U-703 Returns to Hope Island 119
Chapter 6: Operation Gearbox 123
Chapter 7: Operation Gearbox to the Rescue 147
Chapter 8: The Five That Got Through 163
Chapter 9: They Lived to Fight Another Day 205
Chapter 10: Operation FB in Retrospect 217

Appendix 1: Allied Merchant Navy, Armed Guard
    and DEMS Casualty, Survivor and Crew Lists 223
Appendix 2: Ship Details 247
Appendix 3: Letters of Next to Kin 253
Appendix 4: U-Boat Log Book Entries and Insignia 261
Appendix 5: Official Signals and Documents for Operation FB 271
Appendix 6: German Aircraft Involved 283
Appendix 7: Allied Crew Documents and News Accounts 285
Appendix 8: List of Merchant Ships That Sailed to North Russia
    Between August 1941 and the End of the War in Europe 299

Appendix 9: Russian Convoy Details 313

Appendix 10: Allied Escorts/Covering Forces on the
  North Russian Run, 1941-45 325

Appendix 11: Chronology of Events Operation FB 337

Appendix 12: Soldier — Sailor — Survivor: Doug Meadows 347

Addendum: Jack Albert Billmeir 353

Dedication

I would like to dedicate this work to my dear long suffering wife Jean, who complainingly (correct) puts up with me spending long hours alone in my study, writing to and telephoning charming ladies, dashing off here, there and everywhere to research, but without whose love, help and devotion over many years, I would have foundered long ago.

Harry C. Hutson
Grimsby, 1997

Acknowledgments

I would like to thank the following for their generous help, without which this book could never have been written. The list is deliberately random.

The World Ship Society; Ian A. Millar, Trident Archives, U.S.A.; Robert W. Wishart; Horst Bredow; The Office of Records of Shipping and Seamen; Mrs. C. H. A. Johnson; Naval Historical Branch; Georg Hogel; The Rhodes family; Mrs. Mitchell; The Russian Central Naval Museum; St. James Parish Church, Grimsby; Mrs. W. Evans; *The Stornoway Gazette*; Mr. Colin Langley; *Hull Daily Mail*; Mrs. Edel Rising; *The Manchester Guardian*; Franz Selinger; Paul Preuss; Lt.Cdr. A. Hague, RNR; Donald J. Macleod; John Macdonald; Mrs. Marjory Williams; The Commonwealth War Graves Commission; Mr. Peter Anderson; The Jennings family; *Grimsby Evening Telegraph*; Mr. Arthur Hopkins; Mr. John Maclean; BBC Radio Humberside; Mrs. D. Y. Sharp; Mr. Fred Hortop; *The Shetland Times*; Mrs. E. Shadlock; Mr. Ralph Urwin; Mrs. Cilla Robinson; Gordon W. Long; Mr. Ernest Ballard; United States National Archives; Grimsby Central Library, Reference Section; United States Coast Guard Marine Inspection Office; San Francisco Maritime National Historical Park; Tom Worrell; Norman Pickles; Gus Britton; Richard S. Watts; Donald Smith; L. A. Sawyer; Joseph J. Sheehan, U.S. National Archives Mid-Atlantic Region; Cdr. J. R. H. Bull, RN (Rtd.); Robert G. Herbert Jr.; Mike Gillen; Kalevi A. Olkio; John Bunker; Cdr. R. Raikes, RN (Rtd.); Captain W. S. Lewis; William Grady; Russell U. Archutt Jr.; Dennis Roberts; Peter Clothier; Bernard F. Cavalcante, Operational Archive Branch, Department of the United States Navy; Mr. Herbert Rushby; Mrs. Frank Carlisle; Hilary C. Makowski; Mr. Nat Woods; Joseph E. Hecht; Charles A. Lloyd; Charles B. Cox; Vincent Cartabona, Esq.; Clifford O. Peterson; Selvin M. Lien; Anthony Spinazzola; Frank Priore; William D. Sweet; Dr. Arthur Banks; Raymond W. Williams; Harrison O. Travis; Len Phillips; Rudolph J. Langston; John R. Thompson; Wallace William Hand; Edward R. Rumpf; Fl.Lt. S. P. Rennison, BA, RAF 120 Squadron; W. Canner, DEMS, SS *Empire Gal-*

liard; Steve Attwater; R. E. Stoackley; D. L. Woolliams, O.S., SS *Empire Galliard*; Terry Carraghan, Cabin Boy, SS *Empire Galliard*; Ted Coulman; Adam Liddle; Les Wightman; Ian R. Fraser; Graham Watson, Museums Officer, Ross and Cromarty; F. Tarry, 3rd Engineer, SS *Daldorch*; Cdr. Sir Alexander Glen, KBE, DSC; Per Kyrre Rheymert; Kiell Y. Riise; Lt. Morten Andersen, Royal Norwegian Air Force; Captain Hilmar Snorrason; Jon Hialtason; Albert Wray, RN, DEMS Gunner, SS *Daldorch;* Peter Steer; Pat Cannings; Susan Barr, Norsk Polar Institut; Mr. and Mrs. Bill Scott; Allan Burke; R. A. Robinson, HMT *Northern Spray;* Victor G. Sievey; G. Wasp, HMT *Cape Palliser;* Mark Westcott; Harry Pallett; J. J. Watterson, HMT *Cape Mariato;* William G. Harsley, HMT *Northern Pride*; Fred Jollings, SS *Briarwood*; Russian Maritime Museum, St. Petersburg.

The author has made every effort to trace copyright holders for the few pieces not credited but this has proved impossible, mainly due to the time span. Opinions expressed are those of the author, except where stated otherwise. All photographs and drawings were supplied by the author; where known, the source has been given for each. The maps were prepared by Ray Merriam mostly from maps and sketches provided by the author.

Publisher's Update

Harry Hutson passed away in 2002. The year after Harry's death a new edition was produced primarily to enlarge the text and make other format changes to make the book easier to produce. At that time I was doing the printing and binding myself. This also made the page count higher than the original edition.

In late 2005 I started having all of my books produced by an outside source, still using print on demand methods. These new editions use standard industry trade paperback and hardcover (with dust jacket) bindings. This new 2006 edition was completed in October 2006 and made mostly very minor format changes to conform to the new printing/binding methods and to improve the illustrations where possible.

One notable correction to this 2006 edition is in Appendix 7, Allied Crew Documents and News Accounts. The first item had originally been attributed by the author to Ned Hecht. In March 2005 I received a letter from Clifford O. Peterson that the material attributed to Mr. Hecht was actually from his diary and included copies of his diary as proof. That correction was made to that edition and my apologies to

Mr. Peterson for the error. Knowing the diligence with which Harry researched and prepared the material for this book, I'm sure he would have been quite dismayed to learn he had not given proper identification to the source of the material he had used.

With the one exception noted in the previous paragraph, and except for typographical errors that have been weeded out with each new edition, all editions retain the same text and illustrative content.

Ray Merriam
October 2006

Glossary

A	Area time (used in W/T signals)
AA	Anti-aircraft
AAAA	I am being attacked by aircraft (W/T signal)
AS	Able Seaman
Bdr.	Bombardier (Corporal of artillery)
bo's'n	Boatswain ('Foreman' seaman)
CBE	Commander of the British Empire (decoration)
C.O.	Commanding Officer
DEMS	Defensively Equipped Merchant Ship
D/F	Direction Finder (radio apparatus)
DSM	Distinguished Service Medal (decoration)
fo'c'sle	forecastle (part of crew accommodation)
GCT	Greenwich Civil Time
GMT	Greenwich Mean Time
Gnr	Gunner (private of artillery)
GRT	Gross Registered Tons (of a merchant ship)
H/F	High Frequency (in radio terms)
HMT	His Majesty's Trawler
KL	Kapitänleutnant (Kriegsmarine)
L/Bdr	Lance Bombardier (of the artillery)
Lt.	Lieutenant
mm	millimeter(s), 1,000th part of a meter
MN	Merchant Navy
MOWT	Ministry of War Transport
NCO	Non-Commissioned Officer
OBE	Order of the British Empire (decoration)
OL	Oberleutnant (Kriegsmarine)
PAC	Parachute and Cable (AA device)
P.Off.	Pilot Officer (Royal Air Force)
POW	Prisoner of War
RAF	Royal Air Force
RCAF	Royal Canadian Air Force
RMA	Royal Maritime Artillery (Regiment)
RN	Royal Navy

RNR	Royal Naval Reserve
RRRR	I am being attacked by surface raider (W/T signal)
R/T	Radio Telephone
SBNO	Senior British Naval Officer
SNO	Senior Naval Officer
Spiv	Slang for a mild form of racketeer
SS	Steamship
SSSS	I am being attacked by submarine (W/T signal)
Sub.Lt	Sub-Lieutenant (RN)
S1c	Seaman first class (USN)
S2c	Seaman second class (USN)
USAG	United States Armed Guard
USN	United States Navy
USNR	United States Naval Reserve
USSR	Union of Soviet Socialist Republics
VG	Very Good (Seaman's discharge rating)
W/T	Wireless Telegraphy
W.Off	Warrant Officer
Z	Zone (Time)

Introduction

AFTER the disastrous losses to convoy PQ-17 and the not so disastrous but nevertheless terrible losses of PQ-18, convoys to Russia were suspended temporarily. There was of course the excuse of the North Africa landings requirements necessitating the withdrawal of heavy naval units from the northern theater to be used in support of this invasion. There is no doubt that there was a requirement, but I feel sure it was a convenient face-saver. The battle for Stalingrad was underway and the situation for the Russian armies was desperate. Perhaps this had been considered and played some part in the decision to go ahead with Operation FB.

Most of the supplies taken to Russia during the war years by Allied merchantmen were put to good use by the hard-pressed Russians but their disappointment in the quality of some of our tank designs was painfully obvious. Many British and American tanks were no match for the German Tiger and Panther, indeed they were not even as good as some of the Russian designs. For this reason alone many hundreds went unused, kept in reserve for a last-ditch stand which never came. The Matilda in particular, however, was well liked by the Russians and is often quoted as having played a leading role in saving Moscow.

There were only four possible sea routes available to the western Allies for supplying the needs of war to Russia. When the Germans reneged on their treaty with the USSR in June 1941 the might of the United States was still officially neutral. The early efforts to take supplies to the hard-pressed Russians fell upon the equally hard-pressed British.

One of the four routes would have been to use the eastern Pacific ports such as Vladivostok, Sovietskaya, Savan or Nicolaevak. Perhaps even the naval port of Petropovlovsk The Japanese were not yet at war with the United Kingdom or Russia. The passage would have involved traversing the Atlantic, through the Caribbean to the Panama Canal, and across the Pacific, followed by a long overland haul to the fighting front. Imagine how many ships would be tied up to maintain a steady supply from the United Kingdom to Russia. It was already proving very difficult to find enough shipping to supply our own needs at this stage of the war. Hitler's U-boats were still sinking ships more than twice as fast as we could build them. The Mediterranean route through the Dardanelles was totally unusable, and has therefore not even been considered a possibility. The Baltic route to Russia was totally out of the question though part of this route was later used for a time and for a different purpose, by five converted fast motor gunboats, manned by British merchant navy crews to make overnight runs from Hull to Lysekil in southern Sweden for ball bearings desperately needed by British aircraft factories.

The second possible route, which was used to a considerable degree, was via the Cape of Good Hope and through the Indian Ocean to Abadan in the Persian Gulf, where the cargoes would then be transferred for the long railway journey across Iran to Russia. Once again this involved committing a large amount of shipping for the long haul around South Africa. In late 1942 some sixty United States ships were tied up on this route alone. In an effort to increase supplies to the Soviet Union in 1942 the United States were considering using the route from the west coast of the U.S. through the Bering Straits to Murmansk/Archangel. This route was already being used by the Russians in the open season and later the U.S. Government turned over a regular supply of merchant ships to the Russians for use on the same route. All the ships were Russian manned.

By far the most practical route, in terms of distance, numbers of ships required to maintain a steady supply and escorts to give protection, was from Iceland or Great Britain, by way of the inhospitable Arctic to either Murmansk or Archangel. On the negative side though, this route was the most dangerous because in addition to the weather and other natural hazards, almost all the route was within range of the Luftwaffe, U-boats, and German surface naval forces stationed in Norway. Most of the possible routes involved a long rail journey from the port to the fighting front.

The Arctic winter cannot be dismissed in a single sentence, nor can it be fully described in a volume. It really has to be experienced to be appreciated, though appreciated is not really the correct word. In this context it falsely implies a pleasurable experience. The howling winds, frequent blizzards, mountainous seas and almost total darkness are slightly offset by the magnificence of the Aurora Borealis and a gala of stars seldom seen in the more polluted temperate latitudes. Fine weather and calm seas are not always a comfort either, often they herald fog or black frost as an alternative to storms. These changes are frequent and usually with little or no warning.

This relatively short sea route was the one chosen to sail forty convoys totaling over 850 merchant ships to North Russia between August 1941 and the end of the war in Europe. Thirty-five convoys were sailed in the opposite direction, over 750 merchantmen. A total of ninety ships were lost, a figure which includes five sunk while in harbor in Russia. It can be seen from the list of merchant ships at the end of this book, that many did not even complete the outward leg to North Russia, while others made the successful nightmare round trip up to as many as five times.

An appraisal of North Russian ports and their cargo handling capabilities was carried out by the Americans, with the following results. Archangel, Russia's oldest port dating from 1594, could only accept ships with a maximum draft of 22 feet because of the sandbar. Several ships grounded on this obstruction due to excessive draft. It was difficult to compromise fully between loading a ship in say New York, to its maximum capacity for a particular draft requirement and to allow for the difference in the density of sea water on arrival at say Archangel.

There were seven berths available, five with 21.6 feet draft and two with 17.6 feet draft. All seven ships could be accommodated at the same time alongside the wharves. Dockside facilities consisted of one 20 ton gantry crane, two 7½ ton railway cranes, one old but usable 25 ton floating crane and one 150 ton naval crane. Warehousing amounted to some 10,000 square yards. Murmansk could handle about 100,000 tons of imports a month, had berths for five general cargo vessels of 22 feet draft and two of 19 feet. There was room for one tanker to discharge into ten tank cars simultaneously, about 300 tons daily. There was warehousing for some 20,000 tons of dry goods. The railway was capable of carrying 2,400 tons of goods away each day. Of the three smaller ports, Bakaritza and Ekonomia each had eight berths and Molotovsk could handle up to fifteen ships a month at her five berths. In order to maintain the American contingent of fifty ships a month clearing U.S. ports for North Russia in 1942, some 260 of their merchantmen were tied up in this trade. Comparable British figures are not available but would be somewhat less than the American commitment.

Great Britain was quick to react to the needs of her Russian ally after Hitler's invasion. It was considered absolutely vital that Russia should not be allowed to crumble under the blitzkrieg. The first convoy was code-named DERVISH and consisted of seven merchant ships, six British and one Russian. They left Reykjavik on 21 August 1941 carrying arms, ammunition and twenty-four crated Hurricane fighters. The old aircraft carrier, HMS *Argus* carried a further twenty aircraft to be flown off. A heavy covering force consisting of H.M. Ships *Victorious*, *Furious*, *Devonshire* and *Suffolk* together with the destroyers *Inglefield*, *Icarus*, *Achates* and *Anthony* protected them. The convoy arrived safely without any interference from the enemy on the 31st.

Six more convoys, numbered PQ-1 through to PQ-6 sailed at fairly regular intervals and all forty-five merchantmen arrived in North Russian ports loaded to the limit with supplies for the Soviet Union. The smallest of all the Russian convoys, PQ-7, consisting of only two merchant ships, was the first to sustain a casualty, but now the Germans were alerted to the situation.

Succeeding convoys continued to reach Russia without loss, only one merchantman being damaged until unlucky PQ-13 set sail. By now the Americans were in the war, too, and ships of the United States Merchant Marine began to swell the ranks of the convoys. PQ-13 lost five merchantmen on passage and others were sunk by air attacks after arriving in Russia. From this point on and until convoys to north Russia were suspended temporarily, every convoy that sailed was attacked and suffered losses. The returning convoys numbered up to QP-9 had also escaped with light casualties, only one ship being lost. QP-10, however, was not so lucky and it lost four merchantmen.

Between October 1942 and January 1943 twenty-nine ships were sailed independently from Russia to Iceland and only one of these was lost. Another report states that a further nineteen ships sailed independently and without loss to Northern Russia during November and December 1942. We do know for certain that thirteen fully laden merchantmen were assembled and sailed for North Russia in roughly the same period—this is the story of those thirteen independents. Independent sailings to North Russia had been carried out previously, for instance on 11 and 12 August 1942, two Russian ships, SS *Friedrich Engels* (11th) and *Belomorcanal* (12th), were sailed and both reached their homeland safely after a long passage. Whether these two sailings were a prelude for Operation FB or merely opportunity sailings is not known. These sailings were of course in the period between PQ-17 and PQ-18.

Convoys to and from Russia were resumed in December 1942 and the first seven outward bound, now numbered from JW-51, suffered no losses at all. The returning convoys, now numbered from RA-51 were not quite so lucky but in all the remaining Arctic convoys until the end of the war in Europe, losses never approached the dreadful summer of 1942.

The Arctic weather is very unpredictable, except for almost continuous daylight in the summer and the reverse in winter. The lack of any definite distinction between day and night for most of the year makes time, in the accepted sense, seem of very little real value to those unaccustomed to the phenomena. It is indeed very strange to sit down to lunch at about noon when outside it is totally dark or conversely to change watches at midnight in bright sunshine. On top of this the weather changes very quickly indeed and with very little warning. Grimsby deep sea fishermen, who were very familiar with these waters in peacetime, be it summer or winter, would if consulted most likely answer, "It's raining now but just hang on five minutes, it will then probably snow or the wind will increase to half a gale, but if you are really lucky it could do both." Navigation in those latitudes has always been hazardous. Magnetic compasses are prone to disturbance due to heavy lodestone deposits which occur naturally in those regions. It is often very difficult to get an accurate sight for days (or nights) on end, leaving ships masters with only 'dead reckoning.' Even in peacetime before the war there were very few radio beacons to assist the navigator and in wartime they were mostly silent. After leaving Iceland there were no more friendly ports around until the destination was reached. Protective air cover from land-based aircraft was limited, while carrier aircraft often had to fly in atrocious conditions. Although Admiral Arseni Golovko stresses that air cover for the Russian convoys was supplied during the final stages of passage, little mention appears in British and American records.

Throughout the period of these convoys to Russia, Joseph Stalin gave not one word of praise or thanks to his Allies for their efforts on his behalf. Only in the very recent past has the devotion to duty shown by the men of the convoys, been recognized by the Russian administration. They have taken great pains to seek out and award a medal to as many men as possible who made that nightmare journey all those years ago. The Soviet Ambassador in London in 1945, N. Ivan Maisky did pay a short sixty-one word tribute after the war, to all men who had taken part in these convoys.

Great Britain, however, was quick to sing the praises of her merchant seamen and, quite correctly, to award them medals, after the onset of war, despite the unfulfilled promises of World War I. Before that conflict the British merchant seaman was exploited beyond belief, but in spite of this treatment he served his country well throughout those years. Promises of improvements in his treatment and working conditions 'when the war is won,' flowed freely from the lips of the politicians and owners. In 1919, however, after the end of the 'War to end all wars,' few of these promises materialized. Much of the merchant fleet was laid up and many thousands of men lost their jobs. History repeated itself before, during and after World War II and now our once very proud merchant navy has been run down to a few hundred ships and a few thousand men, and is still in decline.

Chapter 1

The Ships, the Men and Their Adversaries

ALL thirteen merchantmen involved in this drama were dry cargo vessels. All the American ships were wartime built standard Liberty ships of just over 7,000 gross tons. All were built in 1942 and four of the five were on their maiden voyage. The Russian ship was British built and originally British owned; she was the oldest ship taking part. She had been built in 1903 and was the only twin screw ship of the thirteen. She, too, was of just over 7,000 gross tons. The seven British ships were a mixed bunch, four were wartime built standards, all prefixed *Empire*, two being 7,000 tonners and two slightly smaller at 6,000 tons. The remaining three were all pre-war vessels, two of 5,000 tons and one of only 4,000, all built in the 1930s.

The tonnage of a merchant ship can be confusing to the uninitiated, 7,000 gross register tons is in no way related to the deadweight of the ship or to the displacement. It is a figure based on the total enclosed spaces including accommodation and machinery spaces whereas the net tonnage roughly speaking, is the carrying capacity given that one hundred cubic feet of cargo space equals one ton of cargo.

The American ships were probably capable of about 11 knots at best, the British ships a little less at 10 knots, but many other factors determine the practical top speed in a given situation. All would be fully loaded and carrying deck cargo, too. The general tramp steamer would usually have four or five cargo holds, two or three forward and two aft with the machinery space in between. Some would have 'tween decks, an extra space between the hold proper and the main deck. The purpose of this was two-fold. It allowed extra space for 'light' cargoes such as baled cotton, thus allowing the vessel to carry approximately the same tonnage of cargo, be it cotton or heavy mineral ore. A further use was to allow for the stowage of cargo to be unloaded at an early port of call without having to unload half the hold to reach it. All our ships were steamers, the American ships were oil fired water-tube boilers while the British were coal fired smoke tube Scotch boilers.

The American ships were all brand new and although they were mass-produced the accommodation was very good, everyone was housed amidships, there were 'kick-in' panels between cabins and alleyways to facilitate easy escape should doors jam after an attack. All the cabins had running water, each ship had domestic refrigerators. The use of wood was reduced to lessen the fire risk but it was still used for furniture. There were economies in the fittings though. They did not have direction finders and although they had a gyro room there was no gyro compass fitted! They had steel lifeboats but initially no lifeboat radio, though this was fitted later.

The accommodation in the British wartime built ships was not to the same standard, though it was better than the average pre-war tramp. The *Daldorch* for instance was typical. She had a foc'sle to accommodate her seamen and firemen, ABs on the port side, firemen on the starboard. Each side had a small washroom/w.c., both totally inadequate. There was also a small messroom in this accommodation, which was right forward in the 'sharp end'! There was hardly enough room to swing a cat for the sixteen men living there in two-tier bunks. The deck of this accommodation was carpeted throughout—with coconut matting! A mattress of straw, two blankets and one pillow were supplied.

Officers and petty officers were housed amidships in two separate sections divided from each other by number 3 hatch and two bunker hatches. The forward section was part of the bridge superstructure and housed the master on the lower bridge deck and below that was the deck officer's saloon, engineer's saloon, deck officer's cabins and the chief steward's cabin. Beyond number three hatch were the cadets, bosun, carpenter, cooks and engineers cabins. These cabins were supplied with two pillows, two sheets, three blankets, two pillow slips and half was changed on a weekly basis. The ship had also been fitted with a gyro compass immediately before her first trip to North Russia, together with echo sounder and direction finder. The ship had also been insulated in her accommodation. Warm clothing had been provided, too. Gunners were probably housed in the same way as they were in other British tramps, accommodation being built for them in the 'tween decks. *Chulmleigh* on the other hand had very well appointed accommodation.

The Russian ship carried the largest number of crew, over eighty persons, while the British *Briarwood* had only fifty-eight. Some eight hundred Allied seamen (including gunners) sailed on this operation and of that number about two hundred and eighty men lost their lives.

Prior to the outbreak of war many merchant ships were idle 'laid up' because their owners could not find cargoes for them to carry. The merchant seaman had once again been forgotten by the government, ship owners and public alike, despite his achievements in the Great War. It is probably very difficult for the general reader to appreciate the conditions under which the pre-war British merchant seaman lived and worked, twenty-four hours a day, seven days a week, on and off duty. The miner could do his eight-hour shift in dark, damp and dangerous conditions, but at the end of his shift he could return to the relative comfort and safety of his own home for the next sixteen hours of each working day.

Five of the seven British ships were relatively new, two were about twelve years old but facilities for the crews were still generally poor. Food varied considerably from company to company and a few of the pre-war tramp fleets were dubbed with appropriate titles. Generally speaking the better the class of ship and the more modern she was, the better the food and accommodation, though this was not a hard and fast rule. The Board of Trade laid out minimum rations for each man per day but for the unscrupulous ship owner so inclined, the regulations could be bent in his favor and there was very little the crew could do about it. There were scores of anecdotes in circulation about the food and the cooks on pre-war British ships. Two examples are: Master to crew, "Who called the cook a ——?" Crew to master, "Who called the —— a cook?" or "God sent the grub, the Devil sent the cook."

Improving conditions for the merchant seaman constituted a net loss to many tramp ship owners, in no way did it improve profits and was therefore of little importance. Imagine coming off watch and having to bathe in a bucket of water, usually heated by a small exhaust steam jet, after having spent the last four hours shoveling coal into furnaces, cleaning fires and disposing of ashes in stokehold temperatures of up to 100 degrees, or after trimming coal in the ship's bunkers and being covered in coal dust and good honest sweat. Firemen and trimmers in the old coal burners had to do this at least twice a day. Washing of working gear was done in the same way. One consolation on this point was that drying the laundry was not usually a problem for the black squad.

Our average British tramp steamer of pre-war years would have a crew of between thirty-five and forty men comprising: Master, 1st, 2nd and 3rd Mates, radio officer, two cadets or apprentices, carpenter, bosun, five or six deckhands, some of whom would be ordinary seamen with less than three years experience at sea, one or two deck boys, and perhaps a lamp trimmer. The latter being a left over from the days when ships used oil or acetylene gas lamps, before the arrival of electricity. There were still quite a few ships flying the Red Duster during

World War II without a dynamo and therefore without many of the benefits that relied on this basic facility. They were mainly coasters, saved from the scrap heap on the outbreak of war. The lamp-trimmer usually assisted the bosun and gradually this position disappeared from ships articles.

The black gang would be made up roughly as follows: chief, second, third, fourth, and sometimes fifth engineers, one or two donkeymen, and six to eight firemen/trimmers. The catering section of the crew would consist of two cooks, two stewards, a galley boy and a cabin boy.

The British merchant seaman had a normal working week of sixty-four hours before overtime was paid. This was seventeen hours more than his shore counterpart. In 1943 the working week before overtime was paid was reduced to fifty-six hours, still some nine hours more than the shore worker.

The pay of British merchant seamen before the outbreak of the war in 1939 was, £3.12s.6d. a month for a deck boy, £4.16s.3d. for an ordinary seaman and the princely sum of £9.12s.6d. for a fully qualified able seaman. The monthly pay of crews increased progressively as the conflict continued. To quote the pay of a fully qualified able seaman then it increased as follows; 15th September 1939 £12.12s.6d., which included a £3.0s.0d. war risk payment; 1st March 1940, £15.12s.6d.; 1st January 1941, £17.12s.6d.; 1st May 1942, £22.12s.6d.; and by 1st February 1943, £24.0s. 0d. A first mate who held a foreign going masters certificate would earn about £23.0s.0d. per month. Typical figures for 1942 were: 1st mate, £27.0s.0d.; 3rd mate, £19.0s.0d.; carpenter, £13.15s.0d.; bosun, £12.10s.0d.; able seaman, £10.12s.6d.; cadet, £2.10s.0d.; chief engineer, £36.0s.0d.; fourth engineer £18.0s.0d.; fireman/trimmer, £11.2s.6d., and cabin boy, £4.10s.0d.

The pay of a master is not quite so easily defined. There are no entries on the ships crew list to give any clues, however, there are several other published examples. For instance, one very experienced master received a letter from the directors of the company he had served well for many years before and during the war. "We are pleased to inform you that in view of your excellent record for this company we are increasing your basic monthly salary from £42 to £47 with immediate effect," so one can see how over generous ship owners were to their loyal servants who held responsibility for ship, cargo and crew, twenty-four hours a day for months on end. Each man eventually received a flat rate of £10.0s.0d. per month war risk money. Food and accommodation was supplied by the ship owner.

For this particular voyage all merchant navy crew members were interviewed while the ships were at Hvalfjord. They were told basic details of the impending voyage and given the option of signing off. If they signed off then they would be kept in 'quarantine' until the completion of the operation. If they decided to make the voyage then they would receive a £50.0.0 bonus (£100 officers) on sailing and in addition their specified next of kin would also receive payment of £50.0s.0d. the day after the ship had sailed. Survivors memories after more than forty years are somewhat clouded but all agree that inducement payments were made. Mr. Richard Watts, then a cadet on board SS *Daldorch* well remembers receiving his £50 bonus from a Mr. Bilmere, a shipping agent, while the vessel was still in Hvalfjord.

By comparison the American merchant seaman at this time received the following payments: U.S. $105.00 per month basic pay for a fully qualified able seaman; $105.00 per month war bonus; $125.00 single payment for ships coming to the United Kingdom; $60.00 single payment for ships coming to Iceland; $125.00 single payment for ships coming to Russia, plus $100.00 from the Russian authorities. The Americans were reluctant for their merchant seaman to accept this money from the Russians and openly discouraged the practice, without a great deal of success. The exchange rate at this time was approximately $4.20 to the pound sterling. The comparative basic rates for other crews of American merchant ships at this time was: first mate, $237.50; radio officer, $172.50; third mate, $167.50; carpenter, $120.00; bosun, $112.50; deck cadet, $92.50; chief engineer, $375.00, and steward, $146.00.

The United States Armed Guard crew received approximately $21.00 per month, plus 20% for sea duty. This was much better than his British counterpart but, as can be seen, much less than his mercantile shipmate. From the available reports it seems there was a great deal more animosity between the merchant crew and gunners on the American ships than on the British ships. Perhaps this was partly due to the differing messing and/or chain of command.

Wartime changes to the merchant ship were generally geared towards defense rather than offense. Anti-submarine guns, varying in size from 12 pounder to 4.7 inch were fitted on the poop, machine guns and later 20 and 40-mm anti-aircraft guns were also fitted. Nearly all merchantmen were fitted with degaussing gear against magnetic mines. A few carried depth charges, too. There were other less effective weapons in her total armament. Extra lifesaving equipment was carried and gradually every ship received at least one lifeboat emergency transmitter and receiver. Protective slabs were fitted to bridge structures and essential blackout facilities were fitted. Perhaps the biggest change was in manning levels, the greatest numbers being in the ranks of Army or Navy gunners allocated to each ship. These men signed articles as 'deckhands' and were provided with a civilian suit on joining their first ship. They received only their service pay and allowances and a nominal one shilling a month for signing Merchant Ship Articles which brought them under the jurisdiction of the ship's master as well as Kings Regulations.

Most British ships now carried three radio officers in order to keep a twenty-four hour listening watch. A crash program of training was introduced to turn out junior radio officers with restricted certificates, in order to try and fill all these new found vacancies. Many of these recruits were youngsters of 15 to 19 years. They were required to serve in a junior capacity until they had sufficient sea experience before being allowed to sit for the higher examinations. It must be remembered that the merchant navy man was still a civilian and that a large number were well over military age while many others were well under military age. There were no conscripts in the merchant navy.

Regulations for promotion were certainly relaxed during the war years; that is evident from the age of some masters (before the war many young masters had to serve as first or sometimes even second mate for several years before being offered a command), but throughout the war years there was still a hard core of very experienced seamen among the crews. The British mercantile marine during the war years had its problems with deserters and troublemakers, just as it had in peacetime, but by far the majority of men served their country exceedingly well throughout that conflict as we shall see in the following chapters. All American merchant ships carried a large number of 'Armed Guards' to man the guns and our five were no exception. British cargo ships however did not normally carry as many gunners as they had on this voyage.

The role of the British DEMS gunners and the United States Armed Guard was the same—to defend the ship against attack, but the conditions of just how they achieved this were totally different. On British merchant ships (except the big liners) the senior DEMS rating would almost invariably be an NCO and he and his men would at all times be under the direct orders of the ship's master. His American counterpart, however, was almost always a junior officer and the Armed Guard were under his orders at all times, not the masters. The USAG totaled some 145,000 men at its peak and included signalmen, radio operators and medics among its numbers. One thousand nine hundred and ten lost their lives during World War II and only fourteen of twenty-seven men taken POW survived. The force was made up of mainly USN and USNR personnel but other services were included in their numbers. They did not sign ships articles at all.

The British DEMS gunners were a mixture of RN, RMA and Marines and all were signed on as 'deckhands.' They could often supplement their service pay by doing extra work on board ship, at the discretion of the master or perhaps by standing as anti-sabotage guards while the ship was in port. British DEMS totaled at its peak some 36,000 men, almost exactly two-thirds to one-third by numbers Royal Navy/Royal Maritime Artillery. Two thousand seven hundred and thirteen RN and 1,222 RMA men paid with their lives. The merchant navy crew had all been on short gunnery courses, the majority on only a two- or three-day course which covered the light machine guns. It was usual, however, for the second mate and other deck officers to have completed a course on the 4 inch anti-submarine gun and 12 pounder. When at action stations the merchant navy crew not on watch or other essential tasks would act as ammunition bearers, belt feeders, etc.

Each ship had been modified to cater for the atrocious Arctic weather conditions, exposed water tanks and pipes had been lagged, extra heaters fitted and additional anti-aircraft guns had been fitted, too, as the threat from aircraft was considered a greater risk than that from U-boats or surface craft in this instance. At least three of the British ships were no strangers to North Russia—they had already made this dangerous voyage in convoy on at least one previous occasion. There had been plans to fit all the ships with high frequency transmitters and receivers but it is not known if in fact this was done. There would be no point in fitting the ships with the additional transmitter if it was not going to be used at some stage either as a routine or in case of emergency. The American ships carried only one radio officer and therefore could not keep a twenty-four hour watch on any other frequency than the international distress frequency of 500 kilocycles (now kilohertz), though it is quite possible that some of the Armed Guard on this voyage were extra radio operators. Judging by the armed guard list for SS *William Clark*, however, it would seem not.

All British merchant ships would have an auto-alarm receiver which was pre-tuned to the international distress frequency but depended for its operation on the receipt of a special signal preceding the actual distress call. Ironically, most British merchantmen carried three radio officers and kept a 24 hour manual watch, whereas most American ships were not fitted with an auto-alarm and carried only one radio officer. This signal would set alarm bells ringing, calling the off watch radio officer to duty. Very often, however, in wartime situations of distress there was insufficient time for this preliminary signal to be sent. The reader will, however, see further interesting reference to this signal in the following pages.

It may seem to the layman that the difficulties in locating a small ship sailing on a very large ocean are insurmountable, bearing in mind the limited aids available in 1942, and indeed this could be so especially in wartime when ships did not stick to normal shipping lanes and were in open ocean. However, on our Arctic route to North Russia, which was well known to the Germans, our navigators and planners did not have a great deal of choice and the enemy was fully aware of this. Given these limitations and coupled with the information received from agents in Iceland the chances of getting ships to North Russia from Iceland without being detected was indeed a problem.

In 1942 Iceland was occupied by British and American forces, but the Icelandic government still insisted on its neutrality. The Icelandic government continued to administer the needs of the population. British and Canadian forces had first occupied the island in May 1940 and at that time there were many German sympathizers. There were also over two hundred German nationals on the island, 166 of them in Reykjavik. This figure included sixty crew members of a German merchantman sunk three months earlier. Quite a number of the Germans fled to remote areas and it took some time to round them up. There are records, too, of U-boats landing agents in the country. *U-252* landed an agent on 3 April 1942 and *U-279* another in September 1943.

Many of the amateur radio transmitters were still active. Iceland's ships continued to use their radio. The powerful transmitter at the German consulate in Reykjavik had been dismantled and smuggled to a hideout in the early stages of the occupation. It was not discovered throughout the occupation. The Americans took over control in April 1942, but in reality the hand-over was quite complex.

The obvious route from the Icelandic anchorage of Hvalfjord on the southwest coast would be to sail ships up the west coast to Cape Horn (North Cape), which almost cuts the Arctic circle. From the navigator's point of view this part of the journey would be reasonably straightforward, since the vessel would seldom be out of sight of land. It was ideal from the planner's point of view, too, because there was least danger from enemy aircraft, submarines or surface craft. The leg from North Cape to Spitzbergen, however, would not be easy. In 1942 there was a large Allied minefield off North Cape and the ice barrier restricted movement even further. It was essential for the navigator to fix his position accurately before departure from the proximity of, in this case, the North Cape of Iceland, before setting out on the journey of several hundred miles across open sea. This would give his 'dead reckoning' navigation the best chance of success should he be unable to fix his position by sun or stars during the passage. No navigator would willingly attempt to make a landfall on a barren and inhospitable coastline without putting to best use all the aids available to him, from eyesight to electronics. Unfortunately some merchant fleet owners thought that equipment like echo sounders and electric logs were luxuries they could not afford. Regulations then in force did not demand these instruments and after all ship and cargo were covered by insurance!

The Germans knew that the North Cape of Iceland would be the most likely departure point for ships bound for North Russia, whether they be in convoy or sailing alone. It also made sense that the ships would pass between the desolate island of Jan Mayen, dominated by the 6,000 foot peak of Mount Beerenberg, and the northern ice barrier, rather than sail closer to the Luftwaffe bases by passing to the east of that island. The same was true of the 120 mile Spitzbergen/Bear Island gap instead of the 230 mile Bear Island/North Cape of Norway gap. While this still left a very large amount of Arctic Ocean to be kept under surveillance, it eliminated an even larger area. It is not surprising therefore that nearly all our thirteen merchantmen were detected, aircraft being the usual means in most cases.

The Germans had at their disposal for surveillance of these Arctic wastes, aircraft, U-boats and surface ships, backed up by intelligence information from agents and/or decrypted radio traffic. We know for instance that one such agent had been landed in Iceland by a U-boat during May 1942. Aircraft were the most widely used of course. They could cover large areas in a relatively short time and there was very little in the way of opposition from Allied aircraft in late 1942. The obvious areas to cover regularly and most likely to give best results for effort expended were Jan Mayen to the ice barrier and Bear Island to Spitzbergen and from a study of the positions of ships attacked or sunk from this operation, this proves to be the case.

All German U-boats southbound on their maiden operational patrol from the Fatherland had to pass between Scotland and Greenland to reach the Atlantic Ocean and then their French base. It was standard practice for some of these U-boats to be ordered north of Iceland and then to sail through the Denmark Strait between Iceland and Greenland in order to reconnoiter these areas at fairly regular intervals, to send weather and ice reports from there before proceeding south. During September 1942 for instance *U-610*, *U-620*, *U-253* and *U-255* were all in this area. *U-255* (Kapitänleutnant Reche) was attacked by Catalina 'U' of 210 Squadron RAF (F. Sgt. J. W. Semmens). The U-boat was damaged and forced to return to base. *U-253* (Oberleutnant Friedrichs) was lost with all hands at this time and it is thought that she struck a mine in the North Cape field. In the middle of October 1942 *U-212* and *U-586* were patrolling off Jan Mayen while *U-377* was patrolling off Spitzbergen after putting the 'NUSSBAUM' weather party ashore on Spitzbergen on the 13th of that month.

The four main types of German aircraft used in this theater were the Junkers Ju 88, the Heinkel He 111 and 115, and the Focke-Wulf Fw 200, though other types were used, too. Some of the aircraft were long range reconnaissance, others were torpedo bombers. All were based in northern Norway.

The U-boats were all Type VIIs and their numbers were never very large and at the time of Operation FB there were only three or four at sea in the whole Arctic. Dönitz, Hitler's Chief of U-boats was as hard pressed to cover all sea areas with his limited number of submarines as were the Allies with their escorts. It was usually a case of robbing Peter to pay Paul by both sides at this stage of the sea war. In an effort to counter the North Africa landings for instance a large number of U-boats were diverted from the Atlantic to the Gibraltar area, while the Allies had pulled escorts from the Atlantic and other areas to cover these same landings.

The conditions endured by the Arctic U-boat crews must have been extremely hard, their only comfort probably lying in the fact that at least they could escape from the weather occasionally by diving! The surface naval forces in Norway were an ever present threat and could not be ignored. They did make several forays against our shipping but their strength was in their threat, which normally kept a large part of the Home Fleet on the alert and many Allied reconnaissance aircraft tied up checking on their whereabouts. During the war we were led to believe that the Luftwaffe were not very good when operating over the sea, after all we were told, they had never been trained on maritime operations. Examination of post-war records, however, proves this to be totally untrue. Aircraft sank a large amount of Allied shipping, both mercantile and warships, they laid a great number of mines and carried out a great deal of maritime reconnaissance, weather reporting and maritime rescue missions. It was the general cooperation between the

Luftwaffe and the Kriegsmarine that left a great deal to be desired, together with the fact that there was virtually no naval air arm.

We have often been told by historians that cooperation between the Luftwaffe and Kriegsmarine was never very good throughout the war but it seems to me that in Norway it was much better than average. The greatest threat to our lone merchantmen was therefore from the air and this had been foreseen by the Allied planners and all the ships had extra anti-aircraft guns installed before departure. Some of the German aircraft were fitted with a primitive radar and once a ship or convoy was detected by any means, the aircraft would climb, report to base and send D/F signals in order that the position could be fixed from shore and attacks organized. U-boats, and indeed all submarines of World War II were really submersibles. That is to say they spent most of their time at sea on the surface. The time they could remain submerged was relatively short, measured in hours rather than days, and it depended on two main factors, battery power and air.

In the latter stages of the war U-boats were fitted with a schnorkel, a device enabling them to bring in fresh air and to exhaust fumes, thus enabling them to use their diesels when submerged. It required accurate depth keeping to avoid the automatic shut off valve closing if the head dipped under the surface of the sea for any reason. Such an event would quickly cause great distress to the crew. The U-boats mentioned in this narrative, however, were not yet fitted with this device. In fact in late 1942 there were no operational U-boats so fitted. All our U-boats were type VIIs, the standard attack type of U-boat, an efficient fighting machine but with little comfort for her crew. There were five torpedo tubes, four forward and one stern tube. A total of fourteen torpedoes could be carried. Deck armament was an 88-mm gun while anti-aircraft fits varied according to availability of various weapons. The main choice was between twin or quadruple 20-mm fittings and 37 mm.

Life on board for the crew of any U-boat must have been very hard but for those of the Arctic Flotilla then the prevailing weather could only add to their misery. Unlike their comrades in the large ocean-going U-boats making voyages to the warmer climates, there was very little chance of them exercising on deck or perhaps a swim while in a 'safe' area. Perhaps the only consolation for them was that their patrols were usually shorter in duration than those of their North Atlantic comrades. U-boat crew numbers varied considerably, but a reasonable average figure for the type VIIs mentioned would be about forty-five officers and men.

In order to detect and find their targets the U-boats had to rely on visual sightings, intelligence information and by diving and listening on their hydrophones, which under favorable conditions could pick up propeller noises from ships at twenty miles or more, and a bearing on the source of the sound could be taken, too. The Germans knew that with very few exceptions any ship sighted or detected was an enemy vessel, while the merchantmen could also be fairly sure that most aircraft sighted would be hostile. The weather was impartial, treating everyone with utter contempt whenever it chose to do so. Since German surface naval forces took no real part against the eastbound ships of Operation FB, except for an unsuccessful search, there is no real point in reviewing this formidable force.

SS *Chulmleigh*, sunk by *U-625*.

SS *Briarwood*.
[World Ship Society]

Cadets Richard Watts, left, and Donald Smith, right,
with the Carpenter of SS *Daldorch*, November 1942.
[Richard Watts]

Commissioning ceremony of *U-586*, 4 September 1941,
Blohm and Voss, Hamburg.
[Paul Preuss]

U-586 alongside the depot ship *Stella Polaris*,
Skjomenfjord, near Narvik, Norway, 1942.
[Paul Preuss]

Chapter 2

The First and the Last of the Few

THE first convoy to North Russia had sailed from Iceland in August 1941, less than three months after the Germans had invaded. It was a small convoy by North Atlantic standards, only seven ships, but all arrived safely after a ten-day voyage. The convoys continued to sail at almost regular intervals and up to the middle of March 1942 only one merchant ship had been lost. The adverse weather conditions accounted for as many ships as the enemy until the fateful PQ-17 in June and July of that year when twenty-three of its merchantmen were sunk by German forces. PQ-18 was badly mauled, too, losing thirteen merchantmen from a total of forty. Convoys were stopped for more than three months at this point but the Russians still pressed hard for sailings to resume.

The Admiralty in their wisdom decided to compromise and came up with a scheme to sail ten merchant ships independently from Iceland to North Russia, hoping that in the vast Arctic waters they would escape detection by the enemy. The plan was to sail each vessel at roughly 200-mile intervals. They would keep strict radio silence but four armed trawlers would be interlaced between the merchant ships and two submarines would be stationed along the proposed route further east to rescue survivors or render other assistance to any ship that fell foul of the enemy or weather.

There were four British anti-submarine trawlers in North Russia at this time. They had arrived with convoy PQ-18 and were enjoying the dubious delights of a North Russian autumn/winter. Only three of these ships were seaworthy. HMT *Daneman* had run out of coal, dragged her anchor in bad weather and drifted ashore. It took the Russians a week to re-float her, but she was aground for some three weeks before that eventual rescue. On examination it was found that there was damage to her hull and she had lost some blades from her propeller. She was dry-docked in Archangel for repairs. Two of the remaining trawlers, *Cape Argona* and *Cape Mariato* were detailed for duty as rescue ships for Operation FB.

HMT *St. Kenan* had been an original choice but she was experiencing extreme steaming difficulties due to her Russian bunker coal. She was withdrawn from the operation because of this difficulty.

Two Russian trawlers and two Russian submarines, *S-101* and *S-102* were also detailed. The trawlers were to be stationed in the Barents Sea while the two Russian submarines were stationed to the east of Spitzbergen. One of the Russian trawlers was sunk in an air attack, the other was damaged but reached port safely. The S (Stalinets) class of Russian submarine were considered the best of the medium-sized boats in service. Only a year after taking part in Operation FB, *S-101* sank *U-639* on one of her Arctic patrols.

Many Russian trawlers of the Arctic Fleet were lost during the war to aircraft, submarines, surface ships and the weather. The records available in Britain on the losses to this class of warship are very thin in detail and it has proved impossible to identify specifically the two Russian trawlers involved in Operation FB. This role of rescue ship could at best be only a token gesture because the chance of survival for men for any length of time under such conditions was pretty slim indeed and the risk to the crews of the trawlers was almost as great as that to the merchant crews.

Telegraphist Les Wightman of HMT *Cape Argona* recalls,

> We left Ekonomia towards the end of October 1942 and headed through the White Sea to Bucaritza, a small harbor with extremely limited facilities. We coaled ship (300 tons) by hand using wheelbarrows. It took three days. We then sailed to our allotted station and commenced W/T and Asdic watch, then moved to our next station and did the same, seven days out then seven days back. We then returned to harbor for bunkers, etc., and repeated the routine before returning, this time to Murmansk. It was during one of these two patrols that we were attacked by a lone Fw 'Condor.' The aircraft dropped about twenty bombs, in twos, but never came within range of our AA guns. On the second of these two patrols we were caught in a force 7 to 8 and we iced up and developed an alarming list. We were kept very busy chopping ice and shifting coal for about seventy-two hours to try and get the heavy list reduced. Throughout these two patrols we kept radio watch on the merchant navy distress frequency but we heard nothing.

The reader may well have noticed that the RN trawler's endurance was extremely limited. He may also wonder how in peacetime they managed to fish these Arctic waters without having similar problems. The answer lies in the conversion from fishing trawler to warship. In peacetime the main cross bunker, of about 200 tons capacity, was supplemented by carrying anything up to 140 tons of extra coal in the after/middle fishrooms. Access to this coal was via a watertight tunnel from the stokehold, through the bunker, to the after fishroom. These fishrooms had been converted to crew accommodation, etc., in the RN trawler and only the normal cross and wing bunker space was then available for carrying coal. This reduced the steaming range considerably. They tried putting more coal on deck but more often than not it was lost to the weather.

It is not clear exactly whose idea Operation FB originally was. Some sources say British but there is documentary evidence to the effect: "British have agreed with us that on the next suitable phase of the moon we have a reasonable chance of getting ten ships through... Have agreed to match the British in numbers not to exceed five..." The American authorities called for five vessels to be selected from ten already loaded with high priority supplies for Russia. The basis of their selection was to be:

A. General suitability and speed of ship,
B. Experience and character of Master,
C. Defensive armament,
D. General cooperativeness and atmosphere of merchant crew, and
E. Priority of cargo.

All the crews would be volunteers and anyone not wishing to go could sign off but would be kept in Iceland incommunicado until the operation was completed. Some ships were to be held in reserve.

It was decided to sail the ships alternately, American, British, American and the Russian was to be sailed as number three and the ships finally sailed as follows: *Richard H. Alvey* and *Empire Gilliard* on 29 October; *Dekabrist*, *John Walker* and *Empire Gilbert* on 30 October; *John H. B. Latrobe* and *Chulmleigh* on 31 October; *Hugh Williamson* and *Empire Sky* on 1 November; *William Clark* and *Empire Scott* on 2 November, and finally the last two British ships, *Daldorch* on 3 November and *Briarwood* on 4 November.

Northern Spray, *Northern Pride* and *Cape Palliser* left the Clyde at 1900 on Friday, 23 October 1942, bound for Reykjavik. They arrived at 1730 on Wednesday, 28 October and immediately took on stores and water. They then sailed for Hvalfjord to coal throughout the night, finishing at about 0600.

Northern Spray was the first of the four rescue trawlers to sail from Iceland, leaving at 0900 on 29 October. She was a large (655 GRT) German-built ship. There were, before the war, fifteen of this class, all built at Bremerhaven in 1936. They were then all London registered and initially fished from Fleetwood but in 1937 all were transferred to Grimsby. All of course were requisitioned by the Admiralty in the weeks leading up to the outbreak of war in September 1939. Two had already been lost by U-boat action when *Northern Spray* put to sea in late October 1942. *Northern Rover* was torpedoed and lost with all hands while on contraband control duties in October 1939 and *Northern Princess* suffered the same fate while on passage to the United States, to help 'Uncle Sam,' in March 1942. Both these losses remained an unsolved mystery until after the war in Europe ended and German records were examined in detail.

Northern Spray was patrolling in the area near Jan Mayen on 31 October 1942, waiting for the merchantmen to pass safely through. The trawler was under the command of Lt. F. A. J. Downer, RNR. Sub. Lt. Allan Burke was his Asdic officer and Leading Seaman Gardiner was the Asdic operator on duty. An Fw 200 Condor was sighted that day but it did not attack. It flew up from astern and down the starboard side before departing.

The first two merchantmen of our thirteen to sail, *Richard H. Alvey* and *Empire Galliard* must have been quite close to this position by this time, having left Hvalfjord two days earlier. At 1225 hours *Northern Spray* sighted a U-boat on the surface in position 7021N 1416W (west southwest of Jan Mayen). The trawler chased the U-boat, which then dived. *Northern Spray* attacked with depth charges but in the resulting explosions cracked the condenser door in the engine room (part of the steam recycling system), and was forced to abandon the chase and return to port for repairs. The U-boat escaped but at least the Allies were now aware of U-boats in the area but it seems they did not warn the merchantmen of this threat. *Northern Spray* took no further part in Operation FB. She was ordered to return to Reykjavik via Seydisfjord. She damaged her rudder in Reykjavik and spent two weeks in the floating dry dock at Hvalfjord under repairs before returning to the United Kingdom.

This U-boat was in fact *U-212* (KL Helmut Vogler) a type VIIC on her first war patrol. Examination of the log of the U-boat shows that she had sighted and identified *Northern Spray* long before she herself was detected. The submarine then prepared for a submerged torpedo attack on the armed trawler. The Asdic officer of *Northern Spray* disagrees with the log entries of *U-212*. He states categorically that there was no Liberator in the area at any time. He also states the depth charges had been set 'shallow' and must have exploded above *U-212* not below her. Only one attack was made because of the self-inflicted damage. Only two rounds from the 4-inch gun were fired. Firing ceased when it was obvious that the range was too great and since their best speed was now only 3 knots, there was no chance of catching the U-boat.

After the war *Northern Spray* was returned to fishing and, just as during the war, she was always in the action. While fishing at Spitzbergen in 1947 for instance, she rescued the entire crew of the Fleetwood trawler *Red Gauntlet* which had ironically struck a reef very close to where *Chulmleigh* had done just a few years earlier. Only three years later, in December 1950 she herself stranded twice during heavy snowstorms in Isafjord, not far from the North Cape of Iceland. Fifteen days after stranding she was safely refloated and after repairs returned once again to fishing. Thirteen years later, however, she again ran aground, not far from her previous strandings, while trying to run for shelter. Fortunately their was no loss of life in any of these strandings, but this time she could not be salvaged. It is most interesting to note that several engineers who sailed in *Northern Spray* were unanimous in saying that of all the pre-war German built '*Northerns*,' *Spray* was the one with the best turn of speed. Even after the war they claimed, she could out-run many of the new post-war trawlers from Grimsby. *St. Elstan* was the next rescue trawler to sail, followed by *Cape Palliser*.

Several Telegraphists from the British cruiser HMS *London*, then in Hvalfjord were seconded to some of the trawlers for temporary duty during Operation FB. This would allow the trawlers to keep continuous watch on the merchant distress frequency as well as the RN control frequency. Victor Sievey and G. Waspe were sent to HMT *Cape Palliser*. Bill Humphries was sent to HMT *Northern Pride*.

HMT *Northern Pride* was the fourth trawler assigned to rescue duties on this operation. On the morning of 4 November 1942 she was patrolling north of the North Cape of Iceland. She received the distress call from *William Clark* and proceeded at once to the position given in the message. Although she searched the area throughout the remainder of that day and night as well as part of the following day, she found no sign of any survivors from the American merchantman. The trawler then turned north to search along the route the freighter should have followed. All her lookouts were keeping an extra careful watch.

In the forenoon of 6 November one of her lookouts observed an unidentified object ahead and the 4-inch gun was ordered into action. After a few rounds brought no reaction whatever from the object *Northern Pride* steamed cautiously towards it. All her guns were manned and trained on the target, fingers on the triggers. The object was soon identified as a seaplane float. It was examined and found to be of German manufacture. It appeared not to have been in the water very long. Could this have been from one of the aircraft damaged by *John H. B. Latrobe* the previous day? Nothing further was seen and *Northern Pride* resumed her patrol.

During the passage of PQ-18 plans were already in hand for loading and assembling the next two Russian convoys, PQ-19 and PQ-20. By the time the decision was taken to halt these sailings, some forty ships were already allocated and in various stages of loading and readiness. One such vessel, the m.v. *Taron*, a 9,500 ton tanker fully loaded with aviation fuel was one of several ships anchored in Loch Ewe for some three weeks until on 16 October 1942 she was ordered back to Stanlow to discharge. Even as early as August it was looking doubtful if PQ-20 would ever sail. American ports were becoming congested with shipments from the manufacturers building up there. Further shipments were diverted to inland storage bases until the situation clarified. Archangel had been heavily bombed on 24 August, adding further to the problems. It was, however, not until 7 October that a memorandum dictated that there would be no further convoys to North Russia until January 1943, "due to shortage of escorts and covering forces."

The British authorities had declared that they would supply all ten ships for Operation FB, but President Roosevelt insisted that American ships would partake on a one-to-one basis. The thirteen merchant ships selected for this dangerous journey had begun their voyage from many different ports in the United States and the United Kingdom and had all made for Hvalfjord, near Reykjavik to await orders. For instance the American Liberty ship *William Clark* had sailed from New York on 24 August 1942, called at Boston, Massachusetts, where she joined convoy BX-35 for Halifax, Nova Scotia. She sailed from the Canadian port in Convoy SC-99 and arrived in Hvalfjord on 19 September 1942 dropping her anchor to await further orders, as did *John H. B. Latrobe*, while *John Walker* came to the United Kingdom from the U.S. and was at anchor in Loch Ewe for over three weeks before sailing to Iceland.

Empire Gilbert had sailed from the Tyne to Loch Ewe while *Empire Sky* had sailed from Hull to Loch Ewe. From this Scottish sea loch the British ships had sailed in convoy to Iceland. There is little doubt that at this point in time the crews had made qualified guesses about their final destination port but they would have assumed they would be sailing in another convoy, not attempting the hazardous passage on their own. The operation was planned to commence at the end of October when the Arctic nights would be increasing and the daylight hours diminishing rapidly, and there would be no moon. The weather, seldom very good, would also begin to test its strength for the onset of winter and this would hopefully restrict Hermann Göring's Luftwaffe and Karl Dönitz's U-boats, too. The pre-sailing conference for the thirteen ship's masters was held at Falcon Point, Iceland, base on 27 and 28 October.

From the sketchy reports available it would at first glance appear that only some of the ships were routed by the more sensible north about route, around the North Cape of Iceland, while others went south about and up the east coast of that inhospitable volcanic island. The reason for this statement is that the 6,640 ton SS *Empire Gilbert*, built at Sunderland only the year before by Bartram and Sons for the Ministry of War Transport is recorded in British records as being lost on 2 November 1942 "off the East Coast of Iceland, presumably by U-boat." We know that sixty-three of her crew lost their lives, a figure which includes sixteen DEMS gunners. There were three survivors. If we consult the German records, however, the position they quote clearly puts the vessel well towards the Norwegian coast, but I tend to think this is purely a recording error. It would not be practical to sail some ships in each direction. How, for instance, could only four trawlers cover both routes? The ships that were to be sailed along the east coast of Iceland would have been at greater risk of detection at a much earlier stage in their journey. Time at sea would have been longer and initially they would have had to double back from Hvalfjord for at least a day before being able to head north. The need for two hundred mile spacing between sailings would also have been a waste of effort. All ex-crew members of the ships involved who were contacted during the preparation of this book are quite sure that they sailed by the more sensible route, up the west coast of Iceland.

Empire Gilbert had loaded at Tyneside during the middle of September 1942 and when she sailed from Tyne Dock at 1:30 p.m. on

Wednesday, 23 September 1942, two of her crew failed to join. She made her way up the east coast, across the top of Scotland and down through North Minch to Loch Ewe where she anchored off Altbea. This Scottish town did not see many large ocean-going merchant ships in peacetime, they had no reason to call there, but it served as a very fine wartime anchorage. It was free from prying eyes; any stranger out of uniform in the area would have stuck out like a sore thumb. The crews for the most part remained on board ship awaiting the arrival of the other vessels that made up the British section of Arctic convoys.

The long and unavoidably drawn out process of convoy planning had probably earmarked these vessels to be part of PQ-19 but the decision to halt the Russian convoys for the time being had already been taken, but not promulgated. The surviving ships of PQ-18 had already joined those of the scattered PQ-17 in North Russia by the time *Empire Gilbert*, *Empire Sky* and *Chulmleigh* had reached the starting line at Loch Ewe. During her time at anchor in the Scottish sea loch one young naval gunner from *Empire Gilbert* was put ashore sick and in late October when she had reached Hvalfjord, Iceland, one of the military gunners, 23-year-old Gnr. S. W. Mullen of Newcastle was put ashore on 26 October. L/Bdr. Bernard Wall, a 32-year-old gunner from Eton replaced him on board. All the military gunners were from the 4th Regiment, Royal Maritime Artillery. Her crew, apart from these two changes, was as originally signed on in South Shields some seven weeks earlier.

It is interesting to note that the DEMS (Defensively Equipped Merchant Ship) gunners were all signed on articles as deckhands, irrespective of whether they were Royal Navy or Royal Maritime Artillery men, while Merchant Navy seamen were signed on as Able Seaman, Ordinary Seaman, or Sailor, depending on their qualification in seamanship. This makes it very easy for them to be identified from crew lists. It is often more difficult to differentiate between RN and RMA men though because in most instances there was no further information on this point. The gunners received only their service pay, much lower than the rest of the crew, though they were fitted out with a civilian suit when they were allocated to their first merchant ship. This was mainly for use in neutral ports and they were under orders to wear civilian clothes only under these circumstances, though exactly how this regulation would be enforced is not revealed. The Armed Guards of the United States Navy carried on their merchant ships did not sign articles and therefore their names do not appear in the crew lists.

Hvalfjord, a good anchorage, well sheltered except from southwesterly winds, is a long but relatively narrow fjord, bounded on either side by high volcanic rock with only the odd remote farmhouse with its brightly colored roof to break up the bleak and barren picture, but it is vast enough to accommodate a large number of ships, is just around the corner from the Icelandic capital of Reykjavik but was not as secure as Loch Ewe. It was, however, the best available in the circumstances. There was a great deal of anti-British feeling in Iceland, rather than pro-German. A few German agents had been put ashore there, too, but it is still a well-kept secret just how effective they were in their activities. They must, however, have received help from some of the local community in order to have operated successfully in such a small place where a stranger not in uniform would be easily distinguished. It is a fact that pro-German swastikas and anti-British and American slogans were painted on walls quite frequently during the occupation.

Merchant seamen of all Allied nationalities during World War II spent many hundreds of hours anchored offshore either waiting to load, unload or join a convoy. Partly to relieve the monotony but mainly to take advantage of the diminished need for shipboard sea-going duties, "Board of Trade Sports Days" were organized and carried out. These consisted of fire drills, lifeboat drills and quite often races between the ships lifeboats to see who was quickest at getting it into the water or raising sail and completing a course. While the crews generally recognized the need for such exercises, the enthusiasm varied considerably.

German records give credit for the loss of *Empire Gilbert* to *U-586* (von der Esche), and they give the position as 7015N 1350E and since the three survivors were taken prisoner of war by the submarine then this fact must add weight to their version of events. Perhaps after all the merchantmen did all sail by the marginally safer northern route. It was not until March 1943 that it was learnt through the International Red Cross prisoner of war sources that there were any survivors from *Empire Gilbert* and on which day she had been sunk. The position given in the U-boat report, however, seems to have been transcribed incorrectly. The German Naval grid square when transcribed indicates the position as 7015N 1330 *West*, not East. This is more in accordance with expectations than is 1350 East. To have sailed *Empire Gilbert* so close to the Norwegian-based German airfields and harbors would have been to invite early detection and subsequent disaster.

ARCTIC INTERLUDE 43

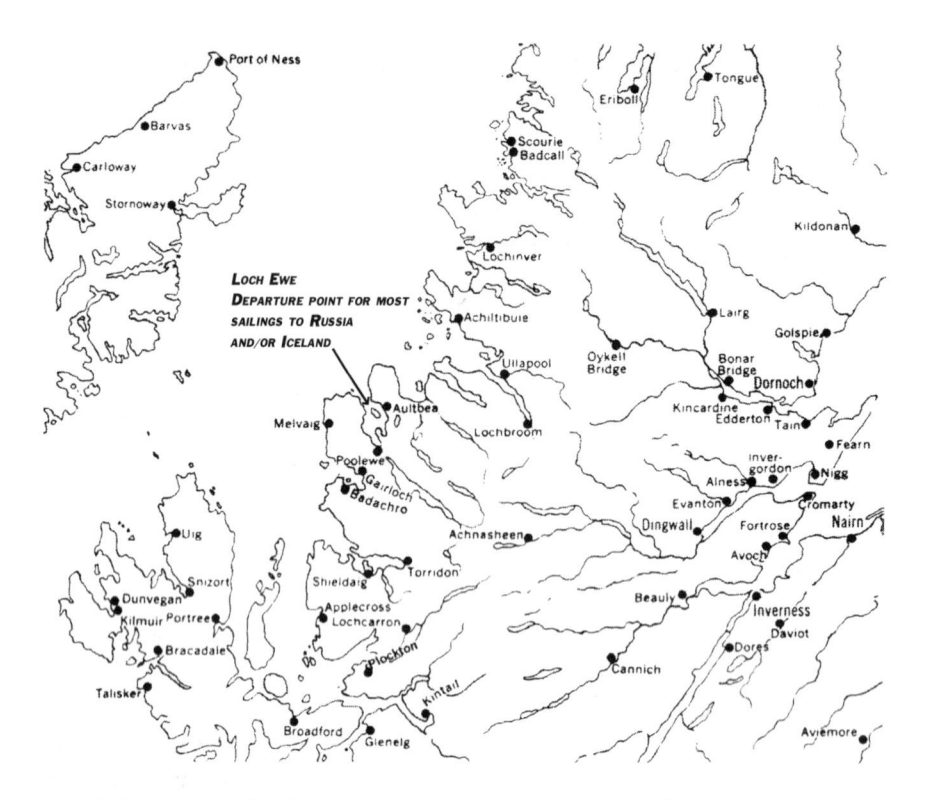

Loch Ewe, Scotland, where most sailings to Russia and/or Iceland departed from.

The crew of *Empire Gilbert* were typical of a British merchantman in time of war. The merchant navy part of her crew tended to come from one area of the United Kingdom, though not exclusively. In this case it was from Tyneside. The large complement of DEMS gunners came from all over the country. There was a strong element of very experienced men in all departments, together with many who were only in their first few years of seafaring.

Twenty-one year old Eric Aisthorpe was born in Boston, Lincolnshire, but the family moved to Grimsby and Eric attended South Parade School there. He was a quiet, conscientious lad and during his youth he learned to play the harmonica and the accordion very well. Work in Grimsby before the war was hard to find and he had set himself up with a small window cleaning round, which would not make him a fortune but earned him enough to live on and it was far better than being on the 'dole.' He was conscripted in August 1941 and joined the Navy, eventually finding himself serving as a gunner on coastal convoys around Great Britain. He was looking forward to seeing more of the world when he joined SS *Empire Gilbert* in South Shields early in September 1942.

Apart from a short visit to Iceland, he would see no more of the world before he lost his life.

Two other young men, John Stewart and Alex Souter, grew up together in Lossiemouth, living only a few doors from each other. They were inseparable friends, sharing all the good times as well as the bad. They even took violin lessons together. After leaving school they both joined the local Seine net fishing fleet. John had hopes of joining the police force in England but this ambition was not realized before war came. Alex was smaller than John and more quiet in nature. He thought very deeply about most things. Whilst he loved the sea he often had a dread of it. As a young boy he had fallen into the harbor at Lossiemouth and was dragged out unconscious and close to death. It was only after long and persistent resuscitation that he recovered. During his fishing days he was involved in an accident which knocked him unconscious during a gale and was washed overboard in that state. Another crew member saved Alex's life by his quick reaction to the situation. He tied a line around himself and did not hesitate in going overboard to attempt to rescue his shipmate. The rest of the crew thought they would lose both men, but not so. John Smith struggled to his unconscious shipmate and seized him while the rest of the crew hauled on the line to bring them both alongside. For his gallant rescue, John Smith was awarded the Royal Humane Society Parchment.

John Stewart decided that he would like to try the big ships of the merchant navy and he had no difficulty in signing on the 8,000 ton tanker *Empire Gem*. On John's return from his first voyage Alex listened to his friend's tales and decided that he, too, would like to join the merchant navy. They both signed on for a voyage to India and back when they had plenty of yarns to spin about their worldly travels while on leave in Lossiemouth. The bond between the two lads was as strong as ever and they both signed on *Empire Gilbert* in South Shields early in September 1942. Soon after this Alex's father was taken seriously ill and the young seaman was sent home for the weekend but before he had reached Lossiemouth his father had died. John had managed to get time off to travel with Alex and he returned to the ship on Monday, pleading with Alex to apply for compassionate leave. Alex, however, wanted to stay with his lifelong friend and would not apply, leaving Lossiemouth a few hours after the funeral to rejoin his ship. The ship had already left the Tyne and he was routed to join her at Loch Ewe in Wester Ross. Soon after re-joining his ship, she sailed for Iceland and then North Russia. Alex and John would lose their lives, too, in the tragedy. Some time later, Alex's sister Marjory remembers, the family received a sum of £50 from a source she cannot remember. This is explained in more detail in another chapter.

Bombardier Arthur Hopkins of the Maritime Royal Artillery had already completed five wartime voyages in merchant ships: two to Canada, one to the United States, one to Freetown and then to the Middle East on a troopship, sailing around the Cape of Good Hope. Arthur Hopkins joined *Empire Gilbert* on the Tyne and he says the voyage to Iceland was uneventful. *Empire Gilbert* sailed as number five from Hvalfjord on 30 October and remained undetected until 1 November when a German aircraft found them but did not attack. It merely flew around, well out of anti-aircraft range, obviously making signals to base. Bombardier Hopkins was on watch soon after ten in the evening when he spotted a U-boat running parallel to them on the port side. He raised the alarm and the ship was brought to action stations immediately, but soon afterwards a torpedo hit on the port side and she sank quite quickly, giving no time for boats to be lowered. Bombardier Hopkins and those around him were forced to jump into the icy sea and he remembers very little else until he was rescued by the U-boat where he found that two of his shipmates were also on board. Bombardier Hopkins is quite adamant, however, that he could hear quite a large number of men shouting in the darkness around him, while he was still in the water. It would, of course, take only minutes for most men to succumb to the icy November water. He was well treated while on board the U-boat, only mildly interrogated but allowed to fraternize with the crew until the submarine reached Narvik and he was handed over to the German Navy. He was further interrogated there for a few days, finally sailing on a German coaster through the fjords to Kiel and on to a prison camp not far from Hamburg.

Ralph Urwin signed on *Empire Gilbert* in South Shields early in September 1942. He was then 17 years old and signed on as deck boy as did two other 17 year olds. Ralph Urwin remembers that speculation was rife as to their destination when the cargo was loaded. It consisted of general war materials, including guns and tanks, crated aircraft and spare parts together with an assortment of ammunition. On deck they carried a cargo of crated aviation fuel and several large crates firmly lashed down. They took a spare crew to Iceland and were due to take them right through to Russia but the powers that be came on board and told the assembled crew about their forthcoming journey, finally saying that they could sign off if they so wished, but no one did. It was considered too dangerous to carry an extra crew to Russia and so these men were taken ashore at Hvalfjord to be returned to the

United Kingdom. After the ship sank, Ralph does not remember a great deal until he awoke on board the submarine and found himself being rubbed down by the German crew to try and bring warmth and circulation back to his numb limbs.

There was a strong smell of cognac, too. He also agrees that they were quite well treated by the crew of *U-586*. He remembers one of the Germans doing a good rendering of the commentary on the pre-war heavyweight title fight between Max Baer and Joe Louis. The third survivor was also a DEMS gunner, 20 year old Army gunner Douglas Meadows of Gloucester.

Paul Preuss was a torpedo mechanic on board *U-586* at that time and he well remembers the three men being recovered unconscious from the freezing water and hurriedly taken down to the wardroom. Their wet clothes were stripped off and they were wrapped in blankets and their numb limbs were massaged until gradually life returned to them. When the men had recovered sufficiently they were given hot drinks and food. For the rest of the voyage the prisoners received exactly the same rations as the remainder of the U-boat crew. He also remembers that they got on very well, despite a language difficulty.

On arrival in Narvik the three survivors were handed over to the Navy and were kept there for about a week. They were then put on board the German coaster *Spree* of Norddeutscher Lloyd Line, she was of 2,867 gross tons and was engaged on running iron ore from Narvik to Germany. The three men were locked in a small deckhouse for most of the voyage but the captain ordered the door to be unlocked for the dangerous Skagerrak crossing from Norway to Germany, 'in order that you will have the same chance as we do if we are attacked.' He did get the men to agree that they would behave themselves during this time. *Spree* landed them and off they went to POW camps. *Spree* continued in her iron ore trade until March 1944 when she was mined off Denmark. She was raised and towed to Stavanger but not repaired until the end of the war. On 6 December 1988 the Russian Ambassador to New Zealand, Mr. Yuri Sokolov presented Ralph Urwin (and eight others) with the USSR North Atlantic Convoy Medallion.

In mid-December 1942, Ralph's mother received a letter from the ship's managers, Turner Brightman & Co. telling her that the ship was overdue and must be presumed lost with all hands. It was not until March 1943 that Mrs. Urwin received a letter from Ralph through the Red Cross, saying that he was well but a prisoner of war.

Examination of the log of *U-586* does indeed reveal that the submarine was running on the surface, closing the steamer. The date is given as 2 November, time 0020 (German time was two hours ahead of GMT).

It is hard to believe that the steamer has not noticed us. Get closer, our course 60 degrees.

0034 Steamer is now 2,000 meters away—torpedo tubes stand by.

0042 Change course to 50 degrees.

0100 Our position is square AA9467 [on the German Naval grid chart].

0107 Change course to 70 degrees.

0117 Start run up, will try with a 2 fan shot from 600 meters.

0119 Torpedoes away—turned off, a blind man should know we are there. The two torpedoes come to the surface a few times but there is a detonation after 31 seconds (450 meters). One hit amidships and another 10 meters from the bow. A high column of black and then gray smoke then after about three minutes there is a heavy underwater explosion. On the water there is a white light and five more going on and off. Nothing was heard on the distress wavelength of 600 meters but at 0140 a German transmitter asked in plain language 'Who sent TTT at 0130?' Nothing further heard.

0140 Went to the place where the lights were and picked up two [sic] swimming Tommies off a plank and saw six more on a raft. The first two could not move after being in the water for less than half an hour (temp. 1 degree C) After reviving them their names are: Douglas Meadows, 20 years, service number 5196097, gunner Maritime Anti-aircraft Corps; Arthur Hopkins, 24 years, service number 1496956, Corporal; Ralph Urwin, seaman with the merchant navy, 19 years. The prisoners stated SS *Empire Gilbert*, 7,500 tons, built 1941, on voyage from Sunderland, Reykjavik, to North Russia, exact destination not known. Cargo, food, munitions, 25 tanks and other war material. Sister ships *Empire Sunrise*, 7,459 GRT, *Empire Mist*, 7,250 GRT. Left Reykjavik 30 October. 66 crew members. Weapons, 1 cannon, 4 × 2 AA guns. The lookout could not see the U-boat very well.

The following day *U-586* sent a brief signal to her headquarters giving details of the sinking.

The short signal TTT mentioned earlier is most interesting indeed. I can think of only three occasions on which this combination of the letter T would be used in radio telegraphy. The first situation can surely be discounted in this instance. There are three classes of emergency signals in international wireless telegraph regulations. SOS, the highest priority, XXX, the urgency signal, second priority, and TTT, the safety signal, third priority. This safety signal is primarily used for urgent navigation or weather information. I cannot envisage a situation where any merchant ship of a belligerent nation would break radio silence to transmit such a signal.

All the British merchant ships of Operation FB carried three radio officers and could therefore keep a 24-hour manual watch on the international distress frequency. They would also be fitted with an auto-alarm receiver. Maritime radio regulations then in force meant that the single operator ships would certainly be fitted with this device. American marine radio authorities at that time, however, considered the equipment was unreliable. They said it caused more problems than it solved. It was not therefore a compulsory fit in United States single operator ships. The equipment would have allowed the ships to keep a 24-hour watch on the distress frequency. Just before going off watch the radio officer would switch on this receiver and check it for correct functioning.

The radio officers of *Empire Gilbert*, Richard Caddick James (Chief), Wilfred Sandford (2nd) and Thomas Beard (3rd) would almost certainly be aware that the American and Russian ships carried only one radio officer. From personal experience I would gamble that the anchor watch on the bridge of *Empire Gilbert*, while in Hvalfjord, had noted the departure of *Richard H. Alvey*, *Empire Galliard*, *Dekabrist* and *John Walker* prior to their own departure. This was standard practice for any such bridge watch. It helped to relieve the monotony and made the watch appear to pass more quickly. All the ships would be easily identified by experienced seamen, not necessarily by name, but certainly by nationality. There was no mistaking the outline of the two Liberties, nor the silhouette of *Empire Galliard*, that is for certain. There would be no problem either in identifying the Russian steamer.

In the normal course of shipboard gossip these facts would soon be known by everyone. The Chief Radio Officer, Mr. James, was 52 years old and one can therefore assume with a good degree of certainty that he was a pre-war radio officer of vast experience. Indeed, if he had begun his career in his youth then he must have served on some of the first merchant ships to be fitted with wireless. He was, by tradition, allowed to choose his watchkeeping period. Although one cannot be certain on the point, it is very doubtful if he would have chosen the middle (graveyard) watch, midnight to 0400. This usually fell to one of the junior radio officers for obvious reasons. Most chief radio officers chose the forenoon and late evening watches.

Empire Gilbert was fitted with the less common IMR (International Marine Radio Company) equipment and was manned by radio officers from that company. The author knows that for certain all three names are in the company's Roll of Honour, working for the same company himself at that time. Marconi equipment and radio officers far outnumbered IMR fitted ships. The IMR Company was, however, very up to date in its designs. The author knows that IMR fitted ships were being supplied as standard fitting with a small clockwork device which, when activated would automatically key the transmitter with a continuous stream of very accurate four second dashes, spaced at one second intervals (i.e. T T T T etc.), until it was either switched off or the spring ran down. The radio officer on watch, probably Mr. James, would have run up the transmitter, ready for immediate use, as soon as any warning was given by the bridge or look-outs. Could this have been the reason for the strange signal "Who sent TTT on 500Kc/s at 0130?"?

We know that *Empire Gilbert* was torpedoed at about 2330 GMT (German time was plus two hours). Bombardier Hopkins tells us that the U-boat was seen only a short time before the torpedo struck. It is very likely that in that short time the alarm bells were sounded to bring the ship to full alert. It is very probable that the chief radio officer, Mr. James, was on watch at this time and I feel sure that such an experienced officer would have run up his main transmitter, without waiting for orders, all ready to transmit at a moment's notice. It is quite possible (but doubtful) that he may have transmitted the three T's as part of his fine tuning in order that the transmitter would be working at full power. This procedure could be done on the 'dummy aerial,' a special non-radiating device for just such a purpose, but, since the ship had already been detected there was no real need. The main aerial could have been used.

Another possible explanation is that knowing the nearest ships to him were all single radio officer vessels, Mr. James decided to transmit the auto-alarm signal to alert them to *Empire Gilbert*'s plight. The auto-alarm receiver would respond to any five consecutive, correctly transmitted dashes/intervals. Perhaps the torpedo explosion cut short this transmission. We shall never know for sure because neither the master, who would have given the transmission order, nor any of the radio officers who would have carried it out, survived. Single radio officer ships had been ordered to keep manual radio watch at certain pre-specified times (see appendix).

U-586 was a Blohm and Voss built type VII-C. She had been launched on 10 July 1941 and commissioned by Oberleutnant Dietrich von der Esche on 4 September 1941. The emblem on her conning tower was a shield in black, red and gold upon which was a clenched gauntlet. The U-boat and her crew served initially in the Arctic, then made one North Atlantic patrol before being ordered to the Mediterranean where she was bombed and sunk in Toulon harbor by U.S. bombers, on 5 July 1944. She sank two merchant ships during her operational life and damaged one other. Dietrich von der Esche had, during his time in command of *U-586*, had the unusual experience of taking over command of another U-boat at short notice, for one patrol. His own boat was undergoing repairs. Oberleutnant zur See Hans Klatt of *U-606* had been forced to return from his first patrol because of ill health. He was admitted to hospital and Dietrich 'Titus' von der Esche was ordered to take over for one patrol. The new CO brought ten of his most experienced key personnel with him from *U-586*. The patrol was fruitless and lasted only thirteen days, chasing convoy PQ-18. 'Titus' von der Esche went on to command the large ocean going *U-863* only to lose his life in her off Brazil in 1944.

SS *Empire Sky*, too, was only a year old and she also had been built in Sunderland but by J. Thompson and Son Ltd. She was, at 7,455 tons, a larger vessel than *Gilbert*. In British records she is shown as sunk 'off Murmansk,' cause unknown. There were no survivors from her crew of sixty. The vessel was listed as 'missing' from 14 November 1942. There must be some significance in the authorities quoting this date. Perhaps she was due to arrive in North Russia then or perhaps she should have made some report at this time. She was one of the ships ordered by the Admiralty to remain west of Spitzbergen until given the order to proceed. The date of the signal delaying the ships is not known but the signal ordering them to proceed is dated 11 November. It seems very likely that *Empire Sky* did not receive the first signal because the vessel was just to the southeast of Spitzbergen when she was torpedoed on 6 November, although an American signal transmitted between London and Washington states that "*Empire Sky* and *Empire Scott* have arrived at Spitzbergen".

This signal must be based on either the vessels (*Empire Sky* and *Empire Scott*) having made a report to that effect. A probable use for the H/F transmitter installed at Hvalfjord before sailing. Another possibility is that they had been sighted by some friendly force, air, sea or land, and a report had been made by this third party. A highly unlikely happening. The official signal made a categorical statement about the arrival at Spitzbergen, which, by inference seems proof positive. There is no element of doubt in the signal at all.

German records, however, show that *U-625* (Oberleutnant Hans Benker) reported sinking the SS *Bangalore* in position 7620N 1730E on 6 November 1942. There is no doubt that Hans Benker was incorrect in his identification because the 6,067 gross ton SS *Bangalore* of the Hain Steamship Company was already on the ocean bed, many thousands of miles away. She had been built in Glasgow in 1929 by Barclay Curle and Company and remained in the service of her first owners until late July 1941. At this time she was bound from London to Hong Kong, via Trinidad and Table Bay with a full general cargo which included aircraft and horses. She was on the Trinidad to Table Bay leg of her journey, just north of the equator, off the north coast of Brazil when she collided with the SS *Richmond Castle* on 20 July. She was so badly damaged that she had to be sunk by the gunfire of an escort in order that she did not become a hazard to shipping.

No other vessel is unaccounted for in this northern area at this time and historians agree that the vessel was almost certainly *Empire Sky*, the first victim of *U-625*.

Empire Sky had loaded at Hull during August and September 1942 and two young Grimsby lads joined her there. Victor James Jennings, 16 years old, signed on as mess room boy. He was the second youngest of ten children, a very quiet type of boy, who, after leaving school, had begun work at a local cycle shop until he had joined the merchant navy in 1941. After working by *Empire Sky* for some two weeks he was given permission to sign off and did so. He told his family that he had seen rats on board and considered her an unlucky ship. This action undoubtedly saved young Victor's life, but his luck would not hold. He signed on the SS *Almenara*, a much smaller ship than *Empire Sky*. He sailed in this vessel on his 17th birthday bound for the Mediterranean. The vessel was mined off Taranto on 20 September 1943 and Victor lost his young life in the tragedy.

George Rhodes was the other young Grimbarian that had signed on *Empire Sky* at Hull. He had signed on as cabin boy. George, too, came from a large family of ten children. His father, Bill Rhodes, was a ship's carpenter and this left his mother, Ethel May, to bring up the family on her own while dad was at sea. George's first job on leaving school was on a farm but his heart was not in it and there was salt water in his blood and so in 1940 he joined the merchant navy as a cabin boy. He had already been shipwrecked off Australia and had two years sea time under his belt when he signed on *Empire Sky*. He decided to stay with the ship when Victor signed off. This decision was to cost him his life. *Empire Sky* took the north about route to Loch Ewe and dropped her anchor within sight of *Empire Gilbert*. *Chulmleigh* had not yet arrived in the Scottish sea loch. The date was 2 October 1942. The 2nd Engineering Officer, 49 year old Mr. W. F. Stark, suffered a hernia while the ship was off Altbea and had to be put ashore for an operation that was to save his life, of that there is no doubt. There are many hundreds of such instances on record, not only in wartime, where such an event resulted in one person losing his life while another was spared.

Sergeant Edward Edgar Stoackley joined *Empire Sky* at this time too. He was the Senior Army gunner on board. He had moved with his parents from Weymouth to Northumberland when he was a boy. He worked at the Horden coke ovens before joining the Army. He enlisted in the Royal Artillery before the outbreak of war and early in 1941 he volunteered for duty as an anti-aircraft gunner on merchant ships. Sergeant Stoackley's son was about 12 years old when he lost his father. He well remembers his mother receiving £100 danger money soon after the tragedy.

Empire Sky was in Hvalfjord during the last week of October and three men were discharged there. The two firemen were replaced and this is where 39 year old fireman James Carr of Greenock signed on for this fateful voyage. His wife Kate was at home in Greenock with their three children, unaware at this point in time exactly where her husband was. James Carr was probably influenced in his decision to volunteer for this voyage by the prospect of earning the bonus that had been offered to each man. It would certainly help with the expense of raising his family. It was, however, impossible to find another fourth engineer before she sailed (the third and fourth engineers had each been promoted) and no doubt the chief engineer would now have had to take a watch, since there were now only three engineering officers on board. The other two firemen who joined *Empire Sky* at Hvalfjord shortly before she sailed on that fateful journey were Robert Hall and John Murray.

Late in 1942, Mrs. Rhodes was informed that her son George was 'missing' but the terrible uncertainty of his fate remained a burden for her until February 1946 when she received a letter from the ship's managers. The letter said that it had been established from post-war examination of German records that SS *Empire Sky* had been sunk by a U-boat and that there had been no survivors from her crew. Soon afterwards she received a message of condolence from His Majesty King George VI.

Mrs. Kate Carr received a similar message, as did all other next of kin. Throughout the coming years she struggled hard to bring up her three children, often going short herself to make sure that they were well fed and clothed. She never re-married and her lifelong grief was finally overcome when the 764 ton Hull trawler *Arctic Corsair*, the last 'sidewinder' of this famous port, in the distinctive livery of the Boyd Line, scattered her ashes off Bear Island in the summer of 1987. Her dying wish had been to join her husband in his unmarked grave in these Arctic wastes.

Further interesting observations and facts about *Empire Sky*'s final twenty-four hours are revealed in chapter eight by an American Armed Guard Officer and a signalman, both members of *Hugh Williamson*'s crew on that fateful journey.

U-625 was a younger sister to *U-586*. Built at the same yard she was launched on 15 April 1942 and commissioned on 4 June 1942 by Oberleutnant Hans Benker. She was declared operational in October 1942 and served with the Arctic flotilla until November 1943 when she went on Atlantic operations before being sunk on 10 March 1944 by Sunderland 'U' of 422 Squadron, RCAF (Warrant Officer W. F. Morton), while under the command of Siegfried Straub. There were no survivors from her crew of fifty-three although many were seen to take to their dinghies as the submarine sank, the luck of her four leaf clover emblem with '13' and a flash of lightning having run out.

Hans Benker claims to have sunk three merchantmen, two of them from our thirteen independents, *Chulmleigh* and *Empire Sky*. There is, however, a great deal of controversy over the final fate of this vessel. He also sank SS *Goolistan*, a straggler from QP-13. *U-625* also sank a Russian naval vessel. He lost his life while serving in *U-625* on 2 January 1944 while on Atlantic patrol. The submarine was attacked by Liberator 'G' of 224 Squadron, RAF (Pilot Officer J. E. Edwards). This aircraft was damaged and some of the aircrew wounded in the attack but Liberator 'C' of the same squadron, flown by Flying Officer E. Allen was informed and on arrival at the scene found the marine markers left by 'G' and began a search. Soon afterwards *U-625* was spotted and attacked with eight depth charges. Hans Benker and one of his crew were lost overboard during this action, most likely blown overboard when the depth charges from the Liberator exploded close alongside.

Her only success under her new commander was a share, with *U-741* (Oberleutnant Gerhard Palmgreen) in the shooting down of a Wellington from 407 Squadron, RCAF (Pilot Officer E. N. O'Donnell), shortly before being sunk herself. This aircraft and crew had sunk *U-669* (Oberleutnant Kurt Koehl) some six months earlier.

SS *John H. B. Latrobe*, 7,191 GRT, was built in July 1942 as yard number 52 by Bethlehem/Fairfield, right alongside *Richard H. Alvey*. She sailed from Baltimore and called at Philadelphia, New York, Boston and Halifax before arriving in Hvalfjord on 21 September 1942. She had left Hvalfjord bound for Archangel on 31 October as number six of our thirteen independents. She was fully loaded with 6,714 tons of tanks, aircraft, heavy machine guns and food.

While at anchor in Hvalfjord men from the depot ship USS *Melville* brought some special cargo on board, fitted an HF transmitter and receiver and supplied additional 20-mm and .30 caliber ammunition. On 24 October, Mr. A. C. Kerr, a special representative, interviewed the master of *John H. B. Latrobe*, Captain Alonzo L. Hodgdon, and outlined the basic plan to him. Wally Hand had joined the ship at Baltimore and soon identified Able Seaman Oree J. Bell as the ship's sharp operator (every ship had at least one such character). Their cabins were adjacent and when Wally heard the sound of hammering originating from Oree's cabin, he couldn't resist the urge to investigate. Wally caught Oree red-handed, stowing cigarettes in the deckhead cavity of the cabin. He quickly allied himself in the 'spiv' and they became 'business partners' for the remainder of the voyage. Wally Hand recalls,

> We hove up the anchor at about 0645 on 31 October, passed through the net defense half an hour later and left the boring safety of Hvalfjord at precisely 0900. The weather was not good, a fresh to strong southerly wind and poor visibility. We were having trouble with the magnetic compass due to disturbance and so the master decided to anchor for the night in Breidefjord. The hook was down soon after 5 p.m. We resumed our passage at 0445 on 1 November, making about 10½ knots.

This overnight anchoring, of course, would now put the next ship to sail (*Chulmleigh*) in the same vicinity. No mention is made, however, of the two ships sighting each other at this point. Wally continues,

> We sighted the North Cape at 1615 that same day. We had seen several small- and medium-sized fishing boats during the day and just after dark we saw a medium-sized freighter some distance away [*Chulmleigh*?]. In the early afternoon we saw a Catalina aircraft. On 2 November we saw only a few small boats. We passed Jan Mayen at 0500 on the 3rd, about 35 miles abeam, having sighted only one small boat. We had been averaging around 10½ knots all the time we were steaming.

Route from Iceland past the North Cape and the Arctic Circle.

The wind had gradually eased away and on 5 November it was light south to southeasterly. The air thermometer was reading 32 degrees Fahrenheit. At 0855 the lookouts spotted a plane low on the water, dead ahead and heading straight towards us. Another aircraft appeared and General Quarters was sounded. I went to the .30 caliber Browning machine gun on the port wing of the bridge. We had been told that we could expect to see friendly aircraft on this day. By the time I had reached the gun position there were three aircraft in sight. They were soon identified as not American, and probably not English, most likely Bv 139s [sic]. As the aircraft closed, however, we could see that they were two motor He 115s. At this point three more aircraft were reported approaching from the starboard beam, down sun, which was then a large, lazy red ball, resting its lower arc on the horizon. The gun crew on the 5-inch stern gun then reported three more aircraft approaching from dead astern. One of the aircraft ahead seemed to drop a mine or something similar into the water ahead of the ship. It then flew off. The other aircraft all then began to circle us, out of range of our guns at about 5,000 yards, still close to the surface of the sea.

About ten minutes after the first sighting three aircraft formed up and came in to attack from the port bow. Only the center aircraft actually dropped a torpedo, the other two broke away to left and right. The weather and sea conditions were good for a torpedo attack but the vessel was handled well and the torpedo missed. I fired when I judged the aircraft were within range but I do not think I hit any. I do know that I continued firing well after the aircraft had got clear, I just couldn't get my finger off the trigger! Fright I guess.

The dual purpose 3-inch 50 caliber bow gun was firing well, then the 20-mm joined in followed by the light machine guns. There were six attacks in all, each by three aircraft and with only the center one dropping a torpedo each time. Only one of the torpedoes failed to run correctly, it belly flopped, turned over and over and then sank. One torpedo passed within 20 feet of us, another about 15 feet off our stern. The ship was not hit but we did hear one heavy explosion nearby but there was no water geyser from it.

The aircraft always attacked in threes, 20 to 40 feet above the surface of the sea and spaced about 150 feet apart. The two outer aircraft would veer off at about 1,000 yards while the center one carried on to about 500 yards before launching its torpedo. All used their machine guns on the approach. The aircraft used red and white light signals during the attacks. After the final attack they all flew off in a southeasterly direction.

There was no damage to our ship or casualties among our crew from the enemy action but two gunners had been knocked down by blast from our 3-inch and several were rendered deaf for some time afterwards. There were only minor scratches and dents from the enemy machine gun fire and a little damage to the rigging from our own 20-mm guns.

Two of the attacking aircraft were definitely damaged. Most of the gunners saw pieces fly off one of the floats of an He 115 and a large hole appeared in it. The second aircraft was hit near the cockpit and there was an explosion when it was hit. Two other aircraft were hit but no damage to them was observed at all.

One of the aircraft was seen to fly off, still low on the water, trailing smoke and flying erratically. The engagement lasted about one and a half hours. After the attacks the master decided to alter course towards Greenland and we began zigzagging between 270 and 300 degree courses. By sundown the mist had turned into thick fog and this continued throughout 6 November but the winds were still light, south to southeasterly. Navigation was by dead reckoning only. During 7 November we encountered mist, rain and heavy snow and shortly before midnight the master ordered the engines stopped and we lay to for the night until shortly before breakfast on the 9th.

We had to stop again later that day because of fog, rain and snow. We obtained a sight on 9 November and set off again, still westerly. Our position was now off Scoresby Sound, East Greenland. We began to encounter ice flows and at 1430 we struck a small iceberg, more like a big growler than a 'berg but it crushed a plate and split a weld in the bows, flooding the starboard forepeak tank. The ship went down by the head a little and our speed was affected somewhat. By tea-time we were free of ice and 24 hours after hitting the growler we sighted land. It was the North Cape of Iceland.

Soon after 6 p.m. on 10 November we struck a large submerged object. The ship was severely jolted and slowed down by the impact. Two distinct collisions were heard and felt, with about five seconds in between. Nothing could be seen. The vessel was stopped and the anchor dropped in 17 fathoms forward, 22 fathoms on each beam and over 25 fathoms aft. A patch of oil developed nearby and was spreading all the time. Later it gradually dispersed but not before another large patch appeared on the port side. The engineers declared it was diesel oil. Our ship carried no diesel at all, either for our own use or as cargo and we were not leaking oil in any way.

Our approximate position at the time of the collision was 6 or 7 miles off shore, Ritturhuk bore 273 degrees magnetic and Haughild 223 degrees magnetic. On 11 November we hove up the anchor and proceeded towards Isafjord. We passed Straumnes at 2 miles and anchored at 1400 in Isafjord because of heavy snow squalls and strong variable winds. We set off again the next day at breakfast time and we passed Stalberg corner at 1330. We anchored in Brede Bugt in the middle of the afternoon and set off on the last leg back to Hvalfjord next morning.

We had expended more than one third of our 3-inch anti-aircraft ammunition in the air attacks. When Lt. Reynolds, the Armed Guard Officer had first joined the ship in the States he had assembled his men and given them a lecture on the 'typical' American merchant seaman. He painted a picture of them all as lazy, ill-mannered, ill-disciplined, drunken womanizers. He advised his men—almost ordering them, in fact—to have nothing whatever to do with the merchant crew. Most of his men were young rookies on their first ship, and most believed what he said. However, after the air attacks he had the decency to retract his statement and to praise the professional way the merchant crew had handled things before, during and after the attacks. His apology was accepted by most of the men, but not all.

I am myself convinced that some of the Icelandic ships seen by us off Arnefjord reported us in some way. Two of these ships deliberately changed course and closed us in order to observe us more closely. They then veered away. They were not fishing at all, they just seemed to be patrolling, waiting to meet us.

Temporary repairs to the hull were carried out by men from USS *Melville* and further repairs were undertaken by USS *Vulcan*. Wally Hand continues,

After this we sailed in convoy with twenty-one other freighters to Loch Ewe, Scotland. Our escort consisted of HMS *Saladin*, *Winchester*, *St. Elstan*, *Cape Palliser*, *Northern Spray*, *Northern Pride*, *Foxtrot* and *Paynter*. Our destination was changed while we were still at sea to Glasgow. The only incident of any real significance on this journey was the rescue of a lifeboat full of survivors on 30 November by the rescue ship *Toward* attached to our convoy.

We discharged some cargo at Loch Long. Six American seamen deserted ship in Glasgow. They were replaced with British seamen. The master was also replaced, Captain J. Kroon, an elderly World War I veteran taking command.

Wally Hand can recall only one name from the small British contingent, Bill Duncan.

John H. B. Latrobe was put into the next convoy to Russia, JW-51-B. This convoy was split into two parts. The 'A' section sailing five days before the 'B.' The first group reached Russia without any hindrance from the enemy but the latter section of sixteen merchantmen were gallantly defended against German surface forces by ships of the Royal Navy and they too reached Russia without loss. *John H. B. Latrobe* discharged her precious cargo and returned in convoy RA-53 during March 1943 but her misfortunes were not yet over. She suffered heavy weather damage on passage, her propeller was damaged and her rudder chains had snapped. She was drifting into the minefield off Seydisfjord and HMS *Opporture* (Cdr. John Le Barber) was ordered to find her and tow her into Seydisfjord. Heavy towing tackle was prepared in very bad weather. The disabled freighter was found and one and a half days later she was safely in Seydisfjord. Able Seaman Len Phillips of HMS *Opporture* received the sum of £1.8s.0d. for his part in the salvage! Wally Hand, still an OS on the freighter, well remembers the three months the vessel remained in that fjord. The men were not allowed ashore and their sole outside recreational function was to observe the tiny settlement with its large American garrison, through the telescopic gunsights.

The vessel was examined by divers and it was found that part of her propeller and rudder were missing. These repairs were beyond the capabilities of the small fishing settlement. The 135 ft., 479 ton tug *Empire Harry* was sent to tow the Liberty ship to the United Kingdom for permanent repairs to be carried out. The two ships left Seydisfjord on 14 June 1943 and arrived safely in Middlesbrough six days later. The small convoy had been escorted by HMS *Sealyham*. Wally Hand again remembers,

> We were put into an hotel in Middlesbrough while the ship underwent dry docking. We stayed there for almost a month and I bought a bicycle and explored the countryside around. I tried to stick fairly close to the railroad tracks so that when I

got tired I could hop on the train back to Middlesbrough. I thoroughly enjoyed our time there.

Wally was an old salt. He had started his sea career as a bell-hop on the small Baltimore to Hamburg liners in the 1930s. He had married in 1939 and came ashore working at Bethlehem Steel in Baltimore until the United States entered the war. He finally left the sea in 1949 and joined the Maryland State Police Department until he retired. *John H. B. Latrobe* sailed from Middlesbrough on 9 July joining convoy EN-54 to Methil, then to Loch Ewe where she joined convoy ON-193 and arrived safely in the United States on 31 July after a voyage lasting almost a year. She made a further trip to north Russia in convoy JW-56B in January 1944, returning in RA-57 in March of the same year. She also later distinguished herself at the Omaha beachhead soon after D-Day. She continued to transport vital cargoes until the end of the war, was then put into mothballs and entered the reserve fleet until she was finally scrapped in June 1969.

One of the two trawlers accompanying RA-53 was H.M.T. *St. Elstan*, who as we shall soon see was one of the four trawlers forming the rescue chain for the merchant ships of Operation FB. In addition to the damage suffered by SS *John H. B. Latrobe*, one of her sister ships in the same convoy, *J. L. M. Curry*, who had been one of the American 'stand-by' ships for FB, suffered a severe weld fracture in the extremely heavy weather and she broke her back. H.M.T. *St. Elstan* rescued all her crew safely and then sank the wreck by gunfire. This latest rescue brought the total number of survivors rescued by this trawler in the past six months to a staggering 260 persons. The American crew of *J. L. M. Curry* had been reluctant to abandon the vessel and the CO of *St. Elstan* had to give them an ultimatum—abandon now or we will have to leave you. They decided that she could not be saved and so they complied with the stipulation, bringing with them plenty of extra food, the ship's cat and dog, too!

St. Elstan was an old hand on the Russian convoy run. She had battled her way through with PQ-16 during which time submarine detector Herbert Rushby of Grimsby was one of *St. Elstan*'s crew who was busy pulling survivors of one of the sunken ships out of the freezing water. It had become a routine task and he leant over the rail and grabbed another struggling swimmer and hauled him unceremoniously over the side and was about to ease him to the deck before going for the next when a voice said to him "Blimey—of all the places to meet you again." It was Frank Carlisle, a friend of his family, who was serving as a DEMS gunner on the SS *Empire Purcell*, bombed and sunk by enemy aircraft only minutes earlier.

On the return journey with QP-13, all went well until the Reykjavik section approached the North Cape of Iceland. Navigation up to this point had been by 'dead reckoning' and the story goes that the SNO caught a glimpse of what he thought was the North Cape of Iceland and altered course accordingly. It was actually a very large iceberg and as a result the ships ran into the protective British minefield. Several ships were hit within minutes and some of the escorts thought that they were under submarine attack. Some of the first survivors from the merchant ships when rescued declared that their ships had been hit by heavy shellfire. For quite some time total confusion reigned. H.M.T. *St. Elstan* and H.M.T. *Lady Madeleine* picked up asdic contacts, probably on the sinking wrecks, or even on mines, and they carried out attacks with depth charges before rescuing further survivors. *St. Elstan* rescued twenty-six survivors from the Russian ship *Rodina*, including four women. This ship had been carrying a captured German aircraft as deck cargo. It was destined for the United States to be toured and exhibited all over the US to promote war bond sales. After the ship sank the aircraft was seen floating half submerged on the water and this led to further rumors that the sudden attack had come from the air! On this particular voyage *St. Elstan* carried a sick bay 'tiffey,' on passage home after his own ship had been sunk. He worked like a Trojan to make all the survivors as comfortable as possible and to administer the limited medical treatment available to them.

After the war, all these wrecks became well documented on the charts of Grimsby fishermen, each one of them initially claiming several full sets of trawling gear from unsuspecting skippers who had fished these waters without too many problems before the war but now found (the hard way) that many of these grounds were littered with wartime wrecks, which, until they were all charted accurately, would cause them to lose trawls or indeed, as happened on one occasion in bad weather, for the trawler to founder with heavy loss of life when it 'came fast' on one such wreck while towing her trawl.

S.S. *Empire Scott.*
[World Ship Society]

S.S. *Empire Sky*

S.S. *Hugh Williamson*.
[Peabody Museum]

S.S. *William Clark*.
[Peabody Museum]

S.S. *John Walker.*
[Peabody Museum]

S.S. *Daldorch.*
[World Ship Society]

S.S. *Dekabrist*.
[World Ship Society]

S.S. *Richard H. Alvey*.
[Peabody Museum]

S.S. *Empire Galliard*, post-war.
[World Ship Society]

S.S. *John H. B. Latrobe*.
[Peabody Museum]

HMT *St. Elstan*, Londonderry, 1941.
[Dennis Roberts]

HMT *St. Elstan*, 1942.
[Norman Pickles]

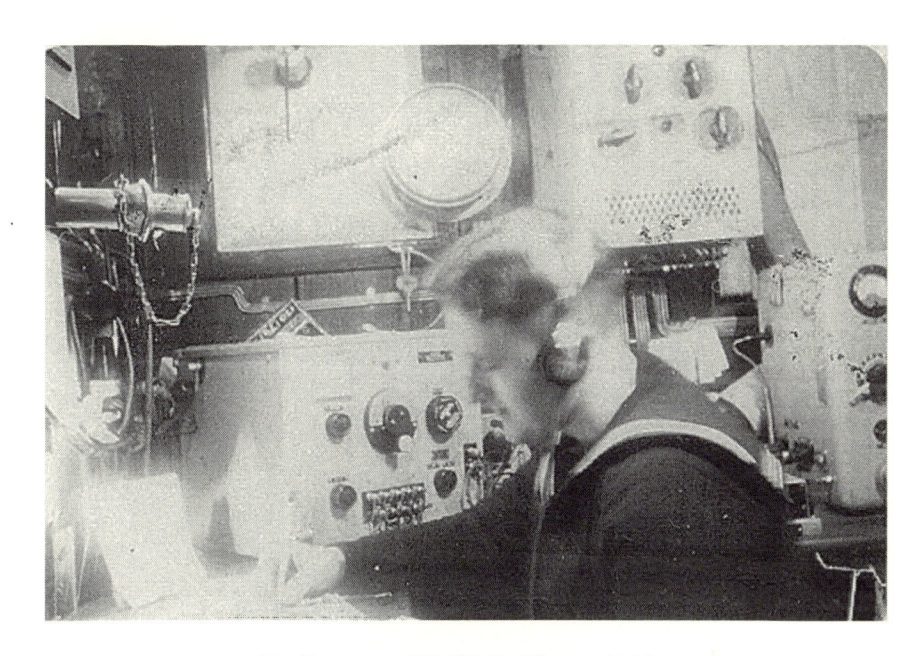

Radio room, HMT *St. Elstan*, 1942.
[Norman Pickles]

Ralph Urwin, Deck Boy, S.S. *Empire Gilbert*, November 1942.
He became a POW when the U-boat rescued him.
Photo taken 1945 on return from German POW camp.
[Ralph Urwin]

Petty Officer Ben Wilson, 2nd Engineman,
HMT *St. Elstan*, 1942. [Adam Liddle]

Adam Liddle, Stoker,
HMT *St. Elstan*, November 1942. [Adam Liddle]

More of HMT *St. Elstan*'s crew, November 1942. [H. Rushby]

S.T. *Cape Palliser* back in her peacetime fishing role.
[*Grimsby Evening Telegraph*]

HMT *Northern Pride*, 1945.

Crew of HMT *Northern Pride*, 1943.

German coaster *Spree* of the Norddeutscher Lloyd Line.

Ex-German *Spree*, 1960.
[World Ship Society]

Able Seaman Gunner Eric Aisthorpe, DEMS gunner, S.S. *Empire Sky*, November 1942.
[Mrs. E. Mitchell]

Bombardier Arthur Hopkins, DEMS gunner and survivor of S.S. *Empire Gilbert*. He became a POW when the U-boat rescued him.
[Arthur Hopkins]

Able Seamen John Stewart and Alex Souter,
S.S. *Empire Gilbert*, November 1942.

ASDIC Rating Herbert Rushby of HMT *St. Elstan*, November 1942.
He rescued his friend Gunner Frank Carlisle, of S.S. *Empire Purcell*,
in a convoy to Russia, when *Purcell* was sunk.
[Herbert Rushby]

Gunner Frank Carlisle, RMA, of S.S. *Empire Purcell*. He was rescued from the sea by his friend Herbert Rushby of HMT *St. Elstan*.
[Family of Frank Carlisle]

W/Sgt. Edgar E. Stoackley, Royal Maritime Artillery, Senior Gunner, S.S. *Empire Sky*, November 1942. Killed in action.
[Family of Edgar Stoackley]

Mr. R. Wishart, Bosun, S.S. *Empire Scott*, November 1942.
[R. Wishart]

Capt. J. N. Stark, Chief Officer of S.S. *Empire Scott*
in November 1942.
[J. N. Stark]

Able Seaman Robert Thomason, S.S. *Empire Scott*. With his family outside Buckingham Palace after receiving his DSM.
[Family of Robert Thomason]

Ensign Platt, USAG, S.S. *Richard H. Alvey*, November 1942.
[Selvin Lein]

Celsas Lester, USAG, S.S. *Richard H. Alvey*, November 1942.
[Selvin Lein]

Ordinary Seaman Wally Hand, left,
S.S. *John H. B. Latrobe*, November 1942.
[Wally Hand]

Able Seaman Oree Jerome Bell,
S.S. *John H. B. Latrobe*, November 1942.
[Wally Hand]

Ronald Lavack, USAG, S.S. *Richard H. Alvey*, November 1942.
[Selvin Lein]

Dewey Lavack, USAG, S.S. *Richard H. Alvey*, November 1942.
[Selvin Lein]

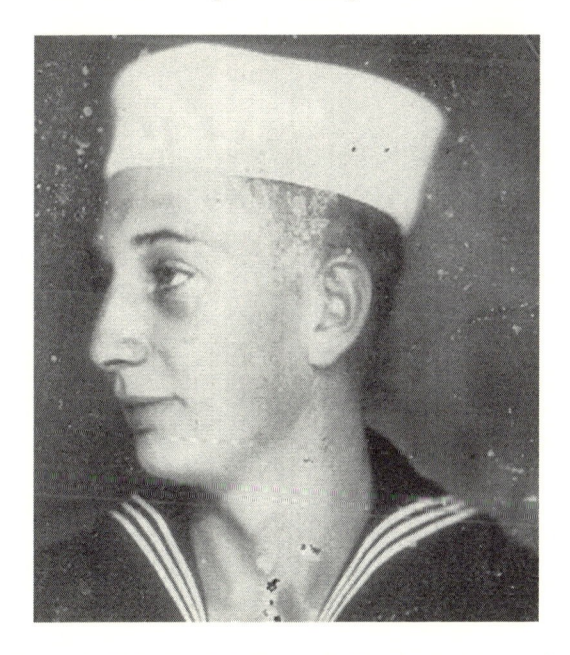

Valmar Lavack, USAG, S.S. *Richard H. Alvey*, November 1942.
[Selvin Lein]

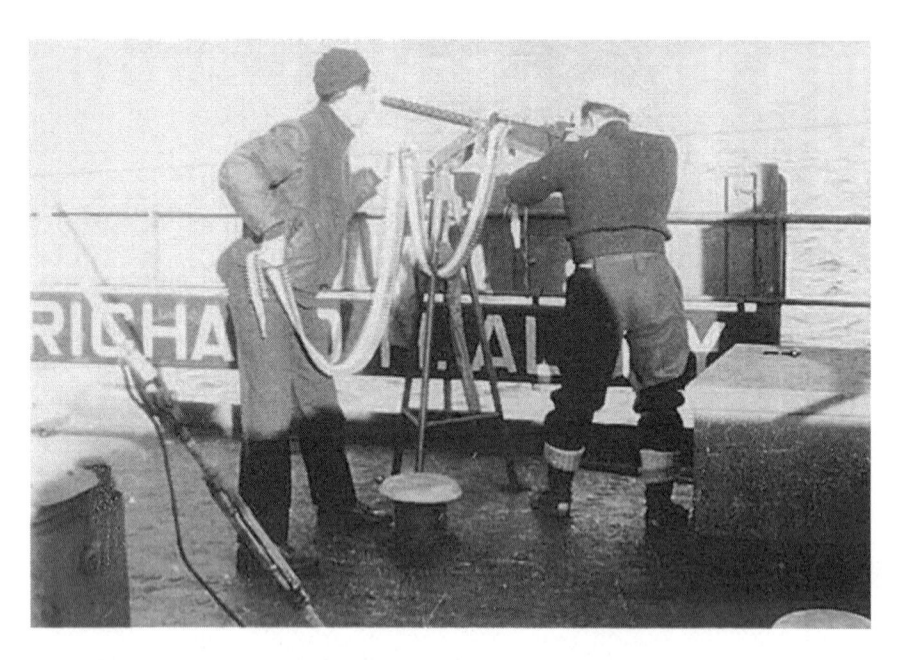

Dewey Lavack and Selvin M. Lein, USAG,
S.S. *Richard H. Alvey*, November 1942.
[Selvin Lein]

HMT *Cape Argona*, Iceland, 1942.
[Ian Fraser]

L/Tel. Ian Fraser and Tel Les Wightman,
HMT *Cape Argona*, November 1942.
[Ian Fraser]

One of two lifeboat transmitters in use from May 1940 but, it seems, not supplied to ships taking part in Operation FB. No mention of them is made by any survivor from *Chulmleigh* or *William Clark*. They had been in production for about two and a half years when FB took place.

Kapitänleutnant Dietrich von der Esche, *U-586*, right, with IWO O. L. Heinz Nagel, Norway, 1942.
[Paul Preuss]

Torpedo Mech Paul Preuss, *U-586*, 1942.
[Paul Preuss]

Kapitänleutnant Hans Benker,
commanding officer of *U-625*, November 1942.
[Horst Bredow, U-Boot-Archiv]

Kapitänleutnant Dietrich von der Esche,
commanding officer of *U-586*, November 1942.
[Horst Bredow, U-Boot-Archiv]

Chapter 3

The Loss of SS *William Clark*

OF the thirteen ships that sailed, three had been forced to return to Iceland for various reasons as we shall soon see. Two other ships had already been lost and only three men from their combined crews had survived so far. For many of the crew of *William Clark*, Lady Luck would smile on them in their hour of need.

SS *William Clark*, like all the American merchantmen on this mission, was one of Henry Kaisers Liberty ships. They were mass produced to standard designs, the first one was delivered on 30 December 1941 and by the end of the war more than 2,700 had been built. *William Clark* had been built as yard number 172 by the Oregon Shipbuilding Corporation, in February 1942. She was owned by the United States Maritime Commission and the Isthmian Steamship Company had been appointed managers. Her maiden voyage took her to Noumea, New Zealand, Australia and Chile while her second voyage was much nearer home—to Trinidad. Captain Walter Edmund Elian was in command for her third voyage and he had a crew of seventy men, which included a large complement of U.S. Navy gunners. Her merchant navy crew were unusually, all non-union men. Like all other ships bound for Russia she had a full cargo of tanks, aircraft, ammunition, trucks, tires and food for the hard pressed Russians, including a deck cargo of ten aircraft and fourteen tanks. The vessel was well armed with a 5-inch stern gun, a 3-inch dual purpose gun forward, nine 20-mm and two .50-caliber anti-aircraft guns disposed throughout the superstructure.

She left the safety of Hvalfjord on 2 November, number ten of our thirteen, sandwiched between *Empire Sky* and *Empire Scott*. The passage from Hvalfjord to the North Cape of Iceland was uneventful. One or two white lights were observed in the distance from time to time, most likely from small Icelandic fishing vessels. Soon after leaving North Cape a British Catalina aircraft buzzed them and then flew off. If it was an RAF aircraft then almost certainly it was one of 330 (Norwegian) Squadron, RAF, based at Akureyri, or one of the very long range Catalinas of No. 210 Squadron, based at Sullum Voe in the Shetlands. The Americans had their VP-94 Squadron of the U.S. Navy, based at Reykjavik and also flying Catalinas. No warships were seen at all. By the morning of the 4 November *William Clark* was in the vicinity of Jan Mayen. Later that same day *William Clark* was struck by a torpedo on the starboard side, in the engine room, all five men on duty in that area were killed instantly and the engines were wrecked. *William Clark* had been on a course north-northeast, steaming at 10 knots and not zig-zagging when at 1135 GMT she was struck without warning by a torpedo. A distress message was transmitted but no answer was received and then the captain ordered her to be abandoned. One lifeboat had been destroyed by the explosion but the remaining three were all launched successfully and were soon well clear of the stricken vessel. At precisely 1215 GMT two more torpedoes struck the vessel on the opposite side to the first one and the vessel broke in half and sank in position 7102N 1320W.

The weather was overcast, sea smooth, wind north-northeast force 3 and visibility was 4 miles. Some survivors state that they had been told by Royal Navy and U.S. Navy personnel in Reykjavik that they would be sighted at intervals of about five hours by an 'escort' and also that no enemy submarines had been in these waters for the past forty-two days! They state that they had seen nothing of any friendly forces for some seventy-two hours before the vessel was sunk.

Inadequacy of lifeboat fittings and equipment were brought to the attention of the de-briefing officer by the survivors. They stressed that the bilge pump fitted to the lifeboat was of insufficient capacity to keep it clear of water, they had to bail at very frequent intervals in order to keep the level down. Rigging and turn-buckles were of poor quality as were the lanterns. The sea anchor was incapable of holding the boat head to sea in rough weather. There was adequate food but not enough water to drink—some of the young inexperienced seamen resorted to drinking sea water and this affected them mentally and physically. They claimed that those of the survivors who were the most active survived with least obvious problems.

The *William Clark*'s hydrophone effect had been detected by the submarine at around 1000 on 4 November and at 1113 the vessel was in sight. The submarine dived at 1311 for a submerged attack and fired three bow tubes at 1333. The submarine was unable to observe the results because while trying to compensate for the loss of weight of three torpedoes, too much water ballast was used and the submarine's periscope dipped under water. *U-354* then went round the stern of the ship which was now stopped but still appeared undamaged. At 1400

Herbschleb fired the remaining bow tube from the opposite side but again without tangible results.

The reader can see from the two above reports, both official, one American, the other German, how discrepancies can easily occur.

U-354 (Kapitänleutnant Heinz Herbschleb) had observed the crew leaving and when they were safely off he sent the torpedo from his stern tube into *William Clark*, watched her break in two and sink, then left the scene at 1600 making no attempt to surface and contact the lifeboats. *U-354* was on her first war patrol and *William Clark* was her first victim.

U-354 was a standard attack type VII-C submarine. She had been built by Flensburger Schiffbau and launched on 6 January 1942. Kapitänleutnant Heinz Herbschleb commissioned her on 22 April and after her working up period in the Baltic she sailed on her first war patrol from Harstad Norway on 30 October 1942 after having made the journey to the Arctic base from Kiel earlier in the month. During her relatively long career of nearly two and a half years before she was finally caught and sunk this U-boat carried various emblems on her conning tower. Perhaps pride of place was however given to the polar bear insignia of the Arctic Flotilla. Soon after sinking *William Clark* she had one crew member washed overboard in heavy weather, he was not recovered. It is surprising just how many times this unfortunate incident occurred in U-boats. All the bridge watch wore retaining harnesses during bad weather, as protection against just such an event, but there is on record one such incident where all the bridge watch were lost overboard in bad weather and the fact was not discovered until watch changeover. *U-354* served continuously in the Arctic, making eleven patrols in all and in addition to sinking several Allied ships this U-boat took weather parties to remote Arctic islands, supplied them and recovered them on completion of their duties.

None of *William Clark*'s lookouts had seen anything suspicious before the attack. There were seven lookouts on duty, one in the crows nest, two in the bows, two on the flying bridge and two on the after gun platform but none saw any signs of the submarine or the first torpedo. With the exception of those killed in the engine room and stokehold areas by the initial explosion, all the crew abandoned ship safely. Number one lifeboat was a motor boat and initially it took the other two lifeboats in tow but due to the danger of them being swamped the towline was slipped after consultation and the captain decided to go ahead in the motor boat in an attempt to bring rescue from Iceland as quickly as possible. With a wave of farewell the motor boat set off on her mercy mission. His boat and all her occupants were never seen again.

According to an American report, Jan Mayen was at this time garrisoned by a small weather party. The USCG also began fitting a Loran navigation station on the island at this time. Once again it is not known if the captains of the merchant ships were made aware of this. *William Clark* was sunk to the west of Jan Mayen. It would have been a much shorter journey for the motor lifeboat but perhaps the master had decided against it because of either weather, or the possibility of missing it altogether.

Number two boat, in charge of the first mate William F. Goldsmith decided, on the strength of the briefing before sailing from Hvalfjord and the fact that a distress message had been sent, to stay in the vicinity for the time being at least. The boats drifted apart and it was only after three days and two nights of extreme hardship from the unrelenting Arctic weather that rescue came for number two lifeboat.

HMT *St. Elstan*, a former Hull fishing trawler, called to arms on the outbreak of war, was one of the trawlers designated to patrol along the route of the independents. She had received the distress message from *William Clark* and had been searching for her survivors ever since. The trawler was under the command of Lt. Roland Roberts RNR, Peter Clothier was his No. 1 and Dennis Roberts was one of her other officers. Leading Telegraphist Norman Pickles was a member of her crew too. He had served in this vessel from August 1940 and would continue to do so until March 1944. The normal complement of three telegraphists had been supplemented by three others hastily drafted to *St. Elstan* for this operation from a cruiser lying at anchor in Iceland. *St. Elstan* had an exceptionally large crew for an antisubmarine trawler. Mr. Dennis Roberts quotes 61 but Asdic operator Mr. Herbert Rushby thinks it was nearer 70. "We carried at least four of everyone, four Asdic ratings, four coders, four signalers, four telegraphists," he says. Unfortunately though, on this particular voyage there was no sick bay attendant. This figure did not include the extra telegraphists seconded from the cruiser for this special trip. These extra telegraphists allowed the trawler to keep a continuous watch on the merchant navy distress frequency of 500 kc/s as well as on the naval H/F W/T frequency.

The trawler was well acquainted with these waters in peace and in war. She had been in the Norwegian Campaign in 1940, then on Atlantic convoy duties with HX-121 from Halifax to the United Kingdom and then with UR-11 to Reykjavik, returning with RU-11, followed by a journey to Russia with PQ-16, returning with QP-13 when she then returned to the Humber for a re-fit, going to Grimsby instead of her home port of Hull, she was accompanied by another of QP-13's escort, HMT *Lady Madeleine*. *St. Elstan* was placed in the very capable hands of E. Bacon and Company, local trawler owners and ship repairers while *Lady Madeleine*'s contract was handled by the yard of J. S. Doig and Company. The six week overhaul in Grimsby was welcomed by three local men among the crew of *St. Elstan*, Sub. Lt. Dennis Roberts, Chief Engineman Len Hack and Asdic hand Herbert Rushby. The vessel and her crew resumed their duties and as we have already seen, November 1942 found her as one of the rescue trawlers for Operation FB.

The telegraphists of *St. Elstan* had received the distress call from *William Clark* and knew she was astern of their own position. The vessel was turned round and steamed at full speed towards the given position. She searched for several days before Able Seaman Anstey, a Newfoundlander who was on look-out aft and like so many of his fellow countrymen he was endowed with exceptional eyesight, sighted the flare sent up by the lifeboat astern of the trawler. There was initially a little confusion over the bearing but this was soon rectified and the trawler steamed off at full speed on the correct course and soon found the Chief Mates boat. The approach of the trawler was such that she was almost alongside the lifeboat before most of the occupants realized it. The joy on their faces was reward enough for all the days and nights of searching by the crew of *St. Elstan*. The lifeboat was some twenty miles from the given position during the day of 7 November, quickly taking the twenty-six men on board, she was under orders to continue her patrol until all the independents were clear of her area and it was not until 14 November that she was able to land the men at Reykjavik. Most of the survivors were in remarkably good physical condition considering their situation, but the Chief Cook, 39-year-old Manuel Alvarez was a big man and he had lost his boots while abandoning ship. His feet were frostbitten and the crew of *St. Elstan* had to assist him from the lifeboat. Norman Pickles, one of *St. Elstan*'s telegraphists recalls, "Many of the American survivors from *William Clark* volunteered as extra look-outs while others helped in the galley and on the messdeck too."

The full story of the ordeal was then told in an affidavit sworn by the Chief Mate of *William Clark* at the American Legation in Reykjavik. On the outward journey from Hvalfjord only two ships had been sighted, both small vessels carrying lights, most likely fishing vessels. After leaving the North Cape only one Catalina aircraft was seen, at about 0900 GCT on 3 November, roughly 150 miles north of North Cape. After the torpedoing the Master ordered the Chief Mate to assess the damage. The main engines had been wrecked, the engine room was completely flooded. He then reported back to the Master, helped him get his briefcase, sextant and chronometer and put them in the motor boat. No alarm bells were sounded as the electric circuits were not working.

Three boats were undamaged and were all launched successfully and soon afterwards the vessel was hit again by another torpedo. There was a huge sheet of flame and the ship broke in two and sank leaving very little wreckage at all. The Chief Mate kept a log of the lifeboats voyage and at first the weather was fine. A bright white light was seen at 2300 on the first night and a flare was fired but it brought no response. At 0300 that same night a red distress flare was seen on the same bearing. The weather turned foggy and very damp during the early morning but still remained calm. An aircraft was heard and could be seen on the horizon and another flare was sent up. The aircraft saw the flare and flew over the lifeboat, signaling 'is that all.' The aircraft was informed that two more boats were adrift and it replied, 'Your companions are about 300 miles away.' This entry is logged as 1400 hours on 5 November, only a little more than twenty-four hours after the ship had been abandoned. It is difficult to reach the conclusion that this second boat could have been either of the other two from *William Clark* when all the known factors are considered carefully, but perhaps the distance given by the aircraft was not correct. *St. Elstan*'s report (see appendix) does indicate that a Catalina aircraft reported finding two lifeboats. Unfortunately no direction is indicated in the log entry. The aircrew of this aircraft, assuming of course that it was Allied, would have reported sighting the lifeboats and no doubt have given a position too, either by radio at the time or on debriefing back at base. The information would have set in motion further rescue attempts and no doubt the rescue trawlers would be made aware of this development.

There seems to be little doubt that Catalina X/330 (Nor.) Squadron, RAF (Lt. Bjorn Tinguistad) was lost north of Iceland while searching for three lifeboats. It is also reasonably certain that these three lifeboats would be those from *William Clark*. Whether or not it was this aircraft that made contact with Mr. Goldsmith's boat at 1400 on 5 November is not known. The aircraft made its last known report at 2036 that same evening and then disappeared. The aircraft had been airborne for around fifteen hours when the last message was received.

Only one other vessel had been sunk up to this point in time, SS *Empire Gilbert*. The Allies were not yet aware of the loss and would therefore not be searching for any of her lifeboats.

Soon after this the weather began to deteriorate and the lifeboat's compass became erratic and so the sea anchor was streamed, but it would not hold the lifeboat head to sea and so it was hauled in and the sail was used instead. The weather improved during the night of the 6th and an aircraft wheel was seen floating on the surface of the sea. Mr. Goldsmith stated that seeing this wheel caused him to believe that the lifeboat was still close to the position where *William Clark* sank, though he gives no reason for this assumption. Early that evening several lights were seen on the horizon and flares were lit, but these brought no response. The weather again deteriorated and the boat shipped water, continuous bailing was necessary to keep the water level down to 12 or 14 inches. It was impossible to gain on that figure. Soon after 0900 on the 7th the lifeboat was alongside the rescue ship and within ten minutes all the survivors were safely on board. Mr. Goldsmith gives great praise to the officers and men of *St. Elstan* for all their efforts to make the survivors as comfortable as possible but he makes the slight mistake of stating that the ship was an ex-Grimsby trawler! She was a former Hull trawler but after the war she certainly landed her catch in Grimsby on several occasions.

The officers of *St. Elstan* in turn gave praise to the way Mr. Goldsmith had maintained morale and discipline among his survivors during their ordeal. Dennis Roberts, one *St. Elstan*'s officers recalls, "The 1st Assistant Engineer of *William Clark*, Joe Peck seemed much more annoyed at losing his favorite 'peter heater,' a woolly jumper knitted for him by his wife, than he did about losing his ship."

Eighteen year old Anthony Spinazzola joined the SS *William Clark* in August 1942, in New York. He had already served as an Armed Guard gunner on board SS *James Gunn* and SS *Valley Forge*. The *William Clark*'s voyage to Iceland he recalls was slow and uneventful. While at anchor in Hvalfjord he remembers being invited on board a British warship for a visit and a meal. It was a large warship, either a cruiser or battleship, but the name of the ship escapes him. The American crew were also taken to U.S. shore bases for short breaks, but they were not allowed to visit Reykjavik at all. While at anchor in Hvalfjord, regular boat drills and general quarters drill were carried out.

"My boat station was with the Chief Mate's crew while my duty station was aft on the 4.5-inch gun, 12 to 4 watch. November 4th was a

ARCTIC INTERLUDE

calm morning and we were about to sit down to chow when the torpedo hit directly amidships, right into the engine room, just below the crews mess hall on the port side. We all rushed out to the port side passageway but the outer door was jammed shut. We went over to the starboard side passageway and had to pass the engine room hatchway by this route. I remember looking down as we passed but I could see nothing but steam, fire and smoke. I did not think anyone down there could have survived that explosion.

"When we reached the deck we looked towards the bridge for some kind of orders, but seeing no one we made for our gun stations. Before I reached my station the abandon ship order had been given. I made my way to my boat station, stopping to pick up some extra warm clothing on the way. The Chief Mate's boat had been destroyed by the explosion and the other port lifeboat was hanging by one of its falls. We crossed to the starboard side but both these boats were already full so we went back to the port side.

"The Chief Mate organized us into getting this boat into the water. The greatest danger was from the water being continuously washed in and out of the hole in the ship's side made by the torpedo. We managed to get the boat launched and to heave on the line fastened to its stern. This kept us clear of the yawning hole. We had to row with all our might when we cast off, but we made it clear of the ship. All three boats came together and the Master said he was going to use his motor to try and reach Iceland to get help for us all.

"The 2nd Mate hoisted his sail and also left. Mr. Goldsmith, however, decided to wait near the scene to see if rescue came. We did not see the submarine at all. The weather got worse and I do not know how we managed to stay afloat. Morale slumped rapidly as the weather deteriorated. We had seen a Catalina while we were in the boat but there was still no sign of rescue. I remember being suddenly engulfed by a bright ray of light which frequently disappeared below the wave tops. We did not know then if it was a rescue ship or a submarine. Fortunately it turned out to be HMS *St. Elstan* and the Captain was warning us to keep clear of the propeller.

"Soon we were all on board the rescue ship and all her crew did everything they could to make us comfortable. Some of us had frozen feet and hands. I cannot remember how long we were on board, but we searched for other survivors, unsuccessfully. When we reached Reykjavik we said our farewells to the rescue ship crew and were taken by ambulance to the Quonset hut hospital. I was there for a month before being taken back to the States on board the USS *Polaris*. I was sent to Brooklyn Naval Hospital for two months until my frozen feet got better and then I returned to sea until the war ended.

"I spent all my remaining sea-time in warmer climates!"

He went on to say "I can relate to some of the faces of the trawler crew, the Captain and another officer along with a couple of the crew. What a shame, someone saves your life and you take it for granted. So much was going on at the time that I am ashamed to say I did not get any addresses."

Anthony Spinazzola was one of several men praised by the Chief Mate, Mr. Goldsmith, in his official report, for the good work he put in and for the excellent example he set while abandoning ship and in the lifeboat.

Frank Priore was another of *William Clark*'s Armed Guard gunners, also joining her in August 1942 in Brooklyn. He remembers the Armed Guard Commander of *William Clark*, Lt. John Daniel Harris of New Philadelphia, Ohio.

> He was a small man, like me, only about 5 feet 6 inches, but a good officer. He kept himself to himself and quite aloof from his men. While we were at anchor in Iceland we had numerous lifeboat drills. I must say I enjoyed getting into the boat, rowing, setting our red sail and having boat races. Our Number 4 boat always shaped up very well. It was in charge of the bo'sun, an old Swede named Lindbloom. We were fitted with extra guns in Iceland by the USS *John Melville*, an old destroyer tender dating back to World War I.
>
> We were told of the impending voyage and that escort ships would be nearby but we would not see them. We worked four hours on and four hours off, rubber suits to be worn at all times and no showers. I was awakened to go to the mess hall for lunch before going on watch. I was having vermicelli soup (my second helping) when I asked the cook the time. As he answered 1137 the torpedo struck amidships port side. All was dark and smelly until I got out on deck and headed for my station on the 3-inch bow gun. I looked towards the boat deck and recognized the Captain and others who were already busy launching their boat. Most people seemed to be heading for the boat deck and so I joined them after going back to my quarters for my sheepskin coat. I passed the engine room hatch on the way. I shouted down but no one answered. I made my way to my boat, Number 3 but Lt. Harris ordered me to go to Num-

ber 2 and help to get it into the water. Walter Butterick and I were on one fall but we managed to get it into the water. We all had one hell of a job to keep the boat from being drawn into the torpedo hole. When the second torpedo struck we had cleared the ship but wreckage rained down all around us, fortunately without doing any injury or damage.

Frank is sure the U-boat surfaced and went to the Captain's boat.

We set our sail and hoisted a lighted oil lamp to the masthead. The weather got worse and we had to bail constantly. What a wonderful sight it was to see that beautiful trawler HMS *St. Elstan* bearing down on us. For about a week we searched for more survivors but one upturned boat was all we found.

The mention of seeing this lifeboat must pose the question—was it possibly one of the lifeboats from *Empire Gilbert*, sunk quite close to this position only about thirty-six hours earlier?

To this day when in conversation pertaining to war, its causes and men, I always tell of the courage and daring of British seamen stuffed into fishing trawlers with very little means compared to our own standards. HMS *St. Elstan* was fitted with out-dated guns and depth charges that when dropped, was like a good kick in the pants. I was fortunate and soon after reaching Reykjavik I went back to the States on USS *John Melville* and after a spot of leave I went back to sea.

St. Elstan made one more run to the Arctic and back in convoys JW-52 and RA-53 before being sent to warmer climes on the UK–Azores–Gibraltar run. She took part in the Normandy Invasion and then spent the rest of the war escorting convoys to and from Iceland and the United Kingdom. Official records show that while escorting convoy RU-124 from Reykjavik to the United Kingdom in June 1944 she attacked an Asdic contact on the 22nd, without any obvious results. The U-boat assessment committee, after examining the subsequent report and Asdic trace declared that the attack had been on a shoal of fish! The CO of *St. Elstan* was most adamant that this was not so! The armed trawler *Brimnes* had been with *St. Elstan*, the weather was not good, visibility was poor with thick fog patches. Only four depth charges had been dropped.

Dennis Roberts, Herbert Rushby and Norman Pickles all agree that HMT *St. Elstan* was always being 'volunteered' for extra patrols, etc., should a sister trawler develop engine trouble or other problems. Whether this was due to their CO or the fact that Chief Engineman Len *Hack* kept the engines in tip top condition is a debatable point.

Two days before *St. Elstan* reached Reykjavik, with her survivors, another ex-Hull trawler, now HMT *Cape Palliser*, landed fifteen survivors from *William Clark* at Akureyri on Iceland's north coast, the nearest port with a hospital. All the men were suffering to various degrees from exposure and frostbite, despite the fact that they were all wearing their rubber survival suits. The crew of *Cape Palliser* had the sad task of landing the bodies of two survivors they had rescued but who had succumbed to the ordeal they had suffered before the boat was found by the trawler. The remaining survivors did not have the strength to cast the bodies of their shipmates into the sea and the commander of the trawler wished to give them a decent burial ashore.

The 495-ton, 169-foot *Cape Palliser* was no stranger to these northern latitudes. She was built by Cochranes of Selby in 1936 for Hudson Brothers of Hull. She had fished all these northern grounds before being called to arms. She had escorted convoys in the English Channel during the summer of 1940 and on 9 August she suffered casualties among her 4-inch gun crew from bomb splinters. Aircraft had attacked the convoy and two merchantmen had been hit. *Cape Palliser* was on her way to assist when she herself was narrowly missed by a high explosive, contact fused bomb. She had seen service with the Russian convoys, being part of the escort to PQ-15 when she rescued the Convoy Commodore Captain H. J. Archer, OBE, and his Yeoman of Signals A. R. Marriott, DSM, from the SS *Botavon* when the ship sank after being attacked.

Another officially recorded incident in her later wartime career while serving in the Gibraltar area was that on 19 June 1944 she, together with HMS *Aubretia* detected and attacked a submerged target at 300 feet depth. The total depth of water was 500 fathoms. Once again the U-boat assessment committee came to the conclusion that it was a shoal of fish, a decision with which the CO of *Cape Palliser* strongly disapproved. After the war she was returned to her former owners and once again sought cod and haddock in these wind swept Arctic wastes until she was scrapped in 1963.

St. Elstan was quite familiar with these Arctic wastes. She fished these waters in peacetime. She had been built in 1937 for the Hull trawling company of Thomas Hamling and she served them well until she was called to arms in 1939. She survived the war with a very distinguished record and was returned to her owners when peace came in 1945. She continued to serve her original owners until scrapped in 1966. But we must get back to our main story.

The third lifeboat from *William Clark* had been in charge of Mr. John Anderson, the second mate and carried seventeen survivors. *Cape Palliser* was among the line of rescue ships stretched across the top of the world and she too had received the distress call and was searching for survivors. Her commander and crew had no real hope of finding anyone alive after the lengthy time they had searched. The survivors in number three lifeboat had endured almost eight days and nights of extreme hardship. All were suffering from exposure and frostbite to varying degrees even though they all had rubber survival suits, similar to those worn by sub-aqua divers of today, and they were resigned to what they considered their inevitable fate of dying one by one in these vast Arctic wastes.

On the morning of the eighth day only hours before rescue came, the second mate, 33-year-old Mr. John Anderson, was found to have succumbed to the terrible conditions he had endured both physically and mentally since having to take to the lifeboat. No one could have tried harder to keep up morale and self discipline among the men in his charge. It was also found that Seaman 2nd Class William Elmus Thomas had died during that night, too. Utilityman Mr. Francisco Domingo had slipped into a coma and was very close to death. The remaining fifteen men could not summon enough strength to commit the bodies of their shipmates and when the keen lookouts on HMT *Cape Palliser* sighted the lifeboat and went alongside, her crew had to jump into the lifeboat and assist to make it fast and to get everyone safely on board. The bodies were recovered too. *Cape Palliser* certainly did not carry a doctor and probably not even a sick berth attendant but all the survivors were made as comfortable as possible and given what limited medical attention was available, while the trawler steamed hard for Akureyri, the nearest town with a hospital.

All the survivors were hospitalized on Iceland's north coast and most had to have amputations. The majority lost only fingers or toes but two men each lost both legs due to gangrene after frostbite. Such was the price that politicians placed upon trying to placate the Russian dictator and such was the price the Allied merchant seamen and gunners paid in full. The men of SS *William Clark* who had died were buried with full military honors by the crew of HMT *Cape Palliser*.

The author tried to obtain a photograph of the American graves at Akureyri, from several friends in Iceland but it appears that the bodies were re-interred after the war. No trace of them could be found by the cemetery supervisor. This again is strange because two of the men who died were American merchant seamen and until a few years ago men of the U.S. mercantile marine were not even recognized as veterans by the U.S. Government. This leads one to believe that any re-interment must have been a private arrangement.

In 1943 another Liberty ship was given the name *William S. Clark* when she was launched. She was luckier than her predecessor and survived the war.

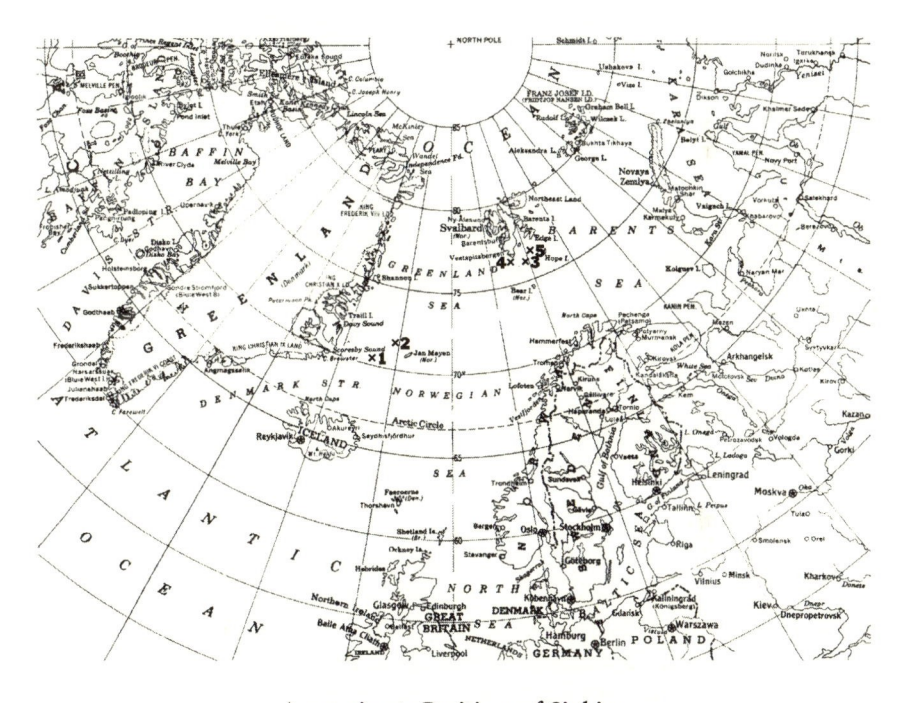

Approximate Positions of Sinkings
1 = *Empire Gilbert*; 2 = *William Clark*; 3 = *Empire Sky*; 4 = *Chulmleigh*; 5 = *Dekabrist*

Anthony Spinazzola, USAG, S.S. *William Clark*, November 1942.
Rescued by HMT *St. Elstan*.
[Anthony Spinazzola]

Frank Priore, USAG, S.S. *William Clark*, November 1942.
Rescued by HMT *St. Elstan*.
[Frank Priore]

Sub-Lt. Dennis Roberts of HMT *St. Elstan*, November 1942.
[Dennis Roberts]

L/Tel. Norman Pickles of HMT *St. Elstan*, November 1942.
[Norman Pickles]

Some of the crew of HMT *St. Elstan*, November 1942. L/Tel. Norman Pickles with the pipe. Depth charge racks in the background.
[Norman Pickles]

The hospital at Akureyri where the survivors of *William Clark* were treated (pre-war photograph).
[Jön Hjaltason]

Kapitänleutnant Heinz Herbschleb,
commanding officer of *U-354*,
November 1942.
[Horst Bredow, U-Boot-Archiv]

Chapter 4

Ordeal and Rescue

THE Russians do not agree that only thirteen ships sailed independently for North Russia in this period. They claim that forty vessels made the attempt, twenty-five of them Russian ships. Ten were lost they say, six Allied and four USSR vessels but the names of the other three Russian ships and the one extra Allied vessel are certainly not listed in the official record of Allied losses for this period. British records are uncertain; one states for instance that during the last quarter of 1942, thirty-seven independent sailings to North Russia were made and twenty-eight ships arrived safely. One thing is, however, certain—one Russian ship did make the attempt and she was caught by German aircraft and sunk. We have to go to German and Russian records to see what happened to the few survivors.

SS *Dekabrist* of Odessa, was built in England by Vickers and Maxim Ltd. at Barrow in Furness during 1903. She was a twin screw vessel of 7,363 grt and was originally named *Anadyr*. Before coming under the Hammer and Sickle she had already been sold by her first owners and re-named *Franche Conte*. Her Russian owners at this period are shown in Lloyds as 'Government, Black and Azov Steamship Company.' November 1942, however, found her bound for her homeland under the command of Captain Beliaev. *Dekabrist* had already made one voyage to North Russia in convoy PQ-6. The convoy had almost reached its destination when on 20 December 1941 six bombs were dropped close to the ship. Two actually hit *Dekabrist* but failed to explode. There was only minor damage and no casualties. She returned to the UK in convoy QP-5.

On this occasion however, she had loaded her cargo in the United States and sailed in convoy to Iceland, originally intended to be part of convoy PQ-19. The lone merchantman was found on 4 November by Junkers Ju 88s of I/KG 30 from Norway and she was attacked several times with bombs and torpedoes, all failing to do any damage to the ship. Aircraft of II/KG 30 also attacked the ship with bombs and machine gun fire. They were driven off yet again by the gunners of *Dekabrist*. One of the attacking aircraft, a Ju 88, number 4D+BM, suffered engine failure on the return flight. Whether this was due to damage or not is not known. The aircraft sent out a distress signal which was picked up by a weather reconnaissance aircraft. This aircraft found the crippled bomber and escorted it to Bear Island where it made a crash landing. All the crew survived unhurt. The weather aircraft reported the incident and next day a Dornier Do 24 air sea rescue flying boat from Tromsoe rescued them all safely, some twelve hours after they had crashed.

Although the rescue was undoubtedly spectacular it was not the first time that anyone had been rescued from that barren island. Almost eleven years to the day, back in 1931, the 19-month-old Grimsby trawler *Howe* had run ashore on the island during a storm. Her fifteen man crew were rescued by men from other trawlers who had landed on the lee side of the island, trekked across to the cliffs overlooking the stranded *Howe* and set about bringing the men off the stricken ship. They had brought equipment with them and set up a breeches buoy. After superhuman efforts they succeeded in bringing all the crew safely ashore and then trekked back to their boats on the other side of the island, finally taking the men off to the trawlers nearby. Several of *Howe*'s crew were suffering from exposure and had to be assisted on the trek.

Soon after the crash landing and timely rescue of the aircrew, their group of the Luftwaffe was sent to the Mediterranean and all this crew were killed in action. The names of the aircrew are not therefore known, but the wreckage of the aircraft is still on Bear Island to this day. We have however digressed from our main story.

The radio operator of *Dekabrist* received a signal from a British ship some 120 miles ahead of them, stating that they had been attacked by aircraft. Only two ships were supposed to be ahead of *Dekabrist*, the American *Richard H. Alvey* and the British *Empire Galliard*, the first two ships to sail. All the other ships should have been astern of *Dekabrist* at this time. That same night, just after midnight, the ship was again attacked, this time by three aircraft, soon followed by five more. Once again bombs and torpedoes were dropped but once again the *Dekabrist* avoided them all until the final aircraft made its attack when one well aimed torpedo struck the vessel in the bows. The Russian crew struggled all day to keep the water at bay, expecting more attacks to come but no other aircraft found them.

By ten o'clock that evening it was obvious to Captain Beliaev that the water was gaining on them at an ever increasing rate. He was forced to admit that the vessel would sink and so he ordered her to be abandoned. She was well down by the head and the foredeck was awash. A final distress message was transmitted 'soon after midnight,' the position given as 7530N 2710E. This distress signal must have been received by the Russians at least because they notified the U.S. and British authorities that *Dekabrist* had been sunk in an air attack. It is also possible that this distress message was the one referred to by Lt. Raikes of *Tuna* as 'SOS followed by mumbo jumbo.' The SOS signal itself was international, but the following text could well have been in Russian.

All four lifeboats were launched safely and there had been plenty of time to stock them with all available food and gear. When all four boats were safely in the water the captain ordered them all to stand off the vessel but to remain in the vicinity, in the hope that rescue would come to them from one of the four rescue submarines. The western trawlers were much further to the south and west, *Dekabrist* being to the east of Spitzbergen when attacked.

The Russian submarine *S-101* received the distress call from the merchantman and made best possible speed to the indicated position. On arrival however there was no sign of the vessel or her lifeboats. *S-101* made a wide search but failed to discover any survivors. Unfortunately, no time scale is indicated in the report and it is therefore difficult to be more precise.

Soon after dawn the crew of *Dekabrist* witnessed the death throes of their ship as another flight of German aircraft found her and sent her to the bottom. The following year the Americans handed over one of their Liberty ships, SS *E. H. Harriman* to their Russian Allies who immediately changed her name to *Dekabrist*. She served them well until in 1972 she was scrapped but they soon built another vessel and gave her the same name too! *Dekabrist* seems to have been a very popular name in Russian shipping circles. The Russian Navy had a submarine of that name. This class had been built in the 1930s and was very prone to diving accidents. The submarine *Dekabrist* was lost in November 1940 while on exercise, most likely as a result of sudden and uncontrollable flooding of a negative buoyancy tank while submerged at depth. This was a known faulty feature of this class.

A thick blanket of fog developed and the four lifeboats soon lost sight of each other. A few hours later the fog lifted and the survivors in the Captain's boat saw land and a hut too. There were people running along the beach waving frantically. One of the other lifeboats came into view too and they closed each other. This boat was under the command of Treticyn (sic) and they confirmed the sight of human habitation. Treticyn's boat managed to land safely through the surf but

Captain Beliaev's boat could not make it through the breakers, the crew were not strong enough to prevent her broaching and so the Captain stood off, his men now totally exhausted. Treticyn had mentioned that they had seen an aeroplane a little while before sighting the Captains boat. He said the aircraft had Norwegian markings and dropped a parcel with a banner attached to it. Nothing further was seen of Treticyn or of any survivor from this boat.

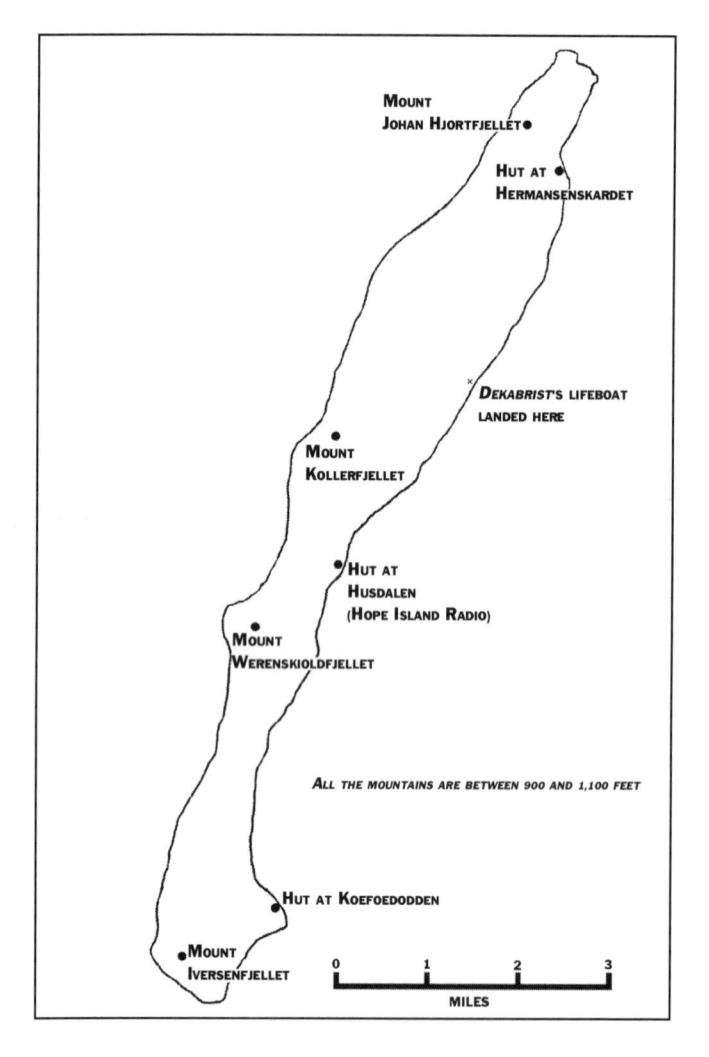

Hope Island

This land was in fact Hope Island, a tiny barren island shaped like a bent forefinger, situated to the east of Spitzbergen. It is roughly ten miles long and with a maximum width of around one mile, with hills reaching about 1,100 feet, just east of 25 degrees east and a little north of 76 degrees north. Before the war the only human visitors to this barren island were Norwegian seal hunters. They had over the years, built a few wooden huts to use as shelter during the hunting season, and these they had stocked with fuel and provisions and had fitted cast iron stoves for heating and cooking purposes. Quite often during the peak of winter, the island was totally surrounded by sea ice. There was usually an abundant supply of driftwood to be found along the shoreline. The sea always took its share of any timber deck cargoes bound from northern Russia to Europe and the New World.

The Master's boat drifted further north with the wind and weather for another four days before the weather changed and they began to drift south again, between Edgoya and King Karl's Land. The crew were in a very bad way and unable to assist themselves. On 14 November they spotted land but had no strength to row towards it, but a few hours later they found themselves washed up onto the beach and all nineteen survivors reached the shore before the next wave smashed the boat and drove it harder on the beach. They had no idea where they were at this point. The conditions in the boat had been very bad indeed, only 100 grams of water each a day and this had to be cut to 50 grams and finally there was only enough to wet their tongues. Food was more plentiful but they all found it very difficult to eat because of swollen tongues and severely cracked lips. They had managed to collect snow in a tarpaulin during a blizzard while in the boat and it certainly helped to quench their thirst. The ships doctor had brought the ship's cat with her into the lifeboat and more than once it was suggested that it should be killed and used as food but she strongly resisted this and the cat was reprieved after long and heated discussions. There is only further brief mention of the cat in the various records and one wonders therefore its final fate.

We know that four lifeboats left *Dekabrist* and we know that the crew numbered around eighty persons. It would be reasonable therefore to assume that approximately twenty people were in each boat. The report of Captain Beliaev and the doctor, both quote a total figure of nineteen survivors in this boat.

All the survivors had great difficulty in walking when they reached the beach. It had been a miracle that no one was drowned when the boat was smashed by the pounding surf. The sails were recovered from the lifeboat and a makeshift tent was erected by the fittest men. Others managed to collect driftwood and light a fire. Everyone then rested, including the cat! Two small parties were organized from the fittest men to search for shelter, one going south, the other north along the shoreline, leaving those incapable in the roughly made tent.

Captain Beliaev's group found a seal hunters hut to the north. From this information and by consulting the map of Hope Island we can see that the boat was washed ashore between the middle and northernmost of the three huts marked. The distance between the huts was quite substantial, at least 9 kilometers, a difficult walk for even fully equipped fit men. As the story unfolds however it will be seen that all three huts were in use at various times by these shipwrecked mariners. All the survivors save the four that were unable to walk set out for the hut. Those left behind in the makeshift tent were the radio operator, Boris Metrovanovich Scherbakov, second engineer, Fedor Gregorovich Gianovski a fireman and the doctor with her cat.

It took a long time to reach the hut as the party had to make frequent stops to rest. The hut was in very poor condition, large holes in the rotting walls, but it did contain an ancient stove minus chimney, and some bunks. The floor was covered in ice. Not long after reaching the hut the weather deteriorated to hurricane force winds and blizzard conditions and before long the hut was completely covered by snow several feet thick. The survivors made a rough chimney from wet wooden boards and this worked well until the boards dried out and caught fire! As soon as the weather moderated sufficiently they dug themselves out and everyone went back to find the tent, the three men, the doctor and the cat that had been left in it. They eventually located the tent but all the men had died from exposure and they were left where they had died. Early in 1945 these bodies were found by members of the German weather station HELHUS during their stay on the island. After the European war ended they were given a proper burial service by the Norwegians.

It was at first thought that the doctor too was dead, there was no reaction from her at all but the cat was still alive and kept close to its mistress. This made able seaman Borodin investigate further and he realized that Nicola, although close to death, was still barely alive and every effort was made to revive her. The efforts were successful and some three days after being left with her unfortunate companions, she was taken to the northern hut. Not long after this Red Navy seaman Kamenskji became very ill and died, most likely from pneumonia, he was soon followed by seaman Frolov.

The desperate survivors had one small stroke of luck when they found that some of the tinned supplies from the lifeboat had been washed up onto the beach and these were eagerly recovered. A routine was soon established, the fittest making daily forages for firewood, others melting snow and boiling water for treating the gangrene victims. The shoreline was generous to the shipwrecked mariners, they frequently found a keg of butter that had been washed up or a sack of flour, some of which was still usable, together with other valuable items of food all of which helped to sustain them throughout the long winter and spring months. The hut had contained meager supplies of flour and butter and there was an ancient shotgun but only a few cartridges. One evening when everyone had settled down for the long night, the flimsy door of the hut was suddenly pounded to pieces by a huge marauding polar bear. Captain Beliaev kept his head however and picked up the loaded shotgun, not knowing for sure whether or not it would fire correctly or explode in his face. He pointed it in the general direction of the bear and pulled the trigger hopefully. There was a tremendous explosion and the bear fell mortally wounded. The body was eventually skinned for the fur, the carcass meat was used for food and the less savory parts for baiting the fox traps. The skins of these foxes made excellent slippers but the survivors had no means of curing them and the stench was terrible. Captain Beliaev had made a wooden needle that could be used for sewing.

During one of the daily foraging trips two men, Lobanov and Borodin, found a flat bottomed boat which had been washed ashore. Captain Beliaev inspected the boat and as he was the strongest he elected to work on it to make it watertight and seaworthy. This boat had been found near the southernmost hut and this could explain why the party was split up between the huts. The distance between each hut, the overall weakness of the survivors and the ration situation would preclude any chance of daily commuting.

When this southern hut was first found and Captain Beliaev saw it he was positive that this was indeed the hut seen from his own lifeboat and also Treticyn's boat. If he was correct in this then it only compounds the mystery of what happened to the men who were seen ashore and also to those from Treticyn's boat since it too was seen to reach this shore safely, several days before the masters boat landed further north on the island.

Captain Beliaev considered the newly discovered boat was large enough for only four people. Lobanov and Borodin were both suffering from scurvy at this time. They both had all the classic symptoms, red spongy gums, bruised skin, painful limbs and listlessness. It was little wonder though in view of their enforced diet. It was a well known problem for ancient mariners. Vasco da Gama lost 100 of his 160 men from it in 1497. It was still a great problem almost three hundred years later. The cure was known but not the cause. It was eventually found to be caused by a deficiency of vitamins.

Death from scurvy can be very sudden but recovery too can take place in a few days with the correct treatment.

The others were still reasonably fit but there is no record of just how long it took for the nineteen original survivors to dwindle to only four in number. The survivors never did get a chance to test the boat because a German aircraft flew over the island, saw some of the four survivors and dropped them a parcel containing bread, butter, cigarettes, bandages, aspirin and anti-septic. A German submarine came to the island and fired a machine gun to attract attention.

> Two armed men advanced through the fog towards the hut and searched it. They then ordered the survivors into the dinghy. Lobanov was half dead. Only Captain Beliaev was kept on the submarine. It was about three months before another submarine came and rescued us.

Captain Stephan Polikarpovic Beliaev confirms the doctor's story in general, stating that Fedorov was in charge of the party that searched to the south. He also relates how the bosun found a container which he was sure contained alcohol. He opened it and drank some of the contents, dying in agony a few hours later. He states that some kegs of butter and a few other provisions were found on the beach, obviously washed ashore from some ship that had been sunk in the area. He also goes on to describe how Borodin and Lobanov found another hut on one of their daily trips. They took Captain Beliaev to see this hut which had obviously been occupied in the very recent past and still contained some supplies, including a large sack with the name of the Canadian province of Manitoba stenciled on it. The aircraft that over-flew the island first was, said the Russian Captain, carrying Norwegian markings! They later explored further and found the hut they had seen from the lifeboat, it was at that time occupied, but by whom they knew not, perhaps the enemy or perhaps shipwrecked seamen such as themselves. There was no sign of Treticyn's boat or its crew. Captain Beliaev agrees with the German version of the rescue. He returned to Russia after the war and died there in 1952. The German story of the discovery and rescue of the survivors is as follows.

On Saturday, 1 May 1943, almost six months after the Russian survivors had first set foot on Hope Island, a Heinkel He 111 (sic) seaplane from Banak in Northern Norway and flown by a Luftwaffe pilot by the name of R. Schutze, had been ordered to overfly the island just in case the Allies had put a weather station ashore during the winter. The aircrew were amazed to see the figure of a man against the white background. The German pilot cautiously flew lower on his second run and the castaway was seen beckoning the aircraft to try and make a landing. The aircraft however climbed and then sent a signal to its base reporting the incident. The reply ordered the aircraft not to attempt to land but to return to base immediately and make a full report.

The discovery caused some hard thinking in the Luftwaffe intelligence headquarters, Norway. It was decided that when the weather next permitted, further investigation must be carried out. The intelligence officers had reached the conclusion that there could be only two possible explanations for human presence on Hope Island. Either the man was indeed a member of an Allied weather party and the beckoning had been a deliberate off putting ploy, or, he was a genuine shipwrecked mariner who had somehow managed to reach the island. The Germans knew that they had sunk ships in the vicinity over the past few months but they found it very difficult to accept that a man could have survived without assistance. This must therefore lead one to the conclusion that the men seen on shore from *Dekabrist*'s lifeboat must have been shipwrecked mariners and not a German weather party. This however gives rise to another anomaly. If this hut had been occupied, presumably by shipwrecked mariners then what ship were they from? what happened to them? had they tried to reach safety in their lifeboat if not then where were they now since no bodies were in evidence. Had it been a German weather party then surely the hut would have been better equipped for survival and there would have been more evidence or the two parties would have made contact on such a small island, and of course the Germans would not have been in any doubt. Perhaps it was not even the same island!

Other aircraft were sent and one reported finding a wooden hut, most likely constructed by seal hunters before the war. The aircraft also reported seeing not one but three castaways, one of whom was almost certainly a woman. None of the survivors had made any attempt to hide from the aircraft, quite the reverse, they all seemed very pleased to have been discovered and all waved excitedly. The aircraft dropped supplies of food, clothing and cigarettes and this caused even more delight among the trio. When the aircraft returned and the crew were debriefed the German authorities decided that they had no other choice than to order a U-boat to make a landing on the island to discover exactly what was going on.

U-703 was one of only a handful of German submarines operating in the Arctic at this time. She was at sea on her eighth war patrol, having spent all her operational life with the Arctic Flotilla. Her first commander, Kapitänleutnant Heinz Biefeld had recently handed over his submarine to his former first watch keeping officer, Oberleutnant Joachim Brunner who had just successfully completed his commanders course at the U-boat school. Oberleutnant Brunner took over command on 6 July and thirteen days later the boat and her crew left Trondheim under orders to lay two automatic weather reporting buoys, one to the west of Bear Island, the other North of Murmansk. The first was laid without problems on 24 July and on that same day *U-703* received a signal from Flag Officer Submarines, Norway. The signal was lengthy and ordered Brunner to take *U-703* to Hope Island, make a thorough search, take off the survivors if indeed they were shipwrecked mariners and to destroy the hut if it was, or had been, used as a weather station. The signal also outlined the background to the order and gave the information that the island was now completely free of sea ice.

U-703 reached the island the next day, Sunday, 25 July and first circumnavigated it at a discreet distance while several members of the crew scanned the barren snow covered rock with powerful binoculars. On this first run they found no signs of human habitation at all and Oberleutnant Brunner then decided to take a closer look. On the second run one keen eyed lookout spotted a wooden hut and a shore party was made ready while other members of the crew inflated the rubber dinghy, checked the 88-mm deck gun and made it ready for immediate action. Light machine guns were mounted on the conning tower and small arms, grenades and ammunition for the shore party was checked. The small well armed group were put into the dinghy and paddled to the shore by two seamen who would remain with the dinghy.

They approached the hut with caution, not knowing exactly what to expect, finally bursting through the door in true Hollywood fashion. The hut was empty but there were signs that it had been recently occupied but not that it had been evacuated at short notice as would have been the case by occupants who had no desire to be found. Very disappointed but somewhat relieved by the anti-climax the shore party returned and reported their findings. They were taken back on board *U-703* and Oberleutnant Brunner conned the submarine further round the island, searching each bay and inlet thoroughly as he went. They soon found a second hut and once again the shore party of four men under the command of Leutnant zur See Heinz Schlott, the second watchkeeping officer, went ashore.

Different tactics were to be employed on this assault. When the shore party were in position surrounding the tiny refuge they signaled the submarine and a warning shot from the 88-mm deck gun on the U-boat was fired. This brought forth a solitary figure, hands crossed behind his head in token of surrender. The shore party advanced stealthily and eventually found that no one else was inside the hut to pose a threat.

Inside the shelter they found an old revolver, ammunition, a few meager rations, old newspapers and skins. They discovered the man was Russian, he could not speak any German and he smelled astonishingly foul. He could however, speak a few words of English and the Germans discovered he was Captain Beliaev of the SS *Dekabrist*. They discovered that his ship had been bombed and sunk as related earlier and the Russian Captain also managed to tell the shore party that there were three other survivors in other huts on the island. No one could discover just why the survivors were not in one group as would have seemed a more natural arrangement in the circumstances.

Captain Beliaev said he would be more than pleased to guide the German submariners to the other huts. He was then taken back to *U-703* where he was encouraged to take a good wash in the engine room, there being no bathroom on the submarine. While he was performing this essential task, Leutnant Schlott was making his report to his commander. Smelling much sweeter Captain Beliaev then showed Oberleutnant Brunner on the U-boat's chart just where he thought the other huts were situated. *U-703* set off, under the guidance of the Russian captain. The first hut was found easily but it was empty when investigated, though once again it showed definite signs of having been occupied quite recently. The shore party was again recovered and *U-703* set off for the next position. It is of interest to note that Captain Beliaev had kept a calendar during his enforced stay on Hope Island and when rescued he found that he was only three days adrift in his calculations.

HM Submarine *Tuna*.
[Royal Navy Submarine Museum]

Lt. R. P. Raikes, RN, commanding officer of HM Submarine *Tuna*,
on the conning tower.
[Royal Navy Submarine Museum]

Lt. R. P. Raikes, RN,
commanding officer, HM Submarine *Tuna*, November 1942.
[R. P. Raikes]

Oberleutnant Joachim Brunner, commanding officer of *U-703*.
Rescued *Dekabrist* survivors.
[Horst Bredow, U-Boot-Archiv]

Chapter 5

U-703 Returns to Hope Island

IN the early afternoon the third hut was sighted and a few short bursts of light machine gun fire was used to attract attention before deciding whether to put men ashore or not. The gunfire brought three people from the hut immediately. Two of them seemed quite fit but the third was obviously seriously ill or injured. Captain Beliaev used the megaphone to instruct the castaways to come out to the submarine in the small boat that could be seen on the shoreline.

The two fit survivors placed the sick man in the boat and then rowed out to *U-703* and were taken on board. Joachim Brunner and his crew were surprised to find that one of the fit survivors was a woman. The Russian captain was pressed into service as interpreter, once again using the mutual limitations of their English. Again great difficulty was experienced in trying to ask and answer even the most basic questions. The sick man appeared to be suffering from severe scurvy.

While the Russians were on board *U-703* being questioned, given food, clothing and facilities to wash, a small party from the submarines crew had gone ashore to examine the hut and is contents. When they returned they reported that the hut was indeed only a refuge. There was no sign of weather or radio equipment at all.

Oberleutnant Brunner then decided that because he still had to lay another weather buoy and because accommodation on the submarine was very limited, he would take only the Russian captain with him. His crew, in common with all other Type VII submariners had to share bunks, there were not enough to go round. When one man came off watch he hopped into the bunk of his opposite number who was just going on watch. Joachim Brunner ordered his crew to assemble a survival kit from the U-boats stores while he explained to Captain Beliaev just what he proposed to do.

When Captain Beliaev translated this to his compatriots their disappointment was obvious on their faces but they accepted the fact that they could have no part in the decision making. They accepted the decision with great fortitude. The survival kit contained medical supplies, vitamin tablets, food, clothes, diesel oil, matches, cigarettes and tools. It was taken ashore and stowed away safely in the hut while others of the submarine crew gathered firewood from the shore and brought it to the hut.

U-703 then set off to lay her second weather buoy. Captain Beliaev was accommodated in the forward torpedo room where he settled down very well. He was allowed to fraternize with the crew, (it would have been extremely difficult to do otherwise) and in turn he carried out many menial tasks without having to be asked or ordered. For the crew of *U-703* his presence made a pleasant change to an otherwise routine existence. The second weather buoy was duly laid and checked before the submarine set off towards Novaya Zembla as ordered, to re-fuel a Bv 139 seaplane that was in difficulties. Shortly after leaving the buoy *U-703* was caught on the surface by an unidentified but obviously hostile aircraft. *U-703* crash dived and depth charges followed her into the ocean depths but caused no damage when they exploded. On 30 July the tables were turned when lookouts on *U-703* sighted a Russian armed trawler and Oberleutnant Brunner dived for an attack. The trawler broke in two and sank within a few seconds of the torpedo striking. The submarine surfaced and when no survivors could be found she set off again for Narvik, arriving there without further incident on 3 August. Captain Beliaev was almost in tears as he shook hands with every member of the submarines crew before being taken away under a Navy guard.

It was during her next patrol that *U-703* once again received a lengthy signal ordering her to return to Hope Island. Aircraft had reported seeing at least two people still alive, nine months after they had first reached the island. The message indicated that the middle hut seemed to be their base and ended by ordering Brunner to bring everyone off the island.

When *U-703* arrived, the shore party found only two survivors in the hut, the woman and amazingly the man who had previously been so ill. He was now remarkably fit and healthy. He had been given the vitamin tablets left by the U-boat. It is therefore reasonable to assume that he had indeed been suffering from scurvy. Without the limited aid of Captain Beliaev as translator communication between the two groups was extremely difficult but they did manage to discover that the third survivor was still alive, living in a separate hut. It was however once again impossible to find out the reason for such an unusual arrangement.

The two Russians were brought on board the submarine, both were encouraged to wash as best they could with the limited facilities available. The U-boat's engineers rigged up a temporary shower using the hot sea water from the diesel cooling jacket. The woman was afforded reasonable privacy by being allowed to use the engine room for this purpose while married Petty Officers were stationed at the fore and aft entrances. *U-703* then made her way to the more remote second hut. The weather deteriorated during this journey, the sea was quite choppy when they arrived off shore. The lone Russian came out of the hut crawling on his hands and knees to meet the German shore party. He was obviously suffering from some serious illness. *U-703* did not carry a doctor. The German version of this part of the rescue is somewhat different.

The shore party from *U-703* went to this hut and found the man close to death in a bunk. They lit a fire, brought him close to it and then signaled the submarine by semaphore asking for advice. The reply received was short and to the point—sort it out for yourself. The shore party melted snow for their patient, gave him what little food they had and when he had improved sufficiently for an attempt to be made they took him to the dinghy. The man was placed in the rubber dinghy by the four Germans and they set off to paddle back to the submarine some little way off shore. They soon ran into difficulties and found they could make no headway against the surf. Oberleutnant Brunner could see their plight and quickly brought the submarine closer. He then managed to float a line to the almost exhausted dinghy crew. They retrieved the line, made it secure and *U-703* went slowly astern pulling the dinghy and its occupants through the turbulence and alongside. The four Germans in the dinghy had been forced to bail continuously throughout this operation in order to keep the frail craft from being swamped. The effort was successful and all five men were brought on board the submarine and quickly taken below while the dinghy was deflated and stowed back into its container on deck.

The five exhausted men were stripped, rubbed down and given dry clothes. Despite this the Russian lapsed into a coma and died a few hours later. Tests for confirming death as recommended by the medical book on board were carried out. All proved positive and the unfortunate man was buried at sea with a formal ceremony. The two remaining Russian survivors, after having had a good wash and fitted out with clean clothes, were now almost unrecognizable, even to themselves and two days later, on 9 October 1943, almost eleven months after first being marooned, they were put ashore at Harstad after expressing their heartfelt gratitude to the German crew.

Almost one year later, *U-703*, still under the command of Joachim Brunner was lost with all hands while on another mission to lay weather buoys. On this occasion one was to be laid off Seydisfjord, on the east coast of Iceland and the second in the Barents Sea. The submarine disappeared without trace but from post war examination of her operational orders and comparing these with the known position of a British minefield off Seydisfjord, there seems to be little doubt that this is where she met her fate.

The orders called for her to take a route which would have meant the submarine crossing the minefield twice while carrying out these orders. She did not report the success of laying this buoy as would have been normal procedure. There is always the possibility of an accident while laying the buoy but this seems highly unlikely. The laying of a weather buoy necessitated the U-boat being made deliberately bow heavy in order to bring the forward torpedo hatch almost into the water. Before this was done however basic precautions would have been carried out. Watertight doors would have been closed, a signal would have been prepared for immediate transmission should any accident occur. All the crew would be at action stations because through-out this operation it was impossible to crash dive the boat. The torpedo hatch would have then been opened and the twelve foot long weather buoy carefully brought up through it, avoiding damage to the buoy, its aerial and its mooring fixtures. Once the buoy was safely in position the hatch would be closed and the submarine brought to an even keel again. No signal was received by U-boat headquarters and no Allied aircraft or ship reported an attack on a U-boat in the area at the time. King Neptune is the only one who knows exactly what happened on that day.

We have, chronologically speaking, jumped ahead of our story about the thirteen independents and we must now return to November 1942 to continue.

Chapter 6

Operation Gearbox

SPITZBERGEN (Svalbard) is a group of islands in the Arctic wastes. The coordinates of 80 degrees north and 20 degrees east straddle the group. There are 122 days of full 24-hour daylight, 115 nights of twenty-four hours when the sun never rises above the horizon, while the remaining 129 days are something between these two extremes. The only natural wildlife are polar bear, Arctic fox, reindeer, elder duck and other migratory birds.

These remote islands at first attracted little attention from either side during the war but when Russia was invaded in June 1941 they took on a more significant role and subsequently received much more attention by both sides.

The small 1,392 ton Norwegian collier *Dagney I* (Captain Olaf Torkelsen) for instance was loading coal in Advent Bay in May 1941 when HMS *Nigeria* and the Polish destroyer *Garland* arrived. The vessel loaded 2,043 tons of coal and was about to sail for Norway. She was ordered to sail for the United Kingdom. She was found by a British aircraft carrier on 31 July and ordered to Thorshaven. HMT *Wastewater* was given the task of escorting her from the Faroes to the Shetlands but German aircraft found the small convoy on 9 August and sank the merchantman.

In September 1941 a British/Canadian force under Admiral Vian evacuated the Norwegian and Russian coal miners and their families, then partially destroyed the coal installations at Longyearbyen and Barentsberg. The mines were left intact. Up to that time the Germans were not unduly worried about the situation there. They received regular weather reports and coal supplies for north Norway from Spitzbergen.

Spitzbergen is a rugged, mountainous and desolate landscape with a few stretches of coastal plain. The mountains are usually white capped throughout the year and there are many glaciers. The whole territory is snowbound in winter and the sea in the many bays is frozen. The western coast is warmed by the Gulf Stream and is free of ice in the summer. Coal mining has been carried out there since the turn of the century. The quality of the coal by British standards is poor, and it was and still is uneconomic to mine it. In 1920 a treaty was signed giving sovereignty to Norway but gave other countries the right to seek minerals there; only two countries did so, Norway and Russia.

In September 1941, the Germans were still confident that the war with Russia would soon be successfully concluded. They were not worried at all by the present scale of Allied (mainly British at this stage) supplies reaching Russia by the northern route.

In London, however, the Norwegians were reacting differently and by the winter of 1941-42 they and the Admiralty became convinced that to leave Spitzbergen unoccupied was to invite German exploitation. If the Germans decided to occupy Spitzbergen then it could prejudice Norwegian sovereignty, too.

In May 1942, a small party of Norwegians set out from Akureyri, Iceland, with two ships, the 437 gross ton icebreaker *Isbjorn* (Captain Ingvald Svensen), and the 166 ton motor sealer *Selis*, to establish a Norwegian base on Spitzbergen. The expedition was under the command of Lt. Col. Elnar Svedrup, the previous director of Longyearbyen. He was killed in the air attack on the two ships.

This second operation was code named FRITHAM. Three British officers, each with polar experience, were attached to the Norwegian party. They were Lt. Col. Wharman, Lt. Col. Godfrey and Cdr. Alexander Glen. Unfortunately, both the ships were sunk by Luftwaffe aircraft at about 2030 GMT on 13 May 1942 before all the supplies could be unloaded. The two ships had left Greenock on 30 April loaded with supplies and carrying ninety-two men to be put ashore under the command of Captain Helgid. The survivors of the two Norwegian ships established themselves ashore and managed to communicate their plight to a Catalina of 210 Squadron, RAF, sent to find out what had happened. One of the survivors of *Selis* was Able Seaman gunner Nils Langbach, who would soon show his fighting ability by shooting down an aircraft that was attempting to attack them again.

The Germans had done exactly the same thing and put a weather party ashore, too, though in a different place on the main island. A series of remarkable flights by a long range Catalina of 210 Squadron, RAF, resulted in the small Norwegian party being replenished with supplies, the enemy base bombed and supremacy for the Allies.

The pre-war Barentsberg was constructed mainly of timber and was built in terraces up the steep rocky shore. Two piers had been constructed, one for coal exports and one for general cargo facilities. There was a small funicular railway from this jetty to the higher levels of the small town. A covered all-weather railway track had also been built to transport men and coal to and from the outlying mines. Facilities for the inhabitants of Barentsberg were essentially basic.

After the war ended Norway and Russia both resumed coal mining on Spitzbergen, mainly for national and political reasons. The monetary losses to both countries is quite substantial. The Norwegians maintain a population of about 1,200 miners and their families at Longyearbyen, while Russia has more than twice that number at Barentsberg where they have built a brick town with all modern amenities.

A great deal of time, money and effort was expended by both sides during World War II on the collection of Arctic and Western Atlantic weather information. The Germans were not quite so well placed to gather this information since they did not command the sea. They had, however, the advantage of air cover and proximity in relation to such places as Spitzbergen. The Germans sent out aircraft to make reports, they sent trawlers to Greenland and established bases there. U-boats, of course, made weather reports, a few were primarily concerned with this task on some patrols, while others laid weather buoys as we have already seen. One U-boat even set up an automatic weather station on the coast of Labrador which remained undiscovered until many years after the war ended. Spitzbergen was another target for weather stations by both sides and Operation GEARBOX was the code name given to one such Allied operation in July 1942. Their task was to remain throughout the black Arctic winter and make regular reports to London. The weather reports, important though they were, took on a secondary priority to the prime task of the ionosphere research installation of Lt. Col. Wharman of the Royal Corps of Signals.

HMS *Manchester* and HMS *Eclipse* landed 150 men, mostly Norwegians, together with 116 tons of supplies early in July, all without any Axis interference. The party was commanded by Captain Ernst Ullring, DSO, RNN, and included one Norwegian Surgeon, Dr. Honningstad. The party were well equipped with short wave radio, defensive anti-aircraft (AA) guns, skis, sledges and ample supplies for winter. Soon after their arrival the Norwegian AA gunner Able Seaman Nils Langback, using his 0.5-inch Colt machine gun, shot down a Junkers Ju 88 that tried to bomb the camp. The German aircrew were Maj. Genst Wibel, Lt. Heinz Wagner, Lt. G. E. Etienne and Sgt. Vobs. None of them survived the crash. Many useful maps and documents were recovered from the wreckage by the Norwegians. The aircrew were buried the next day, with full military honors.

In 1936 Dr. Erich Etienne had led an Oxford University expedition to West Greenland. Not long ago he had set up the first German weather station on Spitzbergen at Advent Bay. Four British minesweepers on passage home from North Russia were ordered to investigate but found the place deserted. The Germans re-occupied the site soon after the British warships had left. They left a four-man team under Dr. Albrecht Mall to operate the station.

The small Norwegian GEARBOX garrison were also subjected to occasional shelling by the odd U-boat that came along. Fortunately no one was wounded in any of these attacks, and the only damage suffered was one storage hut set on fire. This specific attack had been carried out by *U-435* (Kapt. Lt. Siegfried Strelow) while he was returning from an assignment to remove a small German weather party of six men (code named KNOSPE) from Signehamne to the north. They had spent almost a year there and in early August of 1942 had been attacked by a small Norwegian scouting party. The attack by *U-435* on the GEARBOX camp seems to have been in retaliation.

During their early weeks at Barentsberg small scouting parties of Norwegians had stumbled across many pieces of evidence of German presence. One such party had found an aircraft. Almost certainly it was the one shot up by a Catalina of 210 Squadron, RAF, while trying to take off. The Catalina had been on a special long-range mission to Spitzbergen and came upon the German aircraft quite by chance. Another Norwegian scouting party found a fully serviceable automatic weather station of German manufacture. Shortly after this find they found an H/F W/T station, in full working order. Another party found unnerving footprints of one man, in the snow. They searched but could find no answer to this mystery. All these incidents were in August 1942, before the onset of Operation FB.

A small forward outpost of the main GEARBOX camp, housed in camouflaged tents, was set up on 18 July, about two miles east-northeast of Cape Linnie. The small camp was situated in an excellent position to give early warning of any imminent enemy interference. It had a direct link to the main base at Barentsberg. It is not known just how long the outpost remained operational.

In September 1942, HM cruisers *Cumberland* and *Sheffield* took more stores to Barentsberg for the Norwegian garrison. The operation was code named GEARBOX I and the stores included two teams of Huskies and their handlers. For the journey north, makeshift kennels were constructed in the aircraft hanger of *Cumberland*. The two cruisers were accompanied by two destroyers and they discharged their precious cargo on 17 and 18 September. The crews of the ships could observe smoke still rising from the coal mines that had been destroyed by the Allies some twelve months earlier.

HMS *Argonaut*, a 5,500 ton *Dido* class cruiser with a top speed of 33 knots, accompanied by HM destroyers *Inglefield* and *Obdurate* resupplied the base on 19 October and also brought two American civilians with their twenty-four huskies. During November the Royal Norwegian Naval vessel *Namsos* took further supplies from Iceland and a few personnel to replace those who had fallen ill. During the time our thirteen independent merchantmen were attempting to reach North Russia, HM submarine *Tuna* and the Dutch submarine *O-15* were patrolling in the Spitzbergen area, too.

We have already seen how four of the five ships were lost, the British freighter SS *Chulmleigh* had, so far, had a charmed life on this passage. She had been built at Sunderland in 1938 by Wm. Pickersgill and Son for the Dulverston Steamship Company and placed under the management of W. J. Tatem and Company. The vessel was of 5,445 gross tons and had a distinctive cruiser stern. She was registered in London. Chulmleigh is a picturesque village in Devon, about half way between Barnstaple and Exeter, just off the A-377. The owner of the vessel lived there as a child and so it is not at all surprising to find that W. Tatem and Company had no less than five vessels carrying this name between 1900 and 1961. Whether the choice was a good one or not is open to debate because all five ships carrying this name were doomed not to die of old age. The first *Chulmleigh* was sold by the company and with a new name and owner she ran ashore and was wrecked. The second was only a year old when she was torpedoed in 1917 by *U-64*. *Chulmleigh* number three was sold by Tatem and became the *Jalarajan*, only to be torpedoed by the Japanese submarine *I-165* within a few weeks of them entering World War II. The post war *Chulmleigh* had been laid down as *Empire Northfleet* but was completed as *Chulmleigh* in 1946. She served the company until 1961 when she was sold. She ended her days in 1964, being scrapped after being driven ashore during a typhoon in Hong Kong harbor. Our story, however, concerns *Chulmleigh* number four.

The vessel was no stranger to North Russia—she had made the journey in convoy before. Two former crew members, Mr. Bill Lewis and Mr. Bill Grady remember her earlier wartime voyages. In March 1941 she had loaded at South Shields for Takoradi with aircraft in crates and after discharge she had gone to Lagos, Accra and Freetown to load with cocoa beans, palm kernels and mahogany logs for Hull where she discharged her cargo soon after the heavy blitz in May 1941. She loaded a full military cargo there for Reykjavik, where it took some six weeks to discharge in the unfriendly atmosphere prevailing. She sailed from there for New York where she loaded a full cargo for North Russia. She was under the command of Captain Priestly at this time and the chief officer was Daniel Morley Williams. The vessel had been modified slightly to suit Arctic conditions, heaters had been fitted to her domestic water tanks, insulation had been installed to help retain some heat in the well appointed accommodation. Seamen and firemen were all housed aft, there was no foc'sle in the accepted maritime meaning of the word, though it was still referred to as 'aft foc'sle.'

This type of quarters for the crew was quite revolutionary in 1935. It was looked upon with a certain amount of disapproval by the very men who would benefit most from the improved conditions. When midships accommodation for all was introduced in the Liberty type ships this caused even more consternation among the die-hard crew members. The petty officers of *Chulmleigh* (carpenter, bosun, donkeyman) had separate cabins in the poophouse. Able seamen and firemen had double berth cabins aft, too. The cooks, messroom, cabin boys and apprentices lived midships, the former (cooks) had separate cabins, the remainder double. Officer's cabins were amidships and were fitted with hand wash basins with cold water. There were bathrooms/w.c. in all this separate accommodation, too. All the fittings in the cabins and saloons were superior to comparable ships of the era; indeed, Captain Bill Lewis of Gwent who served in this vessel as an apprentice recalls that the fittings and furniture were much better than in many of his postwar vessels. The officer's dining saloon had one main table for six around which were four other tables to seat four. All this accommodation was paneled in mahogany. The ship was even fitted with a small hospital and during the war this was usually occupied by the two senior DEMS ratings.

She sailed to Russia with convoy PQ-6 and stayed in Russia all winter, returning to the United Kingdom in convoy QP-13 in the summer of 1942 with timber, goose feathers, pitch and drums of arsenic which she discharged at Surrey Commercial Docks. The passengers she had brought from Archangel also left the ship here; they were the wife and son of the Russian Ambassador to London and also several British Army officers who had been in North Russia instructing them in the use of the Matilda tank. QP-13 was the unlucky convoy that lost five of its merchantmen when it ran into the protective British minefield off Iceland's North Cape after a huge iceberg had been mistaken for Cape Horn in the bad weather prevailing. *Chulmleigh* was lucky on that occasion, but her luck would not hold. The Chief Officer of *Chulmleigh*, Mr. Daniel Morley Williams, who, as did most chief mates, held a masters ticket, took over the ship for the forthcoming voyage and a new but very experienced Chief Officer was signed on. Comparing the names of the masters of three of the British ships lost in Operation FB, brings to light a strange coincidence. Daniel Morley Williams was now master of *Chulmleigh*, William Williams was master of *Empire Gilbert* and Thomas Morley was master of *Empire Sky*.

One young crewman deserted ship before *Chulmleigh* sailed from London up the east coast of the United Kingdom. Several others had been discharged and replaced. The approximate date of sailing was 15 August 1942. She called at the Tyne to complete loading and once again a few crew members were replaced at this port. By 10 September she was in Leith and then she sailed through the notorious Pentland Firth, along the north coast of Scotland and round Cape Wrath. She continued on through the north Minch to anchor off Altbea in Loch Ewe early in October.

Up to this point in her journey she had firemen of West African and West Indian origin but for reasons not known, all were discharged here and replaced by white British firemen. All the discharged crew received a very good discharge stamp for both ability and conduct. At this point most of the crew must have guessed their most likely destination, though they would think that the journey would be in convoy, no doubt. She sailed from Loch Ewe bound for Iceland, on about 16 October and the journey would have taken between two and three days.

She sailed from Hvalfjord on 31 October 1942 at tea-time with a cargo of 5,000 tons of government stores and sacks of fleet mail for North Russia, the seventh of our thirteen merchantmen. She was quite well armed with a 4-inch anti-submarine gun on her poop, one Bofors, four Oerlikons, two twin and two single Marlin machine guns, four parachute and cable rockets, two floating air mines, all for anti-aircraft defence. Parachute and cable rockets were rather a Heath Robinson affair. The apparatus was situated on the top bridge and when fired, a rocket was propelled into the air and deployed a parachute from which was suspended wires that would hopefully tangle themselves around the attacking aircraft. The floating air mine was a similar device but had an explosive charge at the end of the wire. If the wire was picked up by the aircraft it was hoped that the mine would explode on contact. Perhaps it was fortunate that *Chulmleigh* at least did not carry a Holmann Projector. This potentially lethal device hurled a primed hand grenade into the path of an attacking aircraft, where hopefully it would explode and at least damage the aircraft without scattering fragments among the ship's crew or even drop back on deck before exploding. In addition to her merchant navy crew of forty men she carried nine Royal Navy and nine Maritime Royal Artillery gunners to man her weapons. The gunners were collectively called DEMS (Defensively Equipped Merchant Ship) gunners. All these men were under the command of the master, Captain D. M. Williams.

The vessel crossed Faxa Bay, past Snaefellsjokul ("Snowy" to Hull and Grimsby fishermen, so-called because of its permanent cap of snow all year round). After passing this majestic landmark *Chulmleigh* would steam across Breidi Bay to Stalberg Corner, all excellent fishing grounds frequented by trawlers from the Humber ports in peacetime, and turned into the Denmark Strait. She passed safely through the narrow gap between the protective British minefield and the North Cape of Iceland, crossing the Arctic circle soon after setting her log on her new course, heading for the west of Jan Mayen Island as ordered. Soon after sighting the North Cape of Iceland and setting her course, the weather clamped down and she was unable to fix her position accurately because of overcast skies, haze and frequent snowstorms. She had to rely on dead reckoning.

Chulmleigh had been routed to a position west of Jan Mayen Island where she would set an easterly course. Captain Williams estimated that he had reached this position during the morning of 3 November. Up to this time they had remained undetected by the enemy. He altered course as instructed, allowing for deviation as charted and later that day caught sight of a star and managed to obtain a bearing on it. From his subsequent calculations he then decided that the vessel was steering a course 9 degrees too far to the north and he rectified the error at once.

The new course should have taken *Chulmleigh* some 30 miles to the south of the inhospitable and dangerous South Cape of Spitzbergen. The charts for this area show that dangerous reefs run off for some ten miles from the South Cape. The surveys could not have been as detailed as those carried out in more 'civilized' waters because of the frequent use of 'ND' (not dependable) among the depth soundings given. In his official report, made months later, Captain Williams tells of how during the night of 3/4 November wireless distress messages were intercepted by his radio officers, from American ships to the south. *Hugh Williamson* and *William Clark* should have been the only two American ships to the south of *Chulmleigh*. We have already seen, however, that *John H. B. Latrobe* had anchored for some twelve hours soon after sailing. Some ships steered zig-zag courses while others steered in straight lines. Speeds differed by a couple of knots in some cases. Some ships slowed down in order to reach a given position at the time ordered. Two ships we know for sure had been ordered to wait to the west of Spitzbergen until ordered to proceed. It is more than likely therefore that the ships were no longer in their sailing order.

Since *Chulmleigh* was the next ship to sail it is quite possible that the American ship was indeed now astern of the British ship.

William Clark was not in distress until the late morning of the 4th and then by submarine attack. The messages received by *Chulmleigh* indicated attacks by aircraft. At midnight on 5 November *Chulmleigh* received a message from the Admiralty ordering her to alter to a more northerly course to reach latitude 77 degrees and to make sure that she rounded the South Cape of Spitzbergen during the hours of full darkness. Captain Williams was, understandably, rather reluctant to comply with this order, mainly because he was unsure of his exact position, and he could not rely on his compasses in these latitudes. However, he did alter course as ordered at 0500 that morning. It seems quite probable that this was a similar signal as that sent to the other ship—to wait to the west of Spitzbergen until ordered to proceed.

Five hours later they were spotted by a Blohm and Voss Bv 139 seaplane which circled them, no doubt reporting the vessel to base. The aircraft did not attack at all before flying off. Everyone on board knew that this would be the end of their so far peaceful passage. At noon Captain Williams changed course to get back on to his route and by 2300 that evening he calculated that it was now safe for him to turn eastwards and he altered course. Only half an hour later, steaming at 7 knots the vessel struck a reef. The wind was at this time from the south and only force 2 to 3 but it was snowing very hard. Examination showed that the vessel was hard aground amidships, stern almost out of the water and bows well down with the foredeck almost awash. A distress message was transmitted and was received by an Admiralty wireless station in the United Kingdom. The Admiralty sent the following signal in response, but this would of course be unknown to the crew of *Chulmleigh*.

6.11.42. from Admiralty to *Tuna* and Dutch submarine *O-15* and repeated to Operation GEARBOX—Following intercepted at 0315Z on 500 Kc/s (the International maritime wireless telegraph distress frequency) *Chulmleigh* SOS de GJGM (her peacetime unique International Call Sign), struck reef south of South Cape Spitzbergen, making water rapidly.

Examination of the patrol report for HM Submarine *Tuna* shows that she received this distress signal direct from *Chulmleigh* and she set off to render assistance.

The South Cape of Spitzbergen had already claimed several victims and more would follow in the postwar years. On 16 November 1939 the Russian steamer *Baikal* struck a reef not far from *Chulmleigh*'s stranding. *Baikal* was originally named *Roseworth*, built in November 1919 by Dunlop Bremner and Company of Port Glasgow. She was of 2,554 gross tons, 303 feet × 43 feet. Her original owners, R.S. Dalgleish, sold her to the Russians. The vessel was similar in appearance to *Chulmleigh*. She had a cruiser stern, but she was much smaller. She was a well deck ship whereas *Chulmleigh* was a flush deck vessel.

When she struck the reef she broke in two. The fore part sank but the stern, including the bridge, remained upright and with the main deck awash. She was searched by *U-435* (Kapt. Lt. Siegfried Strelow) on 17 August 1942 and some charts were recovered from her. The wreck was often used by aircraft of the Luftwaffe patrolling these waters as a navigational departure point. As can be seen she had survived the Arctic weather for almost three years as well as Luftwaffe bombs, without breaking up.

One and a half hours later Captain Williams decided it would be prudent to put the crew into the boats and lay off just in case the *Chulmleigh* broke up without warning. All the confidential books were thrown overboard in their weighted bags. Two men were thrown into the water from number one port lifeboat when the after fall was let go too soon. One man was recovered within seconds but the second man, Royal Maritime Artillery gunner Stanley Pepper drifted off. Desperate efforts were made to reach him quickly but in the few minutes that it took he succumbed to the freezing water and was already dead when the lifeboat reached him. His lifeless body was allowed to drift away into the Arctic wastes, the first casualty among the crew.

The master, Chief Officer, Mr. E. J. Fenn, OBE, Lloyds Medal, and the Second Engineering Officer, Mr. R. A. Middlemiss, remained on board the stricken ship to further assess the possibilities of refloating her. Third Officer, Mr. D. F. Clark was in charge of number two starboard lifeboat and her crew. At 0230 the captain, after his inspection, thought that there was no immediate danger of the vessel breaking up and that the crew would be more comfortable back on board. He called the boats back alongside and put this suggestion to the men but they did not seem very keen on the idea of re-boarding the grounded ship. Two firemen volunteered and together with Mr. Middlemiss, the second engineer who had remained on board, they went below and raised steam again. Efforts were made to refloat the vessel but it was a hopeless situation and so the attempt was abandoned.

The chief radio officer was then asked to come on board to transmit a signal saying that the vessel was being abandoned and this he did. By 0400 everyone was off the ship and away from the vessel but it appeared that the lifeboats were surrounded by breakers. They appeared to be in a small lagoon and it was difficult to keep the boats out of the surf. Soon after the Arctic dawn, however, a way out was found and all three lifeboats reached the open sea safely. No sooner had they done this than five German aircraft appeared from nowhere, circled the boats then flew off to make bombing runs over the stranded ship, diving to mast head height before dropping their delayed action bombs. Despite this unopposed action, most of the bombs missed, some by a very wide margin, but two were direct hits and when they exploded a huge column of thick black smoke rose high into the air but the ship did not catch fire. Four of the attacking aircraft were identified as Junkers Ju 88s while the fifth was a Heinkel He 111. After they had all completed their attacks they formed up and flew off without any further reference to the lifeboats.

There can be little doubt that these aircraft were seeking *Chulmleigh* as a direct result of the report made earlier by the Bv 139 aircraft. They would use the South Cape of Spitzbergen as a reference point to begin their systematic search, knowing by simple arithmetic that she must be within 'x' miles of the reported position. No doubt the Bv 139 would have arranged to sight the South Cape of Spitzbergen or the *Baikal* wreck on either her outward leg, the return leg, or both, in order to check her own navigation as accurately as possible.

If the sequence of events, as given in the master's official report, was as stated, then the second distress message must (unless it had been prepared earlier), have been sent in plain language and would almost certainly have been intercepted by the German listening stations, too, thus giving them all the information they needed to find *Chulmleigh* without any bother.

Ships could steam wherever they wished, they could delay or advance their progress as they or the authorities ordered but in order to reach North Russia by this route at this time of the year, they must at some stage pass between the North Cape of Norway and the South Cape of Spitzbergen. The Germans knew that it made sense for the ships to keep as far away from their airfields as possible. Once past Spitzbergen then the merchantmen had much more ocean to play with again, limited only by the land to the south and the ice barrier to the north.

The reluctance of the crew of *Chulmleigh* to return on board, although disobedient, proved justified. The vessel had already been located by the Luftwaffe and in the air over these waters they enjoyed supremacy. They would continue to hunt the lone merchantman whenever the weather permitted flying, and no doubt U-boats would be called in too in an effort to sink her.

The question must be asked however, if the alternative decision to remain on board had been taken, what would have been the outcome? Would the Germans have continued to bomb the stranded vessel or would they have mounted a rescue operation as they did for *Dekabrist* survivors? *Chulmleigh* was still hard and fast and in one piece, when the Luftwaffe photographed her in June 1943, eight months after her stranding. There are no reports of her being boarded at all by enemy forces, but *U-625* claims to have sunk her and is credited with the sinking.

HM Submarine *Tuna* had left Holy Loch and the Dutch submarine *O-15* had left Dundee on 23 October, both under orders to cover the independent merchant ships who would be sailing during the moonless period 26 October to 9 November. *Tuna* was a large submarine, 1,090 tons displacement surfaced and 1,575 tons submerged. She was 275 feet overall with a 26 foot beam and a draft of almost 15 feet. Her top speed on the surface was 15½ knots and nine knots maximum submerged. She was fitted with ten torpedo tubes and carried a crew of fifty-nine officers and men, under the command of Lt. R. P. Raikes, DSO. *O-15*, a much smaller submarine, was built at Rotterdam in 1932, 546 tons surfaced displacement, 704 submerged. She was 199 feet, carried a crew of thirty-one officers and men and her top speed on the surface was 15 knots, 5 knots submerged. *Tuna*'s area of operations for this patrol, according to the report submitted later by Lt. Raikes, covered some 25,000 square miles of sea.

Acting on intelligence information the two submarines were diverted slightly during their passage north, to patrol off Utvaer (*Tuna*) and Stadlandet (*O-15*) on the Norwegian Coast, to look for heavy German surface units thought to be on the move during 27 October. They found no indication of this and the two submarines were then ordered to their respective positions near Bear Island. *Tuna* to 74N 15E and *O-15* to 74N 05E. On 1 November, Naval Intelligence thought that *Hipper* (Captain Hartmann) and her four destroyers (Captain Schemmel), with Vice Admiral Kummetz in overall command, had just passed the Lofoten Islands heading north. This caused the Admiralty to order the merchant ships of Operation FB then at sea on 4 November, to move as far north as the ice barrier would allow. The two submarines were also ordered further north to 7620N.

On 6 November, *Tuna*, in position 7620N 1400E sighted a U-boat in the early hours of the morning. The captain of *Tuna* recalls, "My notes say that we heard an SOS on 500 kc/s at 0045 November 6th followed by a lot of mumbo jumbo. This appeared to be a spark transmitter, estimated bearing 050 degrees so turned on to that course to investigate." [Two ships transmitted distress calls soon after midnight, the SS *Chulmleigh*, a relatively new ship which would almost certainly be fitted with a valve main transmitter but probably a spark emergency set, and SS *Dekabrist* an old vessel built before wireless was carried on merchant ships. She could well have been fitted with a spark set as the main transmitter, there were certainly quite a considerable number of old ships still so fitted during the war years]. Captain Williams (of *Chulmleigh*) in his report, gives no indication of any damage to his main transmitter.

One interesting point arises from the abandoning of both *William Clark* and *Chulmleigh*, since neither were abandoned in great haste. No mention is made either officially or unofficially of any lifeboat emergency transmitters/receivers being put into the lifeboats, or used in them. One must assume from this that the ships were not so fitted. It was the specific task of the junior radio officer to place these items into the designated boat in such circumstances. Had the ships been so equipped, and knowing of the presence of rescuers, surely they would have been used and the possibility of a more fortunate outcome would have been increased. The sets were being supplied to merchant ships as early as May 1940 and they had proved their worth on many previous occasions. The range of the transmitter was between one and two hundred miles. There were two main suppliers at this stage of the war. One wireless company was manufacturing and supplying a spark transmitter while the other company made and supplied a valve set. At least one of the RN trawlers would have been within range of a lifeboat transmitter.

Assuming the rough bearing of 50 degrees, obtained by *Tuna*, was true and not relative, then the possibility that the distress call was from *Dekabrist* is very strong indeed. Lieutenant Raikes continues:

At 0154 we sighted a dark object bearing green 60 and turned towards it. I identified the object as a U-boat, the officer of the watch confirmed. At 0202 fired three torpedoes spread one-third bow, conning tower and one-third stern. The torpedoes were heard to run. Immediately after firing the target went ahead, so I swung to starboard and fired three more using 10 degree angle. U-boat noise estimated 190 degrees, range 3,500 yards and I guessed the speed as six knots. The U-boat then turned towards us and I dived. Explosions were heard 3½ to 4½ minutes after firing but hydrophone effect continued to be heard. The explosions were most likely my torpedoes hitting the sea bed. Hydrophone effect faded and at 0254 I surfaced.

It is interesting to note that *U-625* was the nearest U-boat to *Tuna* but examination of her log does not reveal any record of the incident at all. Is it possible that this was the Russian submarine *S-101*?

Lieutenant Raikes continued:

At 0300 received an SOS from *Chulmleigh*, aground on reef near the South Cape of Spitzbergen and I set course accordingly. At 0710 we sighted an upturned ship, very close, visibility was almost nil in a snowstorm. I now appeared to be in a landlocked lagoon with breakers all around me. Putting my stern to the sunken *Chulmleigh* I proceeded on a reciprocal course and edged into deeper water and waited for daylight. Visibility remained very bad until 1100 hours, at which time there was no sight of *Chulmleigh* or any boats or rafts. The navigating officer reported that the tidal set was to the westward so we proceeded up the west coast without sighting any boats or sign of life. After 1300 the visibility cleared completely so I returned to the position of *Chulmleigh* but sighted nothing at all. Remained in the area until 1720 on November 7th when I received a signal ordering us to a new position some 370 miles to the south.

In his official report, Captain Williams of SS *Chulmleigh* definitely states that the three lifeboats from his ship could not find a way out of the lagoon until after daybreak, which in November in those latitudes would be mid-morning at best.

Lieutenant Raikes is certain that the merchant ships were aware of his presence in the area. He states that his submarine could certainly have picked up a great number of survivors. The fore ends had no spare torpedoes, extra bunks had been fitted and on this trip they carried a surgeon. He puts a figure of eighty on the possible number of survivors they could have squeezed on board. *Tuna* had entered the patrol zone on Sunday, 1 November, and had then set a radio watch on 500 kc/s. She was ordered to remain about 30 miles south of the proposed merchant ship route. He also notes that at 1040 on 4 November a distress message was received from a Russian ship 300 miles to the east.

> 1230. Received an SOS from an American ship to the westward. Heavy explosions were heard all afternoon, all apparently from the northward. I decided to ignore the 30 mile orders and proceeded north. Ships of operation FB had been told to keep north of latitude 77 north in my area and I was moving north to be nearer to them and to investigate the heavy explosions. Stopped about 50 miles south of Spitzbergen. At 2210 [5 November] Asdic operator reported torpedoes running. Nothing could be seen but various alarms were raised in the next hour or so.

On 7 November *Tuna* was ordered to patrol off Soroy to try and intercept *Hipper*, should she try to attack the independents. *O-15* remained in her original position and only left the area on the 9th when her fuel was low. *Tuna* left for home the following day having seen no sign of the enemy in the prevailing bad weather. Lieutenant Raikes and his crew were unaware at this point that on their next patrol *Tuna* would be carrying the canoes and Royal Marine Commandos to the Gironde Estuary for Operation FRANKTON, better known as the 'Cockleshell Heroes.'

Tuna's torpedoes did not miss the second U-boat she met some five months later. Now under the command of Lt. Desmond S. R. Martin she was patrolling to the southeast of Jan Mayen on 7 April 1943 when she detected and sank *U-644* (ObLt. Kurt Jensen). *Tuna* survived the war and was scrapped in 1946.

Hipper and her destroyers were indeed at sea having left Altenfjord on the afternoon of 5 November. They made a wide search to the north and east, reaching 7330N 4230E late on the 6th without sighting anything. They moved further north and at 1330 on 7 November one of the destroyers found the Russian tanker *Donbass*, bound from Russia to Iceland, and sank her. Once it was known that *Hipper* and her two destroyers were at sea, the Russians attempted to recall *Donbass* by radio but either the signal was not received or the ship was intercepted before being able to comply.

The German surface forces then turned south and arrived off Soroy at about 0500 on 9 November, only about 50 miles from where *Tuna* was patrolling. The sailing of the German surface ships was obviously not by chance. The interesting question is why? Were they acting on visual sightings by the Luftwaffe, decrypted radio intelligence or from agents reports from North Russia or Iceland? Were they looking for the eastbound ships, those westbound or perhaps both?

Barentsberg, Spitzbergen.
[Norsk Polar Institute]

Barentsberg, Spitzbergen, 1940.
[Norsk Polar Institute]

Barentsberg, Spitzbergen, 1936.
[Norsk Polar Institute]

Cape Linnie, Spitzbergen, 1936.
[Norsk Polar Institute]

Cape Linnie Lighthouse, Spitzbergen, 1942.

South Cape, Spitzbergen, 1936.
[Norsk Polar Institute]

A party of British sailors going ashore at Cape Linnie, Spitzbergen, in 1941 to destroy the radio station.

The wrecked power plant at Barentsberg coal mine, 1941.

The evacuation of miners and families from Barentsberg, 1941.

The coal stocks at Barentsberg burning, 1941.

S.S. *Baikal* wreck, ashore on Spitzbergen, 1942.
[A. Busch]

HM cruiser *Cumberland*, shown here in 1947.
[Royal Navy Submarine Museum]

The wreck of S.S. *Chulmleigh*, Spitzbergen, July 1943.
Taken by a Luftwaffe aircraft.
[A. Busch]

Korvettekapitän Siegfried Strelow, commanding officer of *U-435*.
[Horst Bredow, U-Boot-Archiv]

Chapter 7

Operation Gearbox to the Rescue

CAPTAIN Williams called a conference and it was decided that all three boats should keep together and try to make Barentsberg, about 150 miles away, further north up the west coast of Spitzbergen, across the open waters of Bell Sound and on to Isafjord. This journey would have been difficult enough in a well equipped ship built for these latitudes, but to make it in an open boat without proper facilities or supplies would need all the courage and skills they could muster. There was, unfortunately, no other choice to be made. It would seem from this decision that Captain Williams was not aware just how close the friendly submarines were, otherwise surely he would have stayed in the area for a few hours to see if rescue came from that quarter before setting out on what he must have known would be an arduous journey. There is evidence, however, to indicate that the master of each merchant ship had received as part of his orders details of safe routes through minefields, and places where food and shelter should be available.

From what we know of the situation it would seem that Captain Williams wisely based his decision on the facts most likely known to him at that time. He was probably aware of the presence of friendly submarines but would not know their precise locations. He could not be certain that his two distress messages had been received since his radio officers had not received any acknowledgment. His ship had already been discovered by the enemy and no doubt they would seek to destroy her (as we know they claim to have done). If his distress signals had been received by a friendly station then almost certainly they had been received by the enemy, too. We know that the Germans were aware of the weather station at Barentsberg, they had attacked it with aircraft and submarines. There was, therefore, no real point in the authorities not telling Captain Williams (and the other ship's masters) of its location. He could not know how long before, or if at all, friendly vessels would arrive at the scene, whereas he had a pretty good idea of how long it would take him to reach Barentsberg. It was the most positive option open to him, though he knew it would require great courage and determination from all his crew.

Courage was certainly not lacking among the crew of *Chulmleigh* as we shall see. For instance, the Chief Officer, Mr. E. J. Fenn, OBE, and Lloyds War Medal for Bravery at Sea, had already proved his mettle. He had been chief officer of the motor vessel *Derrymore* some twelve months previously. *Derrymore* had loaded at Immingham with a full war cargo, bound for Singapore. Mr. Nat Woods of Grimsby signed on her as an Able Seaman, and he recalls:

> The ship was under the command of Captain R. Doyle, a 29 year old Irishman making his first voyage in command. He was a big man, well over six feet and very broad shouldered. He tried to rule by fear and bullying. Mr. Fenn on the other hand was small in stature, a quiet but firm and excellent officer. Two men deserted ship at Immingham and another at Middlesbrough where we had gone to complete loading. She was not a happy ship and trouble was always just below the surface on passage across the Atlantic, through the Panama Canal and on to Melbourne where trouble finally broke surface. The master had decided that he would only allow the men four hours shore leave. Fighting broke out in which the Master became involved and Nat Woods, defending himself, felled him with an excellent uppercut that Joe Louis would have been proud of. Nat deserted ship in Australia because he knew that the big Irishman would not forgive him and he had decided enough was enough. Nat gave himself up after the ship had sailed and he joined another ship, bound for the United Kingdom.

While *Derrymore* was crossing the Pacific, bound for Australia, the Japanese had attacked Pearl Harbor, bringing the Americans into the war and extending Britain's war to the Far East as we have already seen. After arriving in Melbourne some of the crew deserted. They were replaced and the ship sailed for Singapore, arriving at the height of the fighting there, on 2 February 1942. *Derrymore* never did discharge her cargo but took on board a large contingent of Royal Air Force and Royal Australian Air Force personnel and sailed at once for Batavia. Two days after sailing she was torpedoed by a Japanese submarine, ironically on Friday the 13th of February. Chief Officer Fenn was instrumental in organizing and leading one of two parties to construct rafts on which the large numbers on board could stand some chance of survival. The efforts were successful and for this he received the awards mentioned above.

September 1942 saw him as Chief Officer of the ill-fated *Chulmleigh*, and with another desperate situation facing him.

The crew were re-shuffled among the three boats to even out numbers and all set sail. Number one starboard lifeboat was much smaller than the other two and did not sail as well and so after only two hours Captain Williams decided to heave to and wait for her to catch up. He then took all the men off and divided them equally between the two large lifeboats. All the stores and other useful items from the small lifeboat were removed and distributed, then it was cast adrift. There were now twenty-nine men in the master's boat and twenty-nine in the chief officer's charge. Both boats proceeded along the coast making good progress.

During the night of 6/7 November the two boats became separated involuntarily and did not regain contact until the morning of the 9th. Captain Williams had not been unduly worried by this, he knew that his chief mate was an excellent seaman, a born leader, and would take this in his stride.

The weather was very cold but at least it was fine and on one day they even found themselves becalmed. This was, however, the calm before the storm and next day the wind increased to gale force and both boats were forced to stream their sea anchors to avoid being swamped. There was hardly any daylight at all, just a few hours of twilight to break up the otherwise total darkness of an Arctic November. The boats had up to this point tried to sail within sight of the land at all times. The land showed up in the east as an even darker mass of course, however on the morning of the 9th the land was out of sight and each boat was alone in the surrounding seas. Captain Williams ordered the motor to be started in his boat and ran in towards the coast. Some two hours later land was sighted almost at the same time as the other lifeboat hove in sight. Mr. Fenn had also decided to run in until he picked up the coast again. Another conference was called and since all the men seemed quite cheerful, fit and well, despite the bitterly cold weather, it was decided to continue to use the motor in the captain's boat (the other boat was not so fitted) and he would push on ahead to try and reach Barentsberg, still some sixty miles away, for help. The boats had been sailing northwards for about forty-nine hours and had covered roughly half the estimated distance. Things were looking extremely good for the success of this voyage at this stage.

Conditions remained quite severe in the masters boat. All the occupants were covered in frozen spray as were the sails. There was about 2 inches of ice on the outside of the hull above the waterline. It was a miracle that the fresh water tanks were not frozen also, but they were shielded from the bitter wind. The fuel for the motor was now running low and it was decided to use the motor only during the hours of twilight and to resort to sailing during darkness. Again they tried to keep the land in sight at all times but this often proved very difficult.

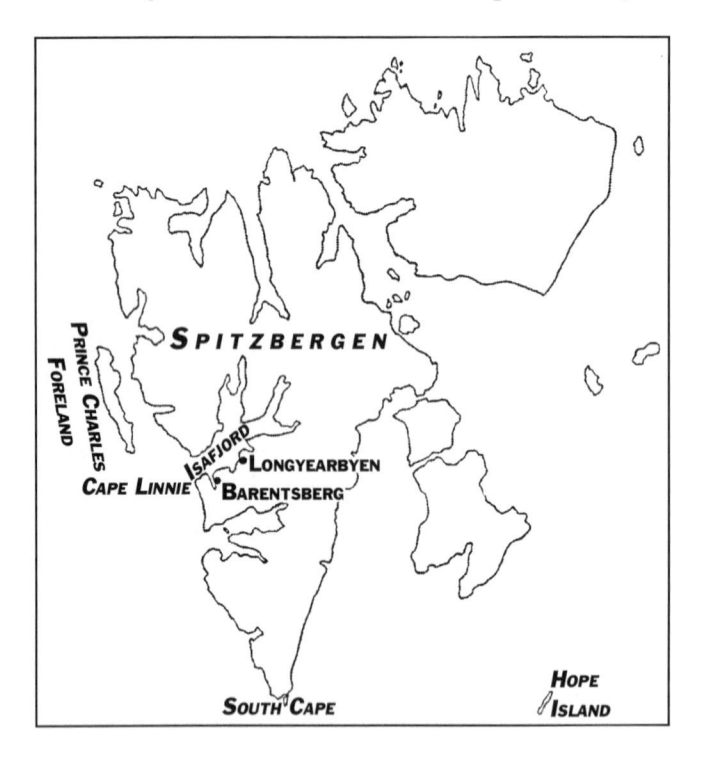

During the afternoon of the 10th Prince Charles Foreland was sighted. It marked the entrance to Isafjord and course was altered towards it. Hardly had the new course been set when the motor decided to freeze up. Repeated efforts to re-start it failed and so it was back to sailing. The first cases of effects of exposure occurred during this night when Mr. J. Suttie, the 34 year old donkeyman became delirious and Captain Williams lapsed into unconsciousness. Third Officer Clark took over command.

All the survivors were now suffering from varying degrees of frostbite, hands and feet were completely numb, nobody was hungry but all craved for more water. Mr. Clark continued to sail towards the inlet having decided that if they did not find shelter soon they would all die of exposure. When the darkness was complete some lights were observed on shore and he decided to try and find a way in.

A miracle happened that night when the lifeboat was washed over a reef and ran up onto the beach. While the boat was crossing the reef through the surf, everyone on board was soaked and the boat was filled with freezing water but against all odds it did not broach. This soaking brought Captain Williams around.

Miracles were in abundance on that stretch of beach that night, 12 November, because the survivors were all still alive after the ducking and they found themselves only about twenty yards from several wooden huts. The terrible hardships of the last few days, however, and the final soaking proved just too much for three of the men, including Mr. Suttie. They all died on the beach before they could be taken to the nearest hut. The remainder managed to stagger or crawl to the hut and once inside they all fell into a deep sleep. By comparison, the unheated hut was warm and it was wonderful to be sheltered from the bitterly cold polar wind. This landing was in fact not very far from Cape Linnie where, it will be remembered, the Norwegians had earlier set up a forward base.

Everyone felt much better physically the next morning but were bitterly disappointed to find that two more of their number could not be roused from their sleep. The date was Friday, 13 November 1942. They had in one night lost the chief steward, a donkeyman and three firemen. Many others were in a bad way, too, and four days later the chief engineer lost his fight for life. During the next week at least one man died every single day, despite the constant attention of the Army gunners.

At twilight, those fit enough emptied the boat of its rations and water, lit the small coal stove in the hut from the stock of wood and coal they found and made hot drinks for all twenty-three men. This raised morale tremendously and soon all were feeling ravenously hungry, the first time for almost a week. They all enjoyed a hearty meal of corned beef and biscuits from the supplies they found in the hut. Over the next few days frostbite began to turn affected limbs gangrenous and several men, including Mr. Clark, became very ill. Captain Williams, however, was recovering rapidly and once again he took command.

Strangely, the four fittest men were all Army gunners, Lance Sgt. R. A. Peyer, Gnr. R. R. Whiteside, Gnr. J. B. Burnett and Gnr. J. W. Swainston. Gunner Whiteside was the smallest in stature and he was the fittest. A Liverpool docker in peacetime, he seemed to suffer no ill effects whatever from his experience to date. These four men carried out almost all the daily chores, collecting firewood, cooking, nursing the sick, collecting snow for melting and many other necessities.

Since *Chulmleigh* had not been abandoned in a hurry, there had been ample time to equip all the lifeboats with charts, sextant, and a watch or chronometer, to assist in navigation. When the master's boat reached the beach, these items were recovered and taken into the hut.

It is not known for sure if Captain Williams had been made aware of friendly forces at Barentsberg; there are arguments to support both yes and no theories. The presence of an Allied force was already known to the Germans, therefore it was not secret, but, did Captain Williams "need to know"—the basic rule usually applied to the giving of such knowledge.

It seems strange, however, that from the outset the survivors had tried to make Barentsberg. They must have known either that it was indeed inhabited or they had decided that their chances of survival and eventual rescue would be better from there.

Although they were not sure exactly how far it was to Barentsberg, using the chart and compass they had brought with them, Lance Sgt. Peyer and Mr. Clark, who had now recovered somewhat, volunteered to make the first attempt to try and reach habitation on foot. They found the going very difficult indeed, rock strewn underfoot, numerous ravines and large stretches of snow and ice to contend with and without the availability of proper equipment and clothing (there was a pair of skis in the hut but no one had any experience in their use). They were forced to abandon their attempt and both men were totally exhausted when they regained the relative safety of the hut.

Most of the survivors, even the fittest, found that they could no longer bear shoes or boots on their feet. Many could not get any footwear on because of swelling, frostbite or gangrene. They had to cut away the uppers and then bind the soles to their feet with rags, twine, or anything else that would do the job. Even this task was difficult for many due to frostbitten fingers.

During the first eight to ten days, despite care and attention from the Army gunners, thirteen men died from gangrene, exhaustion and the effects of exposure. It was impossible to bury the bodies in graves and it took a great effort by several men to carry them to a nearby crevice and to cover them with stones and snow after a simple service.

Meanwhile *U-625* had found the wreck of *Chulmleigh* and, he claims, had completed her destruction with torpedoes and gunfire. Could this have been *Baikal*?

U-625 found the apparently undamaged *Chulmleigh* at about 1400 on 6 November, several hours after *Tuna* had sighted the upturned wreck. The U-boat fired one torpedo in a surface attack at 1559, which struck home, followed at 1601 by a second one that missed. Benker then used about twenty rounds of 20-mm incendiary shells, several of which were direct hits but nevertheless failed to set the ship on fire. He withdrew from the scene at about 1630.

This statement gives rise to yet another anomaly. Lieutenant Raikes of *Tuna* recalls how he went to look for *Chulmleigh* on receiving the distress message and a few hours later found himself in the same "lagoon" as Captain Williams described in his report much later. Lieutenant Raikes encountered exactly the same weather conditions as had Captain Williams. Raikes states that he and his No. 1 sighted an upturned ship in the lagoon, which could only have been *Chulmleigh*. Only a few hours later the commander of *U-625* claims he torpedoed the apparently undamaged ship and also shelled her. Later again the Luftwaffe used her as target practice when no other shipping could be found to attack.

Meanwhile the survivors in the hut had explored a little further afield and they had found a disused lighthouse and a demolished wireless station. There was nothing of interest or of use to them at the wireless station but they thought they may be able to get the light working and so bring help from some source. They broke into the tower only to find that all the vital parts had been removed. They found no food there either and left bitterly disappointed at the outcome. The most likely lighthouse they had found would be that at Cape Linnie. It is within twelve miles of Barentsberg and situated on the south side of Isjafjord. Although it was not a tall stone structure, it only reached a height of some 35 to 40 feet and was built of timber, they nevertheless had great difficulty breaking into the building and had expended a great deal of time and energy. The Royal Navy had destroyed the wireless station in May 1941.

As this event was forgotten and the small band of survivors got themselves fully organized with life's basic necessities their morale rose again. Further attempts were made by small parties, usually made up mostly of the Army gunners and either Mr. Clark or Captain Williams, to try and reach help but all these brave attempts ended in failure, sometimes because of weather, sometimes due to the weak condition of the men themselves but usually a combination of both.

The Norwegian GEARBOX garrison had set up a tented forward observation post two miles east-northeast of Cape Linnie lighthouse when they had arrived in August. It seems totally inconceivable that *Chulmleigh*'s survivors would have remained undiscovered by this forward camp, had it still been in position at this time.

Sergeant Peyer, Gnr. Burnett and Mr. Clark did find a small hut about two miles from their own and in it they found a sack of flour, tinned supplies and cocoa. They decided to abandon their original goal of seeking help at Barentsberg in order to take the supplies back to base where food was now running low. They still managed to collect enough firewood from the shoreline, it seemed to replenish itself frequently throughout their enforced stay. With great difficulty the three men loaded themselves up with as much as they could carry, including the sack of flour. The relatively short journey back to the base hut seemed to take forever but the pleasure on the faces of their fellow castaways was worth all their efforts. They had to make several journeys in order to recover all the provisions but they knew that they now had enough food to feed the group for several more weeks.

Some of the seamen were Shetland Islanders and before they succumbed to the rigors of their ordeal they taught the more able how to make an unleavened bread, just as they had watched their mothers do it on those remote islands.

The remaining petrol had been drained from the lifeboat tank and when the oil for the two primus stoves ran out, although potentially a highly dangerous operation, it was pressed into service as a substitute, fortunately without accident. On the few occasions when there was little wood on the shore the men began to systematically dismantle one of the nearby huts and used the timber for fuel and also to improve conditions for the men in the hut by building more bunks, chairs and tables. There was no shortage of matches, the hut contained dozens of boxes.

The majority of survivors, when asked what they considered had the most demoralizing effect on them, did not reply in terms of food, their injuries, or lack of hope, but that the twenty-four hours of almost total darkness was the most difficult to come to terms with. This was even more pronounced they felt when they ran out of lamp oil and even in the hut, found themselves surrounded by almost total darkness, too. There was very little glow from the enclosed bogey stove.

By the end of December Mr. Clark had again become ill, gangrene was the problem as it was with most of the men. The only medical treatment to hand was hot water but the care and attention given to these men by their shipmates was beyond praise. Nothing was too much trouble in order to try and make them more comfortable and to minimize their pain. The smell in the hut from rotting human flesh was overpowering, but was unavoidable.

The last man to die from the ordeal was 26 year old fireman George Alexander from Kelty, who passed away on Christmas Eve 1942, some seven weeks after reaching the hut. He, too, was laid to rest in the crevice with his comrades.

Captain Williams, Sgt. Peyer and Gunner Whiteside set out on a last desperate bid to reach Barentsberg. To date Gunner Whiteside had been almost totally unaffected either physically or mentally by his ordeal. He had kept up the spirits of the men with his cheerful Liverpool jokes and had performed all tasks necessary for twice as long as any other survivor. When the small party had covered about six miles (about half way, but they were unaware of that at the time) Gunner Whiteside collapsed and was unable to carry on. He had been in excellent spirits when they set out and there was no explanation for his sudden debility. Captain Williams had no option but to return to base. He and Sgt. Peyer had great difficulty assisting Gunner Whiteside. Had he been a bigger man they would almost certainly have failed in their task. They both collapsed from exhaustion on reaching the safety of the hut. Gunner Whiteside was put to bed, the first time he had been in that position during this crisis, except for a normal night's sleep.

With rest, hot food and drinks inside them they all soon recovered but it was quite obvious that they were all much weaker and none had the strength to attempt the journey again. Although outwardly each man tried to be cheerful and did his best to keep up the spirits of his shipmates, inwardly each one knew that his strength was ebbing day by day and that unless help reached them soon, then they would all slowly succumb eventually to this terrible ordeal. These inner thoughts were pushed aside and each man played his part in giving the group hope.

The DEMS gunners remained the fittest among the diminishing band of survivors, throughout, and uncomplainingly they continued to carry out most of the daily chores that were essential for survival, collecting firewood, melting snow, cooking, nursing the sick, and equally as important, keeping morale and hopes high.

On 2 January 1943, almost two months after *Chulmleigh* had run ashore stalwart Gunner Whiteside was out on the beach gathering firewood. Suddenly he burst through the door of the hut looking absolutely terrified and unable to speak. Captain Williams thought initially that he had been chased by a polar bear but only seconds later two more figures appeared, dressed in white camouflage suits. Everyone, including Gunner Whiteside thought that they were Germans and did not consider for one moment that they could possibly be Norwegians from Barentsberg.

Even allowing for the effect of their desperate situation on their reasoning, it makes one ask the question, 'Did they indeed know about Operation Gearbox?' The official report gives no indication on whether the Norwegians jumped to the conclusion that they had stumbled across an enemy camp or if they assumed the man was a survivor from *Chulmleigh*.

We know for certain the commander of the Barentsberg garrison had been made aware by the Admiralty that *Chulmleigh* had grounded and been abandoned and that it was possible that survivors from her would be in the area. It is reasonable to assume that foraging parties and patrols from the Norwegian garrison would be warned of the possibility, though there seems to be no firm evidence that a definite search and rescue operation was organized prior to the chance discovery of these men.

The two men were indeed Norwegians, part of the weather party from Operation GEARBOX. We know that Barentsberg had been informed about the fate of *Chulmleigh* and the strong possibility of there being survivors, but it is doubtful if the Norwegians expected to find anyone still alive after all this time. The two men were out on routine patrol, checking traps and looking for signs of possible enemy activity on shore. They had food supplies in their rucksacks and this was immediately divided out between the nine survivors still alive. The men were also given cigarettes.

When the excitement of rescue had sunk in the two Norwegians set off to bring help. The intrepid Gunner Whiteside and Gunner Burnett convinced the Norwegians that they were fit enough to accompany them. They proved this by walking the twelve miles to Barentsberg without assistance, a most remarkable accomplishment after such hardships.

It was not long before the rescue party from Barentsberg arrived at the hut with sledges, clothing, medical aid and provisions. Mr. Clark and Able Seaman Hardy were the most serious cases and were put on the sledges and taken immediately to the Norwegian base. Dr. Honningstad and two others stayed with the five remaining survivors, looking after them with great care until the following day when twenty men with four sledges arrived to take everyone to Barentsberg.

Every one of the survivors had to be hospitalized in the small infirmary. Dr. Honningstad was an expert on the treatment of frostbite and his skill and care saved several men from major amputations.

A signal was sent to London from the base giving details and names of all the survivors. The signal was later amplified with details of the men known to have died and those still missing in Mr. Fenn's boat. All the next of kin had already been informed that the men were missing, presumed lost at sea, but the latest telegrams brought great joy to the families of nine men of *Chulmleigh*. Eighteen other families who had previously been informed only that their loved ones were 'missing, presumed lost at sea' were now told the sad truth that they had indeed died, but for the relatives of Mr. Fenn and all his boat's crew the uncertainty remained.

Further search parties from Barentsberg were sent out along the coast to search for the chief mate's boat and its crew. The Norwegians had a small motor boat as part of their supplies and it was pressed into service to explore all possible inlets but no trace of the boat or any of the twenty-nine men was ever found.

If we examine the map of Spitzbergen closely, it can be seen just how close to successfully reaching Barentsberg by lifeboat Captain Williams, Mr. Clark and Mr. Fenn came before the cold hand of bad luck played its cards.

On 3 December 1942, Mrs. Violet Swainston, wife of Gunner Swainston, received an official letter telling her that her husband was 'missing at sea.' Three days later another letter arrived, this time from the commanding officer of Gunner Swainston's unit, telling her 'there is very little hope of his survival.'

Some six weeks after that yet another official letter dropped through the letter box. This one brought good news indeed. Gunner Swainston had been rescued but 'no further information could be given.' In April 1943 a further letter from Swainston's commanding officer told her, "Your husband is safe, but he is in a place close to the enemy. We have no communication with this place. Please do not tell anyone about this letter." She heard nothing further until her husband turned up on the doorstep a couple of months later.

Most of the nine survivors spent up to two months in their hospital bed gradually recovering their strength. They were allowed up for progressively increasing periods of exercise until they were all fully recovered. Some took the opportunity to learn to ski during their enforced stay.

On 10 June 1943 HMS *Bermuda* and HMS *Cumberland*, two Royal Navy cruisers, brought fresh stores for the garrison and about fifty men to relieve others who would be returning to the United Kingdom. The two cruisers had picked up the men and supplies at Scapa Flow and then sailed to Iceland where they re-fueled before making the fast run to Spitzbergen with their escorting destroyers.

All the men and supplies had to be put ashore by boat. The destroyers patrolled the entrance to the fjord to make sure that no U-boat could interfere and the two cruisers kept under way except when actually loading into the boats. The crates containing the supplies had been specially made with this point in mind and everything was landed without mishap.

All nine survivors from *Chulmleigh* were taken on board the two cruisers for the journey home that none of them, in the first few weeks of their plight, thought they would ever make, and after spending seven months on Spitzbergen they were landed at Thurso, on Scotland's northern coast on 15 June and were all sent on survivors leave.

It is interesting to note that in accordance with the rules all the merchant navy survivors were discharged in retrospect, on 6 November 1942, the day they had abandoned the ship. It is also interesting to note the payment of wages due. Third Officer Clarke for instance had £27.10.7d due to him, First Radio Officer Paterson received £41.6.5d while the next of kin of Second Radio Officer McVicker received £39.7.2d. and those of cabin boy McDonald £11.11.9d.

After the war the bodies of the seventeen men of SS *Chulmleigh* who had died on Spitzbergen before help had arrived, were removed from the makeshift mass grave and taken to Tromso in northern Norway for re-interment. In one corner of the city cemetery is the plot of the Commonwealth War Graves Commission.

It is not a large area, there was no need for a large cemetery because most of the seamen who lost their lives in that theater have no known grave but the sea. There are only thirty-seven graves, three of seamen still unidentified except that they were British seamen. Almost half the graves in this plot are of men from one ship—SS *Chulmleigh*.

The graves of this, the most northerly British War Grave, are well cared for by the Norwegians. Those men of *Chulmleigh* who have no known grave but the sea are in turn remembered on their respective memorials. The merchant navy men on the plaques of the Tower Hill memorial, the Royal Navy DEMS Gunners on their respective depot memorials such as Chatham, Portsmouth and Plymouth, and the Maritime Artillery gunners on their Regimental Memorials.

There are, however, one or two unexplained occurrences. For instance, Sgt. Charles Gow of the 7/4th Maritime Regiment RA, one of *Chulmleigh*'s gunners, is, for reasons not known, remembered on Panel 77, Column 2, of the Plymouth Naval Memorial, without any reference to SS *Chulmleigh*, the vessel he so ably served. The most likely explanation is that Sgt. Gow was a Royal Marine, but why no mention of *Chulmleigh*?

Captain Daniel Williams never returned to sea; he was invalided out of the Merchant Navy due to the severe frostbite injuries received during his ordeal. He died in 1989, age 92 years. Third Officer Clark was similarly discharged because of his injuries.

Between 6 and 9 September 1943 a German Task force code named ZITRONELLA, comprising the battleships *Tirpitz* and *Scharnhorst* with nine destroyers attacked Allied bases on Spitzbergen. *Tirpitz* shelled Barentsberg, inflicting heavy damage. A further Allied force was landed in October to re-establish the bases.

Capt. Ernst Ullring, DSO, Royal Norwegian Navy,
commander of Operation GEARBOX in 1942.
[Sir Alexander Glen]

HM cruiser *Bermuda*.
[Royal Navy Submarine Museum]

The British Merchant Navy War Memorial, Tower Hill, London.
[Author's photo]

General view of the British War Cemetery, Tromso, Norway, where seventeen men of S.S. *Chulmleigh* are buried. Photos taken in June 1992.

[Kjell Y. Riise]

Chapter 8

The Five That Got Through

THE records of the voyages made by these five vessels to North Russia have, if they were ever recorded, not been preserved. Crew lists for the British ships, together with disciplinary logs are available but there is no mention of weather, actions or sightings at all. It has only been by contacting ex-crew members and listening to their stories that this discrepancy can be partly rectified. Generally speaking, of course, time is not on the side of good memory, but if one can contact sufficient numbers and gather enough stories a general picture begins to emerge.

British merchant shipping and crew records for the period and vessels concerned are excellent and by using these together with the very good co-operation of the media, many contacts have been made, stories obtained and photographs loaned to enable the story of the passage of the two British ships to be told. Despite desperate and very widespread attempts to find similar information in the United States, this has proved almost impossible.

It has, after a great deal of time and effort, been possible to obtain crew lists for the American vessels, together with log books and the odd report but because of the (in my case) restrictions of the U.S. personal information (privacy) laws I found addresses had been blanked out from my copies of the records. Appeals were made through American shipping magazines, union magazines and newsletters but unfortunately most proved negative. For this reason and this alone I have been unable to present many personal accounts of the voyage from American merchant marine sources. If therefore the coverage of the operation from the American point of view seems somewhat less than that from the British, then I apologize. The role played in this operation by the men and women of all three Allied countries was in every way equal, despite the differences numerically.

I have, however, been much more successful in tracing the Armed Guard crews of the American ships. Their excellent cooperation together with the official U.S. Navy reports have enabled me to present an accurate picture of each individual voyage.

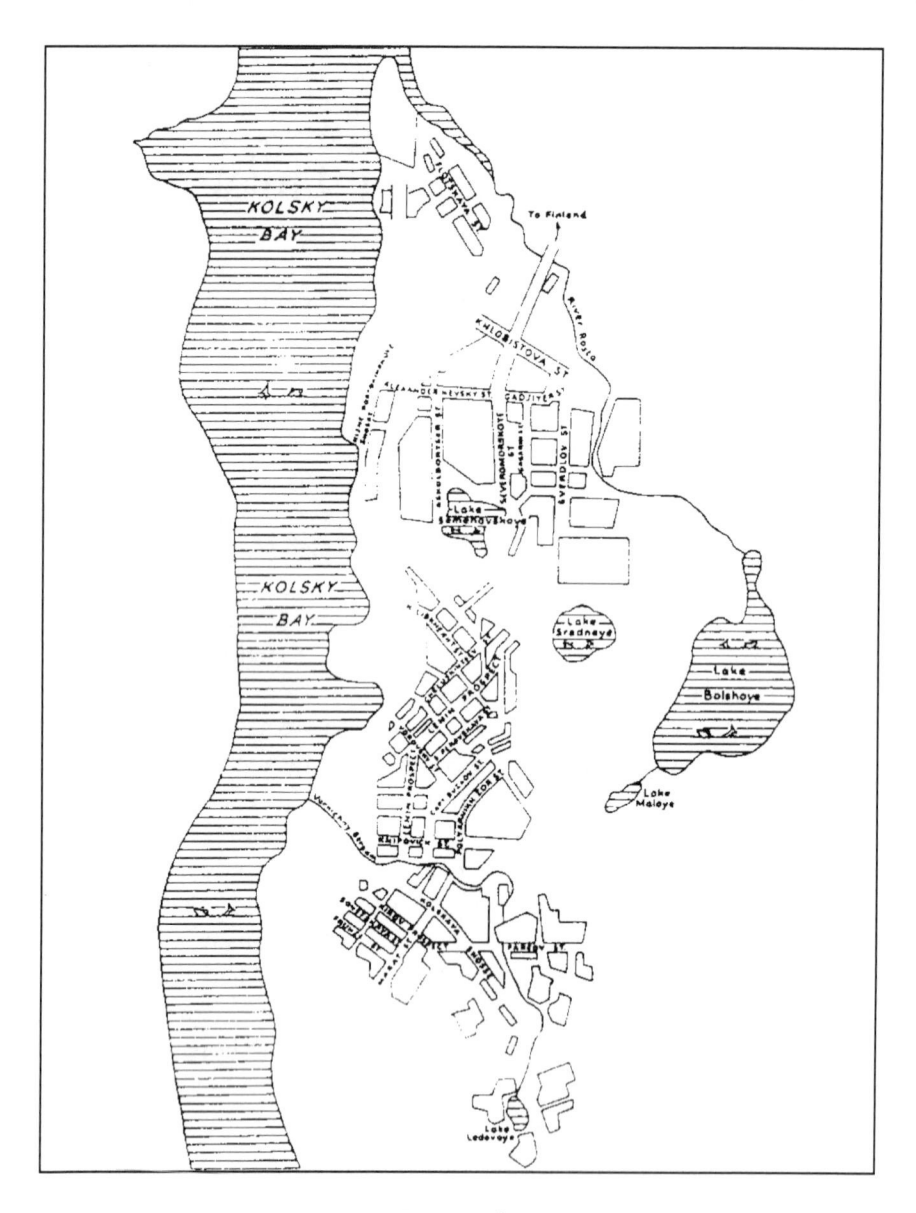

Murmansk

Close examination of the order of sailings and other such factors does not reveal any pattern for a successful (or otherwise) passage. Had the first few ships got through safely and the remainder not then this could possibly have been attributed to surprise, inclement weather or some other common factor, but this was not the case. It looks as though luck played a large part.

The length of the voyage would be in the region of 2,500 miles maximum and if we examine the length of passage for the five ships we see that three of the ships took ten days, one took eleven, while *Empire Scott* was at sea for sixteen days before reaching Murmansk. She was the second of the two ships to sail on 2 November so we can safely assume that if the spacing of some 200 miles was adhered to then it must have been at least in the afternoon of that day when she sailed. The ship that had sailed before *Empire Scott* earlier the same day was the ill-fated American Liberty ship *William Clark*.

The merchant navy crew of *Empire Scott* were mainly Scotsmen but there was a sprinkling of sassenachs among them. The DEMS gunners came from all corners of the United Kingdom. The fact that there were a large number of Scotsmen among her crew is not at all surprising because she had begun her voyage in Glasgow, where most of her crew signed on articles during the first half of August 1942. Most of the crew would therefore have come from the merchant navy pool at Glasgow. Several of them had sailed in the ship on her previous voyage.

Empire Scott was a fine-looking ship, heavily armed and filled with up-to-date lifesaving gear. She was fitted with degaussing equipment against the magnetic mine and she also carried the distinctive 'A' bracket on her bows, which, when lowered into the water gave her protection against the moored mine when her paravanes were streamed.

Before this epic voyage to North Russia, *Empire Scott* had made two previous voyages since delivery from the builders, and on one of them had circumnavigated the globe.

Andrew Crawford and Company had begun the war with three ships of their own and during the conflict they were given the management of six further vessels on behalf of the Government. They paid a heavy price—only two of the nine ships survived the war. *Empire Scott* was one of the ships managed on behalf of the Ministry of War Transport. They had been appointed since the vessel was new from the builders. Her keel had been laid on 23 September 1940 and she was launched on 10 July 1941. She was completed on 26 August that same year and Captain R. L. Barr, a long-standing servant of Andrew Crawford and Company, took command.

Captain Barr had joined the company in 1930 as second mate of SS *Gogovale*. One year later he was appointed Chief Officer of SS *Gretavale* and served in this vessel continuously, being promoted to Master of her in 1940 and then as we have seen, Master of SS *Empire Scott* on delivery from the builders. Captain Barr took *Empire Scott* on her maiden voyage, in ballast, to the United States and brought back from New York the first United States cargo for the new American base at Londonderry. After discharging her cargo the vessel was moved to Glasgow to load for the Middle East.

During loading of ammunition a shell exploded accidentally, killing one stevedore and severely injuring another. She sailed from Glasgow on 3 December 1941 and arrived safely at Port Said on 1 March 1942, via the Cape of Good Hope.

Two Shetlanders, both 29-year-old Able Seamen, John Kay and Peter Anderson had joined the ship when she was brand new in August 1941 at South Shields. Before she reached her destination the Japanese had attacked Pearl Harbor and were fighting their way steadily southwards along the mainland of Asia and it seemed nothing could stop them. Fearing that Australia herself would before long be threatened by the might of the Imperial Japanese Empire, *Empire Scott* was ordered to embark 250 Australian soldiers at Port Said after discharging her cargo and take them to Freemantle, sailing independently. She arrived without mishap after crossing the Indian and Pacific Oceans and as soon as the troops were ashore she sailed south for Geelong to load a full cargo of grain for the United Kingdom.

She then crossed the southern Pacific, rounded Cape Horn where she suffered some weather damage, and crossed the South Atlantic to reach Freetown and then join a convoy bound for home. She had an unfortunate collision with the next ship in the convoy when the steering gear of SS *Empire Simba* jammed and *Empire Scott* could not get out of the way in time. The damage was serious but not fatal and eventually she found herself again on the Clyde.

While she underwent repairs she was fitted out for service to North Russia, exposed water tanks were lagged and other modifications necessary for the forthcoming Arctic voyage were carried out. Additional accommodation for thirty men was built in No. 5 shelter deck, extra guns were fitted, the complement of DEMS gunners was raised from ten to almost thirty. One novel feature fitted on the bridge was a steam hose for keeping the bridge deck free of ice.

During this time Captain Barr became ill and was forced by this to relinquish command. Captain J. Hair, CBE, Lloyds Medal, took over. He had already made wartime voyages in convoy to North Russia. He had been master of SS *Empire Selwyn*, one of the merchantmen of PQ-16 in May 1942. This convoy was heavily attacked for days on end by high level bombers, torpedo bombers, dive bombers and U-boats. Several ships were lost before the convoy reached the Kola Inlet where even then they were subjected to many air raids while alongside discharging or at anchor awaiting a berth.

Captain Hair had seen plenty of action on Atlantic convoys, too. On 20 September 1941 for instance, his ship, SS *Cromarty* was part of convoy SC-44 when a U-boat pack struck without warning. A tanker went up in flames and in the glare the crew of *Cromarty* saw a U-boat on the surface, trimmed down but the foredeck and conning tower were clear of the water. "We opened fire with our Hotchkiss machine guns to give our 4-inch a line of fire," said Captain Hair. "We fired seven rounds and the third and fourth were hits. The submarine disappeared stern first, her bows rising as she sank." Unfortunately the U-boat assessment committee did not credit the merchant ship with the sinking.

While this action was taking place *Cromarty* collided with a submerged object on the starboard side. The collision was clearly heard by both bridge and engine room staff. The vessel lurched to port but nothing could be seen. Captain Hair joined the Lyle Steamship Company in 1943 and took command of SS *Fort Cumberland* and in 1944 the SS *Samtana*.

It was during *Empire Scott*'s time in dry dock that two eager young men from the south of England joined her crew. Both had received initial training at the Gravesend training school ship *Vindicatrix*. Gordon Long had tried to join the merchant navy and the Royal Navy before but had been turned down on both occasions because of slight color blindness. The tests for this problem at Gravesend were not as critical and he got through the medical examination satisfactorily and began his training as a steward boy, receiving a VG discharge for both ability and general conduct on completion. Young Gordon Long and his friend Ernest Ballard traveled north to Glasgow where they signed on the merchant navy pool and a few days later were sent to join *Empire Scott* while she was still in dry dock undergoing repairs and modification. On completion the ship was moved to Princes Dock to load and finally moved to Finneston Dock to load her deck cargo of tanks and to have a special walkway constructed over this cargo to allow access for the crew to and from various sections of the ship.

The vessel left Tail-o-the-Bank on 22 September for Loch Ewe, after compass adjusting had been carried out. SS *Queen Mary* was at anchor nearby, her bows showing damage from her unfortunate collision with HMS *Curacoa*, which resulted in the cruiser being sunk with heavy loss of life. Several troopships were also there having landing craft fitted for the forthcoming invasion of North Africa. *Empire Scott* sailed from Loch Ewe in convoy to Iceland on 15 October. She was obviously a happy ship because no less than twenty-four men did not hesitate to sign articles again for her third voyage. Nine of her crew were from the Scottish Islands, two from the Outer Hebrides, John Maclean, the assistant cook and 20-year-old assistant steward Sydney Evans.

Despite his youth Sydney Evans already had a wealth of sea-going experience under his belt. He had been a very young crew member of the Donaldson liner, SS *Athenia* when she was sunk by *U-30* on the very first day of war between the United Kingdom and Germany. He had also seen action during the Blitz, when his ship was in Londons Docks and received damage from the bombing in January 1941. For his bravery in this event he was awarded The Royal Humane Society Bronze Medal.

The seven Shetlanders had seen their share of action, too. Able Seaman Robert Thomason had already attended an investiture at Buckingham Palace to receive his well earned award, while Peter Anderson and John Kay, who had been shipmates since the outbreak of war, had already been crew members of two ships that had come to grief. In February 1941 they had joined the brand new SS *Empire Knoll* and this ship had run ashore very soon after sailing. They were both rescued by breeches buoy on this occasion.

After a spot of survivors leave, both men signed on SS *Eskdene* in April 1941. The ship was bound from Hull to Buenos Aries with a five-thousand-ton cargo of coal. Having completed the greater part of the voyage without mishap they were found by *U-107*, under the command of Kapitänleutnant Günther Hessler, Dönitz' son-in-law. One torpedo, fired in the early hours, was enough to damage the ship beyond hope and so the master ordered her abandoned. All the crew got away safely in the two lifeboats before *U-107* finished off the ship with gunfire and a second torpedo. The boats reached Brazil safely and after another spot of survivors leave both these young men signed on *Empire Scott*.

Early August 1942 found *Empire Scott* again on the Clyde, loading another war cargo. Thirty-five-year-old Captain J. F. Hair took command on 9 September when the usual captain, R. L. Barr was taken ill and hospitalized. The vessel completed loading and then sailed for Loch Ewe to await convoy to Iceland. She was the third of the seven British ships to arrive in the Scottish Loch. *Empire Sky* had been the first but she had already reached Iceland by the time *Empire Scott* reached Loch Ewe, to find *Empire Gilbert* already swinging on her hook. *Chulmleigh*, *Empire Galliard*, *Daldorch* and *Briarwood* quickly followed and by the last week of October they had all joined the *Empire Sky*, the five Americans and the Russian at Hvalfjord.

According to all the eyewitnesses it was at this stage that each of the British ships was visited by shore authorities and the assembled crews were told of the impending voyage. All were given the opportunity of signing off but none of the crew of *Empire Scott* requested this action. All her Arab firemen had been replaced at Loch Ewe and this had happened in other British ships, too. In the case of *Empire Scott* the Arab firemen went to the Chief Steward to request an interview with the Master. This was granted and they stated that they did not wish to go to North Russia as it would be too cold for them. They were allowed to sign off. The crews were told the basic details and that they would each receive £50 lump sum credited in their pay as soon as the ship had sailed. In addition they were told that next of kin, as given on the crew list, would also receive a lump sum payment of £50 immediately the ship sailed.

Empire Scott left Hvalfjord and proceeded north through the Denmark Straits and after leaving North Cape headed northeast towards the ice barrier. *Empire Scott* was found by a German aircraft about forty-six hours (on the 4th) after leaving Iceland. The aircraft dived to attack the lone merchantman but the heavy anti-aircraft fire from the ship forced the aircraft to break off before actually dropping any bombs and it did not attack again. During the forenoon of the next day *Empire Scott* passed through the area where *William Clark* had been sunk and there was a very strong smell of fuel oil but there was no sign of any lifeboats or survivors.

Gordon Long, the cabin boy of *Empire Scott* is certain that one of the radio officers of his ship received a distress call from *Empire Sky* and that they were ordered to look out for survivors as they passed through the given position. This causes some confusion because the three ships in question all sailed from Hvalfjord within twenty-four hours of each other. *Empire Sky* in the evening of 1 November, *William Clark* during the morning of 2 November and *Empire Scott* during the same evening. Although radio propagation conditions in Arctic latitudes can cause problems, surely another vessel would have received the distress, too.

The rescue trawlers had received *William Clark*'s signals earlier. The U-boat that sank *Empire Sky* did receive her distress call but reported that she had sunk a different ship. It is really a question of dates and positions because *William Clark* was sunk on 4 November while *Empire Sky* survived until the 6th, four days after *Empire Scott* had sailed. *Empire Sky* was posted 'missing from 14 November' by the British authorities and it was February 1946 before her fate was known in the United Kingdom and relatives of the crew were informed of the circumstances of her loss.

If the radio officer of *Empire Scott* received *Empire Sky*'s distress call then he was duty bound to log it and report it at once to the Master. The ships were under orders not to break radio silence to acknowledge such calls, however, the contents of the log should have been brought to the attention of the Senior British Naval Officer when the vessel reached Russia.

Two other points indicate that it was most likely *William Clark*'s distress to which *Empire Scott* responded, not that of *Empire Sky*. *William Clark* was sunk near Jan Mayen on 4 November and she was indeed an oil burner. *Empire Sky* was sunk southeast of Spitzbergen on 6 November and she was a coal burner. *Empire Scott* was ordered to delay passing the South Cape of Spitzbergen until ordered to do so. She certainly remained west of Spitzbergen for several days before proceeding around the South Cape and therefore it would be much more than twenty-four hours after the loss of *Empire Sky*.

The lone merchantman was again sighted by an aircraft the following morning but this time the aircraft made no attempt to attack the ship, circling out of anti-aircraft gun range she was obviously sending signals to her base and no doubt her base was arranging for direction finding cross bearings to be taken to fix the vessel's position. After about half an hour the aircraft seemed satisfied and flew off towards Norway. Soon after this a thick blanket of fog enveloped *Empire Scott* and no other aircraft was seen or heard. The ship pressed on further into the mushy ice and spent several days in this ice to the west of Spitzbergen before making her final run for Murmansk. It is not absolutely clear from information available whether Captain Hair, acting on his own initiative, decided to delay his final dash, or if it was on Admiralty orders, or perhaps a combination of both.

The Admiralty had certainly signaled *Empire Scott* and *Empire Sky* to 'wait' west of Spitzbergen because they sent a signal to these two vessels on 11 November for both these ships to proceed. They were obviously unaware that *Empire Sky* had already been sunk. Official records show that *Empire Scott* was sighted off Sem Island at 1730A on 17 November and escorted in by Russian destroyers. Captain Hair would certainly have known about the attacks carried out on *William Clark* and *Dekabrist* and his radio officers should certainly have received the two distress messages we know for certain were transmitted by *Chulmleigh*. We also know that he was ordered by the Admiralty to a position north of 7730N and east of 0700E and he carried out these orders.

The weather also deteriorated to a gale with heavy snow squalls. Like all of the ship's masters on this nightmare voyage Captain Hair had had no opportunity to take sights at all but he continued to navigate by dead reckoning through the increasing ice. It was not until 14 November that he obtained a fix by observation, enabling him to chart his position with a good degree of accuracy. The weather continued as bad as ever and the ship rolled heavily, shipping tons of water at irregular intervals, adding to everyone's discomfort, but at least it kept the Germans at bay, too, it seemed.

The other four ships to reach Russia all went to Archangel or Molotovuk, which would add at least another day to their passage, compared to that of *Empire Scott* under roughly the same conditions. *Empire Scott* was the only British ship to unload at Murmansk at that time. Mr. Long recalls that the ship was found and escorted for about the last 100 miles, by six naval vessels. Captain Hair was questioned by Royal Navy officers on arrival and he reported that he had not seen *Empire Sky* at all.

The Kola Inlet at its best is a wild and barren place and even in June patches of snow can still be seen in the hills. There is no greenery, only black granite rock and the odd bush-like stunted tree. In 1942 there were foghorns mounted on wooden towers above the steep shores of the numerous small islands. Fog is frequent in this part of the world. Most of the buildings in Murmansk were built of wood, almost all of the modern brick-built blocks had been reduced to rubble in the numerous daily air raids. The streets were cobbled and without pavements. The Russian Naval base at Polyarnoe was off to starboard and Vaenga Bay was on the east side of the Inlet, between the mouth and Murmansk. Murmansk itself was then intersected by two small rivers and was bounded by several small lakes. The Russian dockers, many of whom were women, worked in shifts round the clock, only stopping for the frequent air raids.

As soon as the cargo had been discharged, *Empire Scott* loaded a cargo of chemicals for the ICI works at Middlesbrough and then left the wharf for a slightly safer anchorage. While there she bunkered several British anti-submarine trawlers with good British steaming coal from her own ample supplies. Throughout her stay in Murmansk she suffered no serious damage from the repeated bombing attacks. One fireman had to be hospitalized in Murmansk due to illness and it is interesting to note that his pay and allowances stopped immediately and the balance of pay due to him was withheld until he was repatriated.

Empire Scott returned to the United Kingdom as Commodore ship of convoy RA-51, leaving Murmansk on 30 December 1942 and arriving in Middlesbrough on 19 January 1943, where she discharged her cargo of apatite, a crystallized phosphate of lime.

Empire Scott was a lucky ship, only one month later she sailed again for North Russia, this time in convoy. She was now under the command of Captain J. H. Colvin and she was fully loaded with bunker coal and 4,000 tons of general cargo. The reason for having full bunkers (which meant less cargo for the same draft bearing in mind the sandbar limitations), was that all the escort trawlers needed good quality steaming coal to operate efficiently. Russian coal was of very poor quality and caused enormous problems with fire cleaning on these ships. The full bunkers of *Empire Scott* would enable all the trawlers to replenish their depleted bunkers with good British steaming coal, though it would be a hard and dirty task for all the crews to coal ship by hand.

The two British naval trawlers, *Cape Argona* and *Cape Mariato* sailed from Iokanka to provide rescue services for the independents in the Southern Barents Sea. Both reported steaming difficulties due to poor quality Russian coal. *Empire Scott* spent the whole of the summer months in North Russia, and carried cargoes from Archangel to Murmansk and other North Russian ports, during which time she used all her British coal and had herself to bunker from Russian stocks! This poor quality Russian coal reduced her speed to six knots and when a complaint was made to the Russian authorities they said it was poor firing, not poor coal. They replaced the British firemen with Russian naval stokers for one voyage and the best speed they could produce was five knots! The British firemen were reinstated, needless to say.

She finally loaded a cargo of timber and general and sailed for the United Kingdom in convoy RA-54B in December 1943. She had endured and survived over three hundred air raids during her prolonged stay in North Russia. *Empire Scott* made one further voyage under the management of Andrew Crawford and Company before being sold by MOWT to the Chine Steamship Company. She survived the war and was re-named *Walter Scott* in 1946, *Zafiro* in 1960, *Oriental* in 1961 and was, sadly, scrapped in Hong Kong during 1963.

Captain Thomas Morley of *Empire Sky* and Captain James Mitchell of *Empire Galliard* were both 51 years old in 1942. Both had spent a lifetime at sea and were equally well experienced and skilled in their chosen profession. Thomas Morley and all his crew perished in the

Arctic while James Mitchell and his crew evaded the hunting bombers and submarines to reach Russia safely and so we can rule out experience as being the only factor in success in this venture. It is interesting to note, however, that all eight ships that survived the ordeal, the five that reached Russia and the three that returned to Iceland, all survived the war and went on to serve their owners well until finally being scrapped. Lady Luck must have played at least a small part in this I feel. *Empire Galliard* and her crew of mainly Tynesiders lived up to the dictionary definition of 'galliard'—valiant, stout, sturdy"—as indeed did all the men who set out on this voyage.

Empire Galliard was sighted by Russian aircraft about 100 miles north-northwest of Cape Kanin. Only a few miles away they also found *Richard H. Alvey* and both were escorted in by Russian destroyers. The reader will probably remember that these ships were the first two to leave Iceland.

Mr. Bill Canner, one of *Empire Galliard*'s DEMS gunners, called up at 18 years of age, remembers,

> We were very lucky, perhaps it was bluff. We reached Molotovuk without seeing any action at all on our independent journey. We were not so lucky on the next voyage, this time in convoy to North Russia. We were detected by aircraft and bombed. Several bombs fell close but did no damage and caused no casualties. The weather clamped down soon after the attack and once again we reached North Russia safely.

Empire Galliard's two cabin boys on the independent voyage were both youngsters from Sunderland. Arthur Sproxton was a tall, well-built lad while Terry Garraghan was barely five feet tall. They were nick-named "Mutt and Jeff" by their shipmates. Terry Garraghan, now living in Canada, recalls,

> Tanks, planes and ammunition were loaded at Sunderland South Dock and we left for sea. All the guns were tested. The ship was very heavily armed. All the after 'tween decks had been converted into accommodation for the extra gunners. We also had on board a Russian seaman who was being repatriated. His name I well remember was Nickolai Kapotka. We called at Glasgow because some of the tanks on the foredeck had broken loose in bad weather. While we were at Reykjavik naval and civilian visitors arrived on board. The crew of our ship

were all assembled in the officer's saloon. The visitors then began to tell us about the heavy losses to the previous convoys and explained that the intention was to try and sail ships alone. One of them said that one ship would not be missed from the anchorage by any German reconnaissance.

The question of volunteering and the payment of a bonus was brought up and someone among our crew said that fifty pounds was a reasonable sum. This was agreed by the majority. The officers, however, got more. We were not given any further information and I remember waking up one morning to find us at sea.

Empire Galliard was the second ship to sail, leaving in the p.m. on 29 October. Terry Garraghan continues,

I cannot remember any action during the voyage, but my job kept me indoors for most of the day. We arrived safely at Molotovuk, cleared customs and immigration and then the Russian dockers began to unload the ship. They were a sorry sight indeed, political prisoners we were told. A British armed trawler came alongside us for coal. She had run aground on a sand bank. [This must have been HMT *Daneman*.] They had been bunkered with poor quality Russian coal but we were able to give them good quality steaming coal. One other merchant ship was alongside the quay at this time, the American Liberty ship *Nathanael Greene*. Her crew were a fine bunch indeed.

After discharge of our cargo an icebreaker made a passage for us and we sailed to Murmansk to await a convoy back to the UK. We had numerous air raids during our stay in Murmansk but we were not hit. Our guns were in action a lot. During the passage to North Russia the ship's engineers and firemen did an excellent job. They had to remove some handrails because the excess vibration from the engines running at full speed kept shaking the fastenings loose. They got fed up with re-fitting them every few hours. I can remember too that on the way to Russia we saw lifeboats with lifeless bodies in them. We did not stop, we had orders not to stop for anything at all.

This last remark of Terry Garraghan's is also most interesting. It will be seen that he speaks in the plural when referring to seeing lifeboats. He would, of course, not be in a position to know just where the ship was at the time of these sightings, or indeed if the boats were seen at relatively short intervals of time or over a longer period. Only one boat from *William Clark* was 'missing,' we know for sure. One from *Chulmleigh* and three from *Dekabrist*. All these are definite. *U-625* reported seeing lifeboats from *Empire Sky* after torpedoing the ship, but could see no sign of them later, after the large explosion. *U-586* and the three survivors from *Empire Gilbert* make no mention of lifeboats leaving the ship. We shall never know for sure from which ship(s) these lifeboats came.

Soon after arriving back home, Arthur Sproxton, Terry Garraghan and fireman Andrew Wilson of *Empire Galliard* were each awarded the DSM. Three of the crew of *Empire Scott* were similarly honored for their part in this extremely dangerous mission.

Ordinary Seaman Denis Woolliams of SS *Empire Galliard* has a vivid memory of the ship and her voyage to North Russia.

> I signed on at Plantation Quay, Glasgow on 6th October 1942. She was a well armed ship. Twin 4-inch on the stern, Bofors on the poop, a pig trough, 2-inch rockets on the bridge, six Oerlikons and eight machine guns. We had a few depth charges, too. There was a 60-ton jumbo derrick on No. 2 hatch. The cargo was mixed: Valentine tanks, Bren gun carriers, ammunition, food and clothes. We left Glasgow and went to Loch Ewe were we joined a small convoy of about twelve ships and six escorts to Iceland. This journey was without incident. There were a large number of ships anchored in Hvalfjord, including warships. Several days after anchoring the skipper went ashore and came back with three men.
>
> The master called the crew to assemble and they were asked if they would be willing to sail to North Russia without escort. All the crew would be volunteers. Each man would receive £50, officers £100 and the master £500, to be paid when the ship sailed or when she returned, by personal choice. Only three men wanted to be paid on sailing. No mail could be sent or received until the operation was over. We were issued with Arctic clothing for the trip. We were told we would be the second ship to sail and that the ships would be spaced twelve hours apart.

We made a rendezvous with a trawler on the Thursday [29 October 1942, when *Empire Galliard* sailed, was a Thursday] and we had three further incidents. The first of these was an aircraft that we heard but could not see. The second occurred on about the fifth day after sailing; we heard a very loud explosion but never found out the cause. We saw two German aircraft but they did not attack or even come within range of our guns. The weather grew very cold indeed. We sighted two Russian aircraft and the next day an escort picked us up and escorted us to the White Sea where we picked up a pilot who took us to a small port about sixteen miles from Archangel. The town was two or three miles from the docks. There was a large prison camp between the town and the docks. The only way to get to town was by horse sledge. Not many made the journey twice. There were only three places to go ashore. The Intourist Hotel, the Theatre and the Post Office shop.

There was a ten p.m. curfew ashore and you were liable to be shot if you broke it, though we did. Most of the houses were unlocked and we would nip into the nearest one when trouble reared its head. I made some good friends and used to visit them nearly every night.

I still have a pipe carved for me by donkeyman F. Gencovski, one of our crew. He was classed as a White Russian and could not go ashore for fear of arrest.

The pipe is certainly unique. It has been painstakingly and intricately carved to a very high standard. Mr. Woolliams kindly sent it to me in order that I could fully appreciate the time and effort that went into its making. The pipe has never been used for its prime purpose and is still in pristine condition. It is straight stemmed and round bowled. All the decorative carving is round the bowl. This depicts crossed UK/USA flags immediately above the base of the stem and a large star containing the Hammer and Sickle is at the front of the bowl. On one side, between these two a lone U-boat is shown and on the opposite side three distinctively hostile aircraft. Mr. Gencovski, the skilled woodcarver/donkeyman must have spent many hours shaping and carving this fine piece. Just as on any pipe of that shape, the stem is in two pieces, the joint being about one and a half inches from the bowl.

SS *John Walker* left Baltimore in the middle of August 1942, called at New York and Halifax before crossing the Atlantic in convoy to Loch

Ewe, where she stayed at anchor for more than three weeks before sailing for Iceland. Raymond Williams, one of *John Walker*'s gunners remembers,

> When I joined the ship at Baltimore there were only two or three of the merchant crew on board. There was no food available and we had to eat ashore. It was about two weeks before we were ready to sail for New York.

During her stay in Loch Ewe boat drills and general quarters (action stations) drills were carried out frequently. On one such occasion one of the 20-mm anti-aircraft guns was fired accidentally and because the muzzle cover had been stuffed in the end of the barrel, the first round from the gun exploded on contact with the obstruction, shattering the muzzle of the gun, fortunately without injuries or further damage.

Ray Williams also recalls a typical wartime experience while the ship was anchored at Loch Ewe:

> Some of our gun crew, me included, were ordered to attend a British gunnery school for two or three days instruction on Lewis and Hotchkiss machine guns. This we did and enjoyed it, but our ship did not have any of these weapons on board.

John Walker left Loch Ewe on 18 October, in convoy for Iceland, arriving there without incident on 22 October. She was at anchor there for another week. She had had a rough passage on her way to the United Kingdom, losing a lifeboat in heavy weather, which was replaced at Loch Ewe. She was the fourth ship to leave Hvalfjord sandwiched between *Dekabrist* and *Empire Gilbert*, both of which, as we have seen, were sunk. Despite the heavy overcast weather, *John Walker* was found by three Ju 88s and an Fw 200 on 4 November and attacked with sticks of between four and six 500-pound bombs.

Ray Williams was second in command of the Armed Guard gun crew, and with the commander shared a 12-hour watch and watch about system. He had gone off watch at eight a.m., had his breakfast, turned in and was soon asleep.

> The general quarters alarm gong woke me at 0955. It took me several seconds to gather my thoughts then I grabbed my lifejacket and ran for the gun deck. As I reached the ladder leading

to this deck and began to climb it, the 3-inch 50-caliber gun, close above my head, let go the first round. It shook me terribly but I didn't seem to be hurt so I carried on to my station. It was three p.m. before we secured from general quarters. During that time many aircraft attacked us but we managed to drive them off. We shot down two aircraft for sure.

The official report, submitted in Russia by the Armed Guard commander, sums up the battle as follows.

The aircraft circled the ship at 7-8,000 feet and one aircraft would then dive to attack and then climb immediately after attacking. The aircraft making the third attack was hit by our anti-aircraft fire and broke off the attack with smoke trailing from it as it headed towards Norway. Two more Ju 88s joined the remaining aircraft about an hour later and they, too, attacked. We managed to escape into a fog bank about twenty minutes later. One of the bombs exploded close enough to shift cargo in No. 2 hold. Some of the cargo was damaged and some lower frames in the hull were bent by the force of the blast. Eight attacks were made in which thirty bombs were dropped. The gunners on *John Walker* expended some 35 three-inch shells, 4,000 rounds of 20-mm, and several thousand rounds of light machine gun ammunition. A radio message then ordered her to Archangel instead of Murmansk, her original destination. Later that same day Russian aircraft and naval escorts found *John Walker* and escorted her to harbor.

Rudi Langston, another of *John Walker*'s Armed Guard recalls, "After the attacks we found many spent German bullets on deck, and most of us kept some as souvenirs." When the vessel eventually returned to the USA all her gunners received well deserved citations.

She escaped without further damage and continued her passage only to run aground on the sandbar at the Dvina River and then to add insult to injury she collided with *Richard Alvey* who was also aground at that time! She was refloated on 12 November after pumping 400 tons of fuel oil into a tanker, brought alongside her for this purpose. She then proceeded to Molotovuk where she discharged and her hull was inspected by Mr. J. N. Novak of the USSR Registry of Shipping. The damage sustained was repaired and a certificate of seaworthiness was issued.

Harrison O. Travis, 1st Assistant engineer of SS *John Walker* recalls,

As we approached the Dvina River entrance to Archangel, from the White Sea we had a Soviet pilot on the bridge. We could see a vessel in the distance, obviously a Liberty ship. Captain Jenssen remarked to the pilot that she appeared to be aground. The Russian pilot seemed quite pleased with this remark and volunteered in reply, 'That is the *Richard H. Alvey*. I ran her aground yesterday!' The pilot then proceeded to put *John Walker* aground on the same sandbar right alongside *Richard H. Alvey*. The weather deteriorated during the night and the two ships rolled together at the bows. The bulwarks were badly damaged and two Boston A-20 bombers of our deck cargo were smashed. We pumped all the water overboard and gave some fuel to *Alvey* who was short and then pumped more fuel into a tanker barge before we managed to get off.

Harrison Travis remembers several members of *John Walker*'s crew very well. The Chief Mate, Bruce Rawding,

... an excellent officer and seaman, later in the war he got his own command. Nick Yladesco, the 2nd Assistant engineer was a man in his sixties. [He was, in fact, then 57 years.] He had been at sea during World War I. He had been working ashore on the railroad when World War II came along. He left his job and returned to sea. He was a fine and brave man. Young John Brocklander was my right hand man. We worked long hours together and he had a fine voice. He was always singing, 'Cocktails for Two' being his favorite tune. Walter Hale, an oiler, was a keen observer of animal behavior. The only animal he could observe while we were at sea was the ship's dog, whose name escapes me. Not surprisingly we nicknamed Walter 'Jungle Jim.' He noticed that whenever we were under attack the dog disappeared to the dirty linen locker some two decks below the main deck. Jungle Jim was convinced that the animal knew the safest place on board and consequently he spent many hours with the dog in this shelter. Most of us, however, thought that the dog just enjoyed being with the dirty linen! George Kritzman was the engineering cadet. It was his first trip to sea and he suffered constantly from seasickness. When we got back to the States he promptly joined the Army!

He further recalls,

As 1ˢᵗ Assistant engineer my battle station was in the engine room. The Liberty was known to be slow and was particularly slow when heavily laden as we were. A heavy coat of ice contributed to this. When under attack in order to get more revolutions I had the boiler pressure just under the safety valve setting and the firing rate at a maximum, too. At every stroke of the engine the safety valve would 'pop.' In the engine room, despite the noise, we could hear the 5-inch gun on the stern, the 3-inch in the bows and the eight Oerlikon 20-mm guns firing. When bombs dropped close, the generator would trip out. This often caused a little excitement but no real trouble since no vital machinery was totally dependent on it.

He continues,

When we arrived in Molotovuk a large icebreaker cleared the ice from around SS *Ironclad* and then moved her from the quay. We went alongside and the *Ironclad* was berthed alongside us. This ship was a survivor of the ill-fated PQ-17 convoy and was in a rough shape. It was rumored that some of her crew had mutinied and were ashore in the brig, but we did not know for sure. The engineers from *John Walker* had to go on board her to heat the oil in her double bottoms so that it could be used. It had been allowed to go cold. The steam coils in the tanks had been allowed to freeze up and the oil was too thick to pump. We had to use steam hoses to warm it through. A long and tedious task.

In his report to the U.S. Naval authorities at Molotovuk, Lt. (j.g.) Milton A. Stein complained that all the crates loaded in U.S. ports had been heavily stenciled 'USSR' while all the crew were told repeatedly not to discuss the ship's destination or cargo when ashore!

The ship left Molotovuk just before noon on 14 December with a cargo of chrome ore and explosives. She dropped anchor in the Kola Inlet, some four miles from Murmansk at breakfast time on the 16ᵗʰ. The explosives were unloaded a week later. They consisted mainly of depth charges for British escorts.

She was caught up in several air raids during her stay in North Russia. One of these was on Boxing Day, while the vessel was still at anchor outside Murmansk. Second Mate Joseph S. Baril was the watch officer when the air raid alarm sounded just after 1 p.m. The Master, Captain John E. Jenssen had gone to his cabin to put on his bridge coat and while he was there the ships 'general quarters' alarm was rung by the forward gun platform as they saw an aircraft approaching the ship at high altitude. It was an Me 109 and it was being chased by Russian Spitfires. The German pilot jettisoned his five small bombs in order to better his chances of escape. Two of the bombs struck the water close to starboard, two on the port bow and one on the port beam. All exploded on contact with the water, showering the ship with splinters.

Mr. Baril had climbed part way up the ladder leading from the bridge deck to the boat deck in order to get a better view of the attacking aircraft. Thomas L. Jackson, one of the armed guards whose station was on one of the light machine guns, needed to go up this ladder to reach his station. Mr. Baril stepped down in order to let him pass.

The aircraft dropped a few bombs, only small ones of 50 or perhaps 100 kilograms but they were fitted with instantaneous fuses and exploded on contact with the water. One of these bombs landed close to the ship's side, near No. 2 lifeboat only a few feet from where Mr. Baril was standing. Fragments of this bomb went through the ventilators and also hit the bridge. The other bombs were not close enough to do any damage.

Third Officer Franklyn C. McNaught found Mr. Baril slumped on the deck, obviously wounded. He was taken to his cabin and the master was informed. The master carried out an initial examination which showed that Mr. Baril had a jagged wound about one inch in diameter on his right side, over the kidney. There was very little external bleeding and the master feared it was a deep wound and that his second mate was bleeding internally.

He immediately got in touch with HMS *Gleaner*, lying just ahead of *John Walker* and a British Naval surgeon was sent over at once. Mr. Baril was removed to the British Naval Hospital just outside Murmansk as soon as the air raid ceased. One gunner was very slightly wounded but remained on board. Several further air raids occurred each day over Murmansk but no further damage or casualties were sustained by *John Walker* or her crew.

The ship left Murmansk on 30 December 1942 and Captain Jenssen had seen Mr. Baril the previous day when he seemed to be progressing favorably but unfortunately Mr. Baril's condition deteriorated and he died from his wounds.

John Walker called at Loch Ewe and then crossed the Atlantic again, this time westbound, called at St. John's and arrived in New York on 17 February 1943 to end her six-month voyage. After her Arctic interlude, *John Walker*'s next voyages were to North Africa, Italy and then the United Kingdom.

SS *Hugh Williamson* had begun her voyage from New York at almost the same time as *John Walker* had started her voyage from Baltimore. She made her way via Halifax, Nova Scotia, to Iceland. While the vessel was loading the bo'sun had to be hospitalized in New York and was unable to rejoin the ship before she left. Two men were still ashore when the vessel left the Claremont Terminal, New Jersey, and the ship had to anchor off City Island to await their return. They had gone ashore to make phone calls after overhearing the pilot say that he would not be taking the ship away from the pier until after 11:30 a.m. The men were taken by train to City Island and then out to the ship by cutter. Such happenings were not unusual in the day-to-day running of a merchantman in peace or war.

On arrival the vessel stayed at anchor in Iceland for some six weeks during which time, claims one crew member, there was no shore leave. Ned Hecht says the ship left Hvalfjord at 0730 on Sunday, 1 November. "It was a quiet passage round Iceland. We departed North Cape at 0400 Monday. A British Catalina took a look at us next day," he said.

The reader will no doubt have noticed that there are numerous references by the various merchantmen, of seeing and/or communicating with "a British Catalina." Despite intensive research in an effort to identify the Royal Air Force squadron of which these aircraft formed a part, it has proved impossible to prove the point beyond doubt. The most likely seems to be No. 210 Squadron based at Sullum Voe in the Shetlands. They had the very long range version of this aircraft and definitely carried out missions in this area. They sometimes used Akureyri, in Iceland, as a detached base. Although the squadron was beginning a move to Gibraltar, they were still flying from Sullum Voe on long-range missions during late October/early November 1942. The operational record books for this period in the squadron's history are not very detailed. A typical entry being "Catalina... detached to Iceland for special duties." The other possibility is that the aircraft could have been one of the two Catalinas operated by No. 330 (Norwegian) Squadron, RAF, based at Akureyri.

This same crew member, Ned Hecht, says she was the seventh ship to sail (according to official records she was the eighth) and that the following British ship (number eight he says), nine in fact, *Empire Sky*, overtook his ship. *Hugh Williamson* then overtook the British vessel later the same night and then received a distress call from the British ship saying that she was being attacked by a submarine, "and we could hear explosions." Ensign Roger Philip Wise, the U.S. Armed Guard commander, in his report states,

To comply with a message from the Admiralty to round the South Cape of Spitzbergen at nightfall, we had reduced our speed for eighteen hours. During this time the eighth [actually the ninth] ship caught up with us. She then fell back out of sight as we rounded the Cape at nightfall on the 6th. At 2130 GMT we received an SOS that a ship had been torpedoed just a few miles from our position. Twenty-five minutes later, we saw a huge red flare go up about ten to fifteen miles on our port quarter. This was accompanied by a low rumble and immediately followed by three booms from a 4- or 5-inch gun.

Ned Hecht was a U.S. Navy signalman on board *Hugh Williamson* and he says he exchanged signals with the ship, which identified herself as the British SS *Empire Sky*.

We gave her soundings [depth of water] and our position. At around eleven o'clock that night we received a distress call from her saying she was being attacked by a U-boat. We obeyed orders and carried on. We saw the explosion a little later on our port quarter.

Examination of the log of *U-625* for this day shows quite clearly that after her attack on the stranded SS *Chulmleigh*, the U-bat set off to return to her designated patrol area. An hour later she dived to reload her torpedo tubes and while submerged the sound operator detected propeller noises on a bearing of 150 degrees true at 1830 hours German time. The U-bat surfaced ten minutes later and set off at high speed on this bearing.

Fifty minutes later the lookouts on the U-boat could see a dark shadow off the port bow. They soon identified it as a large merchant ship, steering roughly an easterly course at about 9 knots. The U-boat gained on the ship rapidly and overtook her to get into a suitable attack position. By 2000 hours *U-625* was beginning her run in and fourteen minutes later she fired two torpedoes. Both missed completely.

Hans Benker had most probably underestimated the speed of *Empire Sky*. Benker logs that the ship then increased her speed and began zig-zagging at 12 knots, while he was running hard to get ahead of the ship for another attack. The next attack with two torpedoes also failed and *Empire Sky* turned away, says Benker.

Two hours would elapse before the next attack. Surely, therefore, the master of *Empire Sky*, had he indeed been aware of the first torpedo attack on his ship, would have ordered his radio officers to transmit an attack report. The need for strict radio silence had now gone. The vessel had been detected, her position, course and speed were now known to the enemy. It appears however that except for *Hugh Williamson*, neither friend or foe heard any transmission at this time.

U-625 again increased speed to get ahead of the merchantman, and using his radar once again got his submarine in a favorable position to attack. He then waited half an hour until the sky was quite bright due to the Aurora Borealis. He intended his next attack to be from close range in order not to give the merchantman any time to take avoiding action, should they spot his torpedoes running towards their ship. In the intervening time the forward torpedo tubes had been reloaded and he ordered tubes one and two to stand by. He ordered them to be fired at 2224 hours and observed one hit the bow and the other just aft of the midships superstructure. Benker states,

> The ship is listing to starboard then to port. The bows sink deeper. Transmits a radio message, name of ship not recognized. Boats are lowered. Astern is an aircraft on a catapult. [This must be a mistaken observation. CAM ships (Catapult Aircraft Merchantman) were fitted with a fighter on a catapult which straddled the foc'sle head, not the stern. None of the ships taking part in this operation were CAM ships.] On deck aircraft are lashed and there are large boxes. On the bow and stern there are guns. Ship has six holds. Estimate 6,500 tons. Ship now stopped.

Benker then goes on to report,

> Fire torpedo from tube five (stern tube), hit after 35 seconds. [This would indicate that he had probably only reloaded tubes one and two of his four bow tubes.] Ship explodes in a great detonation, night is brightened to daylight, a fire column rises in the sky, wreckage splashes around in the water, which seems to boil. Many splinters hit our boat. Only a short time later, smoke marks the scene of the disaster. The lifeboats have also disappeared. Return to patrol area.

Examination of the log of the U-boat shows a time span of only two hours between the attack on the stranded *Chulmleigh* and the hydrophone detection of *Empire Sky*. This indicates quite clearly that the relative positions of *Chulmleigh*, *Empire Sky*, and *Hugh Williamson* were all within about fifty nautical miles, using the time factor and the top surface speed of *U-625* as a basis for estimates. The 200 mile spacing between the merchantmen, deemed so important on sailing, seems to have been forgotten, or to have become of less importance at this stage.

It is very likely that *U-625* left the scene of the sinking at a fairly high speed and on the surface, away from *Hugh Williamson*. Had *U-625* dived and listened again on her hydrophones then surely she would have detected the propeller noise of the American ship only a few miles further to the east.

From these two reports it is almost certain that they were both about the same ship, the ill fated SS *Empire Sky*. *Hugh Williamson* was extremely lucky to escape undetected from *U-625*.

Hugh Williamson was attacked by an Fw 200 "Condor" unsuccessfully but did receive some slight damage from a near-miss bomb. Ned Hecht recalls,

> On 7 November the big cargo ship experienced her first bombing of the war. The submarine that sank *Empire Sky* had probably given our position to another foe. The next morning we were found by an Fw 200 four-motor bomber. When he saw we were alone he didn't waste any time. We were plenty scared but we put up a tough battle. He dropped his load and we turned him back. Some of the bombs just missed us.

Friendly aircraft found them on the 9th and a British escort took them to Molotovuk.

Official records show that *Hugh Williamson* was sighted by Russian aircraft near Cape Kanin at 1509 on the 9th. She was met by HM Ships *Harrier* and *Gleaner* at 2230 that night. The two escorts had sailed from Iokanka earlier that day. The records also state that, "The steamer *Hugh Williamson* transmitted numerous distress calls during the concluding stages of her passage." The use of the words 'distress call' in these reports is, I think, an unfortunate choice. I feel sure that they were AAAA (aircraft attack) signals and not distress signals in the true maritime radio definition.

Hugh Williamson was the first of the two ships to leave Hvalfjord on 1 November. *Chulmleigh* had sailed some twelve hours earlier and *Empire Sky* would sail twelve hours later. The log of *Hugh Williamson* shows that she received a distress call on 6 November but unfortunately no other details are given. Only two ships sent distress calls on this date as far as we know, the *Dekabrist* and possibly *Empire Sky*. What a pity that the entry is so limited. It does say that the vessel said it was torpedoed. The report, however, does not state whether by aircraft or submarine attack.

On the following day *Hugh Williamson* was attacked by a four-engined bomber during the morning. The vessel replied with her 3-inch anti-aircraft and eight 20-mm cannon. Bombs landed close to Nos. 4 and 5 hatches on the starboard side but there was no real damage to the vessel nor injuries to her crew. The position is logged as 76N 30E. The vessel was not taking in water. An aircraft attack signal was transmitted at 1045 GMT.

Two days later she was again found by two hostile aircraft but they did not attack. The ship's guns were manned but not fired as the aircraft remained out of range. This time the position is logged as 6825N 4124E, approaching the entrance to the White Sea. Once again at 1135 GMT an aircraft attack signal was transmitted. These aircraft were almost certainly Russian, and they were searching for the merchantmen.

It is very interesting to compare the above report and the approximate positions of *Empire Sky* and *Hugh Williamson* on 5 November, the day when the two ships are reported to have played leap-frog. Without knowing more facts one can only surmise, but it is within the realms of possibility that they did indeed overtake each other as related. It would only need *Hugh Williamson* to have been delayed a few hours while waiting to round the South Cape of Spitzbergen under favorable conditions for *Empire Sky* to have caught up with her. If this did indeed happen then it seems that *Hugh Williamson* was the last friendly ship seen by *Empire Sky* and that she did send a distress signal. What a pity that the log entries of *Hugh Williamson* are not more detailed. From the statements by Ned Hecht, Clifford Peterson and the Gunnery Officer we know that *Hugh Williamson* deliberately slowed down for some eighteen hours, and the notes made by Ned Hecht in his diary at the time indicate that there is no doubt whatever that the ship was *Empire Sky*.

On 11 November while entering Molotovuk at 1315 hours *Hugh Williamson* collided with the Russian steamer m.v. *Volga*, inflicting some minor damage to her. *Hugh Williamson* suffered no damage whatever.

During her stay in Molotovuk Bosun Erik Alvar Johansson became very ill. The port was searched for a medical officer and a Russian doctor from a ship in the harbor came out and administered emergency treatment but was unable to save his life. Two other crew members were less severely ill; they too were treated and fortunately recovered. It was the opinion of the medical officer that these men had consumed inferior alcohol. Ned Hecht remembers,

> On December 9th we had a death on board. One of our merchant seaman crew got loaded while ashore. Once back on board he started to look for more drink. He spotted some antifreeze in the paint store and drank it before anyone could stop him. Two AB's who had been ashore with him also drank some, though not as much. The b'osun died and we buried him in Russia. The two AB's were very ill but they recovered.

The vessel steamed astern of a Russian icebreaker in December before joining her convoy for the United Kingdom and finally arrived back in New York in February 1943. "By which time" says Ned Hecht, "I was skin and bone and looked 10 years older than I was."

Later that same year, in September 1943 she was again attacked by aircraft no less than forty-nine times on this occasion while unloading supplies for the beachhead at Salerno, Italy. She claims shooting down several aircraft and also a glider bomb. She then made a trip to Great Britain followed by two long voyages to Aden and Port Said via Cape Town and Durban.

Richard H. Alvey arrived at Loch Ewe from the United States on 10 September and dropped her anchor. She left Loch Ewe before breakfast on 18 October, bound for Reykjavik in a convoy of about fifteen ships, escorted by five warships. It was a very peaceful trip and they all anchored safely in Hvalfjord at lunch time on the 22nd.

One week later she left the safety of the anchorage, again before breakfast time, bound unescorted to North Russia. She tested her guns the next day and found them all in perfect working order. That same afternoon a Catalina contacted them and wished them luck. Nothing else was seen until 2145 hours on 2 November when a small freighter of about 2,000 tons appeared on the port beam at about one mile. Both ships took avoiding action. The small steamer was going westwards. This unscheduled meeting point was about 50 miles southwest of the South Cape of Spitzbergen. No contact was made with the vessel. "The next day, at 1400 hours the superstructure of a much larger freighter appeared for about fifteen minutes on our port quarter, then it too moved away. On November 4th at about 0900 we sighted the smoke of a steamship on our port quarter but we never sighted the ship at all on that occasion," said Robert B. Platt, the U.S. Navy Ensign in charge of the Armed Guard.

The most likely explanation for these two sightings is that they were the first two of the eight westbound ships of Operation FB, the SS *Mussoviet* and the SS *Azerbaijan* who had sailed from North Russia on 29 and 31 October, respectively. The next westbound vessel to leave, SS *Chernyshevsky* did not sail until 2 November, the day that the first sighting was made.

During the morning of 4 November *Richard H. Alvey* received three distress messages. These were actually aircraft attack signals. They were AAAA de KGBL (*John H. B. Latrobe*) 7447N 0220E; AAAA de WKPA (unknown) 7530N 3130E at 1000 hours; AAAA de YZIM (a corrupt call sign) 7500N 2710E. The first of these messages seems straightforward as the call-sign was as stated in brackets. The second attack gives what should be an American call sign but none of the American ships carried this call sign at all! The third attack is again a mystery. If we examine the call signs of the various ships together with the positions quoted then it seems most likely that this message originated from SS *Dekabrist* (UOML) but the position is accurate. The call sign of *Richard H. Alvey*, the ship receiving the messages was KGIM, an easy corruption of YZIM!

Richard H. Alvey had zig-zagged during daylight and moonlight (moonless period!) but had taken a straight course during the hours of darkness throughout the voyage. When about one hundred miles north of the entrance to the White Sea the ship was met by two Russian escorts and taken to Archangel. *Richard H. Alvey*'s report states that the weather was fine and clear except for the final 250 miles. The temperature was just under freezing throughout. She had been running at a speed of 11.5 to 12 knots without any problems.

Selvin M. Lien, one of *Richard H. Alvey*'s gun crew remembers,

> The most beautiful sight I've ever seen happened on February 3rd, 1943, the sight of the Statue of Liberty as we entered New York Harbor. What a glorious day. There were many times during this voyage and others, when I thought I would never see the United States or my family again. The Armed Guard crew were sent on leave and then to different ships but I did keep in touch with the three LaVack brothers who had made the Russian journey with me. Dewey, the last surviving brother, died last year.

For her next voyage *Richard H. Alvey* was under the command of Captain T. C. Hallum and he remained in command until 1945. Articles were opened on 4 March 1943 and closed on June 6th. Several crew members are mentioned in the log for minor offenses. For the third voyage the pattern is repeated between 30 June and 11 August. Different names this time. There appear to be no records of this nature for this ship prior to 4 March 1943, however.

International Marine Radio Company Limited
Radio Officers : Roll of Honour

ALLAN, BENJAMIN MARSHALL
ANGLO, ALBERT
BARRY, RICHARD JAMES
✖ BEARD, THOMAS WILLIAM
BERRY, KENNETH PETER
BIRD, ERIC
BOOTH, BASIL
BOULTER, JOHN
BROWN, FREDERICK WILLIAM THOMAS
BROWN, KEITH
BURNETT, TRAYTON
CAMERON, KENNETH WILLIAM ROWLAND
CAMERON, LACHLAN
CAMPBELL, EDWARD RUSSELL
CARTMELL, BENJAMIN
CARTON, WILLIAM EDWARD
CHATER, HENRY WALTER JOHN
CHILD, ALFRED GEORGE
COLEMAN, EDWARD ALAN
CROSBY, DANE GEOFFREY
COOK, ALEXANDER
CUNNING, HENRY
DAVIES, FREDERICK WILLINGTON
DAVIES, LEWIS ARTHUR
DAVIES, RONALD LLOYD
DEAN, ALAN
DICKSON, GEORGE EDWARD
DWANE, STEPHEN
EVANS, HAROLD HELLIER
EVANS, NORMAN ALLEN
FARRAR, RONALD
FAULDS, THOMAS ERIC AITON
FERGUSON, CYRIL MILBURN
FRANKS, LEONARD
FULTON, ROBERT
GAFFNEY, JOHN
GARDEN, HARALD DENNISON
GERARD, MAX REGINALD
GLEDHILL, ERIC ROBERTSON
GOLDIE, JOHN McNICOL
GRAYSTON, DEREK HOLLINSWORTH
HARLEY, WILLIAM
HARTLEY, WILLIAM HENRY
HEGARTY, NORMAN WOOD
HELLAWELL, CLAUDE
HENDERSON, KENNETH WALTER FORBES
HENDERSON, LAWRENCE BOLT
HENNERTY, MICHAEL
HERMAN, SIDNEY PHILIP
HILDRED, RAYMOND GURTON
HOWARTH, WINSTON EDGELL
HOWIE, WILLIAM KELSO
HUME, WILLIAM FRANK
✖ JAMES, RICHARD CADDICK
JOHNSON, DESMOND VANE
JONES, HYWEL
KELLY, ALBERT
KIRKBRIDE, JOHN STEELE
LECKIE, THOMAS SPROTT
LE FEUVRE, LEOPOLD EDWARD WILLIAM
LEITCHMAN, JAMES DELVIN
LONG, LAWRENCE DAVID
LOWNIE, DAVID GIBB
McCULLOCH, GEORGE DONALD
MACINTOSH, CHARLES STEVEN
McEWING, IAN McDOUGALL
MARCHI, VINCENT DOUGLAS
MATTHEW, GEORGE
MILNE, HARRY BISSETT
MITCHELL, JAMES WILLIAM KING
MURRAY, ALAN HARRIS
O'SULLIVAN, JAMES
OWEN, JAMES
PHILLIPS, JOHN
PHILLIPS, RICHARD
POMEROY, PETER
PRICE, JOHN LAING
QUIGLEY, JOHN JOSEPH
RAE, WILLIAM
REES, JAMES GILBERT
REGAN, DOUGLAS ERNEST EDWARD
REILLY, ROBERT
REYNHART, VICTOR WALLIS
SADLER, WILLIAM EWART
✖ SANDIFORD, WILFRID
SCOTT, CHARLES NEVILLE
SEBRIGHT, ROBERT RONALD
SERGEANT, ALAN HOWARD
SEVERS, ALFRED LAWRENCE
SHERLOCK, MAURICE FRANCIS
SIBBITT, HERBERT ERNEST
SKEARS, WILLIAM CHISLETT
SMITH, CLAUDE HARRY
SMITH, JOHN BRYANT
SPRIGGS, JACK VERNON
SPRUNT, GEORGE
STOREY, GEORGE ALEXANDER
TAYLOR, WILFRED
THEW, BASIL PAUL
THOMSON, WILLIAM STARK
WARNER, LOUIS MERRICK
WATT, VICTOR RICHARD THOMAS
WEBB, CHARLES BRYDGES NANFAN
WHITE, JAMES
WHITE, JAMES ALEXANDER
WHYTE, WILLIAM C. McA.
WILLIAMS, BASIL TUDOR
WILLIAMS, EDWARD JOHN
WILLIAMS, JOHN PURSEY
WITHAM, SOREN ALBERT TERKELSEN

IMRC

✖ = *Radio officers of S.S. Empire Gilbert.*

ARCTIC INTERLUDE

While on her third voyage after her independent trip to North Russia *Richard H. Alvey* was involved in a relatively minor collision with SS *Nathan Clifford*, one of her sister ships. *Richard H. Alvey* seems to have escaped further wartime damage according to the official records available. Raymond Barba, an ex-USN Armed Guardsman disagrees with the records. He says he was a member of the Armed Guard crew of *Richard H. Alvey* on the voyage immediately following her independent trip to north Russia. The master, he says, was a Swede and that Captain Hallum had been in command during the trip to Russia. He claims that the records have been deliberately 'mislaid' for reasons he does not know about. My own copies of official records, however, show the Master as Captain C. S. Forisland on the independent run, and Captain T. C. Hallum as Master on successive voyages.

After her independent trip to North Russia *Richard H. Alvey* made two voyages to North Africa and then came to Great Britain on her next three trips from the United States. She then made a second journey to the bleak Arctic in convoy JW-56A during January 1944, returning home in March to go back on the North Africa run.

It was on the voyage immediately following her lone run to North Russia that *Richard H. Alvey* rescued seventy-six survivors from two ships which had collided. SS *Alcoa Guard* remained afloat and was towed to safety while the Norwegian motor vessel *Tamesis* sank. The survivors were landed at Bermuda.

Leading Telegraphist Ian Fraser of HM Trawler *Cape Argona* kept a diary during his Navy days. This, of course, was totally contrary to King's Regulations, the Official Secrets Act and probably a breach of at least half a dozen other punishable regulations then in force. It does, however, enable me to be more specific in *Cape Argona*'s involvement in Operation FB.

Cape Argona had been part of the through escort to PQ-18. She had left Hvalfjord with full bunkers and even carried coal on deck. When she arrived in North Russia she had only five tons of coal remaining. Other trawlers of the escort were in a similar plight. They obtained coal from SS *Empire Baffin* and *Empire Morn* but had to top up their bunkers from a Russian collier, too.

On 29 October *Cape Argona* was under orders to keep steam for immediate sailing but the following day she was still alongside No. 19 sawmill berth. Lieutenant Pate attended a very secret conference at Archangel on the 31st and the ship moved to the Dvina Bar and anchored on 1 November. The following day Lt. Pate assembled the crew in the mess deck and outlined their part in the operation. He informed them that they would patrol North Arctic waters and then go to Murmansk. "We will not be home for Christmas," were his final disheartening words.

HMT *Cape Argona* sailed that same day with orders to find merchant ships that had been sailed independently from Iceland and to bring them in. It is quite possible that the Soviet trawlers had been sailed earlier because the first of the eight westbound Russian freighters of operation FB had left North Russia on 29 October, followed at intervals by the rest.

From Ian Fraser's diary we know that on 4 November *Cape Argona*'s lookouts challenged a Ju 88, "which answered correctly." This is a most interesting entry. Why bother to even challenge an enemy aircraft? Perhaps the Russians had captured Ju 88s and were using them as part of their own air force.

On 5 November Ian Fraser's diary shows that as well as chipping ice, HMT *Cape Mariato* was sighted by the lookouts of *Cape Argona*, hull down. The diary also shows that a distress signal from *Empire Clarke* (sic) was received. (No such named vessel is listed in *Empire* ship records). SS *William Clark*, however, had been sunk the previous day. This signal was passed to HMT *Cape Mariato* by R/T. Both ships were much too far away from *William Clark* to be of any assistance. On the following day a signal was received by *Cape Argona* informing them that three of the independents had been recalled to Iceland.

It was on 7 November that an entry in the diary shows that *Cape Argona* was attacked with two bombs, both near misses, dropped by another Ju 88 whom they had challenged by Aldis lamp and had received the correct reply. The trawler set course for Iokanka on this day, too, having seen no sign of the merchantmen.

The first two merchantmen to sail from Iceland, *Richard H. Alvey* and *Empire Galliard*, both arrived in Molotovuk on this day. *John Walker*, the fourth to sail, arrived the following day.

Cape Argona was attacked again by aircraft while returning to port, again escaping without serious damage. she arrived back in Iokanka on 9 November and took on bunkers. On 11 November she was once more under sailing orders. She sailed the following day with orders to look for *Empire Scott* and *Empire Sky*. The weather was very bad, high winds causing very rough seas which carried away the forward companionway and put plenty of salt water on the mess deck. The weather remained bad, *Cape Mariato* was sighted briefly on the 14th. She, too, was under the same orders. The wind increased to storm force and *Cape Argona* was forced to dodge to the weather. The air temperature dropped rapidly and she began icing up. It was back to chipping ice for the crew but they were fighting a losing battle and by 17 November *Cape Argona* had developed an alarming 30 degree list as she made her way slowly back to Iokanka. The alert lookouts of the trawler sighted a small convoy in the brief twilight of the 18th and arrived at Iokanka on the 19th. Her crew of fifty-seven officers and men were all relieved to find themselves alongside the familiar jetty once more.

So ended *Cape Argona*'s participation in Operation FB. It was not, however, her final involvement with the merchant ships of the operation. During December 1942 she was ordered to escort *Hugh Williamson* and *Richard H. Alvey* from Archangel to Murmansk. She then took on coal from *John Walker* and also 75 tons from *Empire Scott* before becoming part of the escort for these ships in convoy RA-51 later that same month.

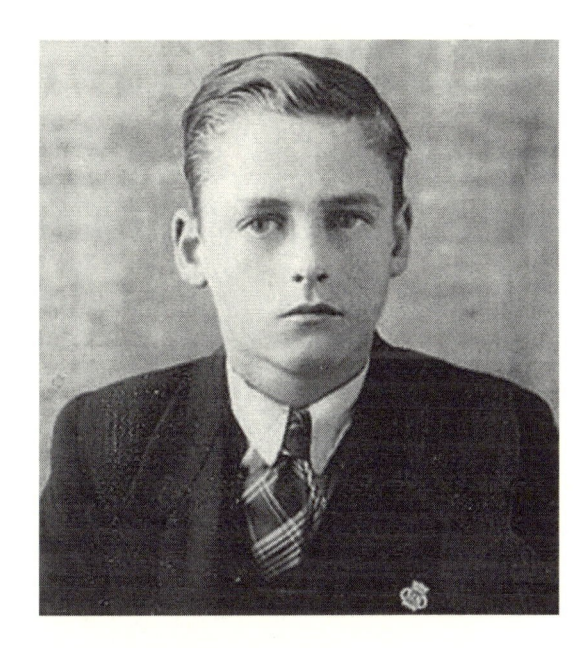

Cabin Boy Terrence P. Garraghan,
S.S. *Empire Galliard*, November 1942.
[Terrence P. Garraghan]

Ordinary Seaman Denis L. Woolliams,
S.S. *Empire Galliard*, November 1942.
[Denis L. Woolliams]

Denis Woolliams' pipe, 1942.
[Denis L. Woolliams]

Capt. J. H. Colvin who took command of S.S. *Empire Scott* after her epic voyage to North Russia.
[J. H. Colvin]

Capt. R. L. Barr. He had to relinquish command of S.S. *Empire Scott* when he fell ill.
[R. L. Barr]

Sidney Evans (and his wife), Assistant Steward,
S.S. *Empire Scott*, November 1942.
[Mrs. Mary Evans]

Peter Anderson and John Kay, left to right, both Able Seamen,
S.S. *Empire Scott*, November 1942. Far right is unknown
but not a crew member of *Empire Scott*.
[Peter Anderson]

Gordon Wilfred Long, Cabin Boy,
S.S. *Empire Scott*, November 1942.
[Gordon Wilfred Long]

Sidney Evans, Assistant Steward,
S.S. *Empire Scott*, November 1942.
[Mrs. Sidney Evans]

John Angus Maclean, Assistant Cook,
S.S. *Empire Scott*, November 1942.
[John Angus Maclean]

Crew of HMT *Cape Argona*, 1942.
[Ian Fraser]

Russian women coaling HMT *Cape Argona*, summer 1942.
[Ian Fraser]

Raymond W. Williams Jr., USAG, S.S. *John Walker*, November 1942.
Photo taken at New York in 1943.
[Raymond W. Williams Jr.]

First Assistant Engineer Harrison O. Travis Jr.,
S.S. *John Walker*, November 1942.
[Harrison O. Travis Jr.]

Clifford O. Peterson, USAG,
S.S. *Hugh Williamson*, November 1942.
[Clifford O. Peterson]

Ned Hecht, USAG, S.S. *Hugh Williamson*, November 1942.
[Ned Hecht]

Armed Guard crew of the S.S. *Hugh Williamson*.
Wilbur D. Sweet second from left.
[Wilbur D. Sweet]

Selvin M. Lein, USAG, S.S. *Richard H. Alvey*, November 1942.
[Selvin Lein]

Bombardier Eddie Shadlock, RMA DEMS gunner,
S.S. *Briarwood*, November 1942.
[Mrs. Eddie Shadlock]

Captain W. Thompson, S.S. *Daldorch*, November 1942.

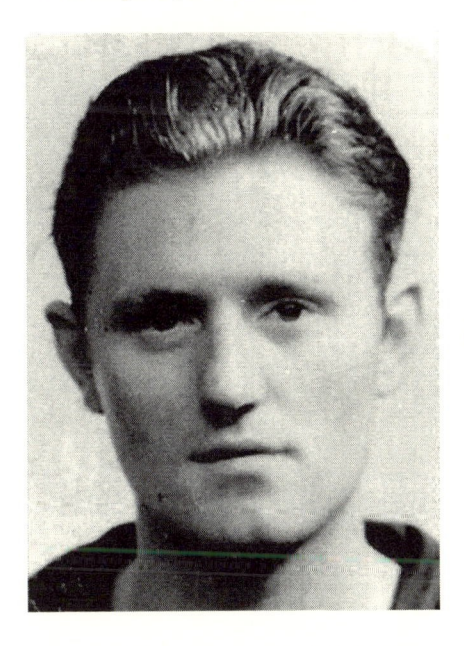

Able Seaman Albert Wray, RN, DEMS gunner,
S.S. *Daldorch*, November 1942.
[Albert Wray]

Chapter 9

They Lived to Fight Another Day

THE sixth ship to leave Hvalfjord was the American Liberty *John H. B. Latrobe*, departing slightly ahead of the ill-fated *Chulmleigh* on 31 October, and we have already seen how she was attacked and then returned to Iceland.

The final two ships to sail were both British and there is a certain amount of mystery surrounding both. These two ships were originally intended to be part of a second wave of independent eastbound sailings. Six American Liberty ships were already at anchor in Hvalfjord for this purpose. There was a third British ship in Hvalfjord but she only had a partial crew. More men would need to be brought from the UK to crew her. There were other British ships in the UK already loaded and ready to sail for Iceland. A signal from the Admiralty ordered *Briarwood* and *Daldorch* to be sailed at once, even "at the risk of upsetting the Americans."

Close examination of their respective crew lists and official logs, when compared to the other British ships leads one to a few possible conclusions. We will first examine in detail the voyage of the last ship to sail, lucky for some, number thirteen, the SS *Briarwood*.

She was, at 4,019 gross tons, the smallest of the baker's dozen. Built in 1930 at Newcastle for the Constantine Steamship Company of Middlesbrough. She was, by tramp ship standards, very well equipped with modern gear: gyrocompass, echo sounding device and radio direction finder. Her first brush with the enemy came on 4 July 1940 while she was steaming down the English Channel, off Portland Bill, in Convoy OA-178. The fourteen-ship, outward bound convoy was attacked and bombed by Ju 87 dive bombers and suffered losses and damage. The convoy was again attacked later in the day by S-boats and suffered further casualties.

After repairs had been carried out *Briarwood* had a relatively quiet war for the next few months until on 5 November 1940 while homeward bound in the thirty-seven ship Convoy HX-84, in mid-Atlantic, the German pocket battleship *Admiral Scheer* (Captain Theodor Krancke) attacked the ships. His Arado spotter aircraft had detected the convoy some 90 miles away, during the early afternoon. The German ship had been informed to expect the convoy, the signal giving the sailing time having been decoded successfully by the German B-Dienst. The Canadian escort had left the convoy some twenty-four hours earlier, leaving only the armed merchant cruiser HMS *Jervis Bay* to accompany it until they were met by the British escorts, which would have been about a further twenty-four hours time.

The fact that Theodor Krancke chose to make his attack just when the convoy escort was at its weakest was not by chance, but by a combination of excellent intelligence information and equally excellent aerial reconnaissance by his Arado spotter aircraft crew. They had achieved almost perfection by detecting the convoy without themselves being spotted.

Unfortunately, however, they had failed to spot the SS *Mopan*, a fast, independently routed merchantman, loaded with bananas, that had overtaken the convoy a little earlier and was to upset Captain Kranke's carefully planned surprise attack. SS *Mopan* had been invited to join HX-84 by the convoy commodore but politely turned the offer down. *Mopan* was steaming at her service speed of 14 knots while the convoy was limited to *Briarwood*'s 9 knots.

As Krancke was closing the convoy he unexpectedly came across *Mopan* between him and his prize and he had to dispose of this vessel first. *Mopan* did not have time to send out an RRRR signal which would have immediately alerted *Jervis Bay*. It was most unfortunate that the first salvo of shells from the raider struck the bridge and wireless room of the merchantman. The ships of the convoy were, however, alerted by the distant gunfire, though they did not know at this stage that it was enemy gunfire.

HMS *Jervis Bay* (Captain E. S. Fogarty-Fegen) put up an heroic battle against overwhelming odds while the convoy was ordered to scatter. Five ships were sunk from the thirty-nine ship convoy and Captain E. S. Fogarty-Fegen and 191 of his crew lost their lives trying to save the merchantmen. He was posthumously awarded the Victoria Cross for his gallantry.

Briarwood was one of the lucky ships that escaped without damage. She was under the command of Captain W. H. Lawrence, on a voyage Halifax to Oban with 6,500 tons of steel and timber. Her crew numbered thirty-four and there were no casualties. It was at first thought that the topmasts, when sighted, belonged to a British man-o-war and Captain Lawrence went below for his tea. No sooner had he reached the saloon when heavy shells began to explode in the middle of the convoy. *Briarwood* opened fire on her adversary, getting off six rounds, but the enemy was well out of the range of her 4-inch gun. After the order to scatter was given all ships dropped smoke floats over the stern at regular intervals and soon the area between the raider and the scattering ships was totally obliterated by a heavy pall of thick black smoke.

Briarwood was the slowest ship in the convoy, only capable of about 9 knots, while most of the other merchantmen could steam at 14 knots. Captain Lawrence ordered the safety valves on the boiler to be screwed down and called for volunteers from the seamen to double up with the firemen in the stokehold. It was not long before *Briarwood* was running at 12½ knots, with bulkheads and fittings vibrating merrily at this unprecedented turn of speed, which she had never before reached.

In August of 1941 *Briarwood* was again under attack. Captain Lawrence was still in command and this time the vessel was bound from Lisbon to New York via Gibraltar. In position 4054N 1916W she was attacked by a four-engined FW 200 "Condor" aircraft. The whole action lasted only a minute or two but fortunately *Briarwood* was not caught unawares because her gun crews were already closed up. L/Bdr. W. C. Halliday was in charge of the 40-mm Bofors gun and Captain Lawrence dashed to one of the bridge machine guns as the alarm was given. Bombardier Halliday withheld his fire, despite the fact that the ship was being raked with machine gun and cannon fire, until the aircraft was well within range. He then emptied several magazines in quick succession at the "Condor," hitting the aircraft several times in the tail region, setting it on fire. The aircraft jettisoned its bombs and turned away, losing height and trailing smoke, but it was not seen to crash.

Three 200-pound bombs dropped only about 20 feet off the starboard quarter of *Briarwood* and the ship was hit by several hundred splinters when they exploded. Several of the crew received minor cuts but no one was seriously hurt. Fifty-four rounds of Bofors and 400 rounds of machine gun ammunition had been fired by *Briarwood*'s gunners in the short, sharp attack. Captain Lawrence also states in his report that the PAC was fired, too, and that it fouled both port engines of the "Condor." Bombardier Halliday received the DSM and Captain Lawrence was invested with the OBE for their efforts in this action.

She made her first voyage to North Russia, in convoy PQ-3 during November 1941. She made her second trip to North Russia in PQ-14. Twenty-four ships left in the outward convoy, sixteen returned with weather damage, one ship was lost and seven, including *Briarwood* reached Murmansk. Captain William Henry Charles Lawrence, OBE, was still in command of *Briarwood* and he was vice commodore of PQ-14. The commodore was taking passage in SS *Empire Howard* and when this vessel was lost Captain Lawrence took over the duties of commodore for the remainder of the passage. There were as many escorts as there were merchantmen when they reached Russia.

He was made commodore of the homeward bound convoy, QP-11 and for the excellent performance of his duties he was made a CBE. She sailed for home in convoy QP-11 with twelve other merchantmen and a strong Royal Navy escort. Off northern Norway the convoy was attacked by German destroyers and after a fierce battle one Russian merchantman had been sunk, one British escort was damaged and one German destroyer was at the bottom of the Barents Sea. The remaining twelve merchantmen of the convoy were brought safely to Reykjavik on 7 May 1942.

Late August of 1942 found *Briarwood* in her home port of Middlesbrough discharging and loading cargo. This must have been quite a lengthy task because she was still in port in late September of that year. Captain W. H. Lawrence was Master of the vessel and according to the articles he had been Master on her previous voyage, seventeen others of her crew also signed fresh articles during August, a good indication of being a 'happy' ship. In an unhappy ship most of the crew would do '11' voyages—'1' out and '1' home! Captain James Shaw signed on the vessel as Staff Captain on 25 August but the articles show that he took over as Master of the vessel in Hvalfjord, Iceland, on 3 November, "On orders of the A.C.I.C. Iceland." No definition of A.C.I.C. is given but I suspect that the initials stand for Admiral Commanding Iceland Command. I have seen in other records the definition given was Admiral Commanding Iceland (C) and Admiral Dalrymple-Hamilton was named as incumbent. The (C) was ordered to be included in the title by Winston Churchill to avoid any possible confusion with Ireland.

There had been one or two minor misdemeanors by various crew members. This was quite normal in any merchant ship in peacetime as well as in wartime. For instance, one man had deserted ship at Middlesbrough, others had been logged for missing a watch or for going absent without leave, a fireman had been put ashore ill, all quite normal occurrences in the day-to-day running of a merchantman.

Fred Jollings was an able seaman on this vessel, at this time and he recalls,

We loaded at Middlesbrough with bombs, cased petrol, Red Cross and medical supplies, small arms ammunition, manila, wire rope, and food. Deck cargo was tanks and crated aero engines. We were told the value of our cargo was over £3 million. We had very bad weather on passage from Scotland to Iceland, some deck cargo shifted. While in Iceland the ship was visited by Ministry of Shipping officials. All hands were assembled and called upon to volunteer for an independent run to north Russia. All volunteers would be paid a £50 bonus (and we were). Anyone not wishing to volunteer would be held ashore until the operation was complete, then return to the UK with no victimisation. Because of storm damage we were put at the tail end of the group. We sailed, but after about forty-eight hours we were ordered to return to Iceland. We returned to anchor and spent about five weeks carrying out various exercises with HMS *Berwick*. For light relief we coaled anti-submarine trawlers at Hvalfjord. We had our midships deep tanks full of coal, intended for the trawlers marooned in North Russia. We finally sailed to North Russia in convoy JW-51B. To the best of my recollections I cannot remember Captain Lawrence ever being in command during this voyage.

I also managed to contact relatives of one of *Briarwood*'s DEMS gunners. Among the Army DEMS gunners that had signed on the ship in Middlesbrough early in September 1942 was 23-year-old Gunner Eddie Shadlock of Grimsby. Five of his fellow Army gunners had sailed in the same ship as Eddie on their previous voyage, the SS *El Mirlo*. Eddie was a hostilities-only soldier, he had attended South Parade School in Grimsby and on leaving school at fourteen he had become an errand boy for a prominent local butcher. He later went to work in Grimsby's Wintringham's Timber Yard and Saw Mills until he was called up in 1940 and joined the Royal Artillery, later transferring to the Royal Maritime Artillery. He had already been torpedoed once while serving as a DEMS gunner on a tanker. On this occasion he and his shipmates spent an uncomfortable week in the lifeboat before being rescued.

Eddie's humble background was quite typical of many of his fellow DEMS gunners of World War II. Despite the significant differences in pay between the DEMS gunners and the merchant seamen there was very little animosity between them, and the gunners did their job well. A contributory factor to the general goodwill enjoyed by all was perhaps the fact that the full Army/Navy discipline was relaxed to a great degree in these ships, it was not necessary. Merchant navy food was marginally better than service messes and there was usually a good chance of earning some extra money on board.

According to some official reports *Briarwood* sailed from Hvalfjord on 4 November, returning on the 6th, but the official log of the vessel shows an entry on 3 November giving the ship's position as Hvalfjord. A similar entry on the 5th does likewise. She is not listed in official records as being damaged at this time so perhaps she was recalled to Hvalfjord on Admiralty orders.

We do know from these records that the ship was back in the United Kingdom at Loch Ewe on 14 December, finally sailing for North Russia in Convoy JW-51A as Commodore Ship the following day. This was the first convoy to sail for North Russia for more than three months. All the ships of this convoy arrived safely in Murmansk on Christmas Day, some ships carried on to Molotovuk, arriving two days later. The *Briarwood* made the return journey to the United Kingdom in convoy RA-52 and discharged her cargo of Russian timber for Wintringham's Timber and Saw Mills at Grimsby on 13 February 1943. She also brought back eight crew members of the SS *Empire Elgar*, a heavy lift merchant ship that had gone to Russia for a long stay. She was one of about three such ships that were sent to help speed up the discharge of tanks, locomotives and other heavy machinery, supplementing a very limited service in Murmansk. Eddie Shadlock was pleased that he did not have to face the usual long rail journey to go on leave, a five-minute bus ride would suffice this trip.

It is interesting to note that there were no large changes to the crew during the period we have been discussing and the only change made on the instructions of the A.C.I.C. Iceland was that of the Master. The situation with the twelfth ship is totally different. A few changes to crew in the other British ships had been made on the instructions of this official, mainly changing Arab, West African, West Indian or Chinese firemen and crew for a white British equivalent. No reason is ever given and the discharged men received 'Very Good' discharge records. Sometimes the changes were made at Loch Ewe, before the vessel sailed for Iceland, sometimes they were made at Hvalfjord, Iceland. The number of changes in the case of *Daldorch* are exceptionally high and it appears that there was either some confusion or there was a desperate shortage of firemen at Hvalfjord.

It is known for certain that there was a hospital ship stationed there where seamen could receive treatment and be hospitalized. Almost certainly there would be an accommodation ship, too, where spare crews would be available as replacements. According to one crew member of *Empire Scott*, they brought out a spare crew from the United Kingdom. This crew was intended to go through to Russia but the orders were changed and they were left at Hvalfjord.

SS *Daldorch* was also built in 1930 for the Campbell Steamship Company. She was later purchased by Paddy Henderson and Company of Glasgow. She was a slightly larger ship than *Briarwood* but still small by comparison to most of the other ships of our group. She was in Liverpool during September 1942 when articles were opened and a full crew signed on. The firemen were mainly West African. She completed loading in Liverpool and sailed for Loch Ewe, arriving there on 14 October. Forty-four-year-old Captain W. S. Thomson was in command. While the ship was at anchor off Altbea (Loch Ewe) all the West African firemen, donkeymen and greaser and the Chinese assistant cook were discharged and replaced by mainly Maltese men, on orders from HM Government. The ship then sailed for Hvalfjord, in convoy, arriving there in late October 1942. Three seamen were discharged here on 26 October due to misconduct, and were replaced. On 1 November all the Maltese crew were 'withdrawn by order of the A.C.I.C. Reykjavik' and Captain W. H. Lawrence (late of SS *Briarwood*) initialed the log entries to this effect! They were replaced by mainly British nationals on the same day. On 3 November, however, all these men, too, were discharged 'on the instructions of A.C.I.C. Reykjavik' and the Maltese firemen were re-instated with pay going back to their original signing on day! It makes one wonder if this was because there were no more engine/boiler room ratings available in the pool there! Many of the log entries for *Daldorch* at this time are not in chronological sequence, again strange.

Daldorch was still in Hvalfjord on 3 November and the next positive date in the records is 17 November, still at Hvalfjord. There is no evidence of damage by enemy action and so the full details of her sailing from and returning to Hvalfjord remain a mystery. According to official information she sailed on 3 November and returned on the 6th, but no reason is given. Mr. Richard Watt, who was a young apprentice in 1942 and a member of her crew, recalls quite certainly that she did indeed sail as ordered but after about thirty-six hours at sea she was recalled by wireless signal, no reason being given.

The American VP-84 Squadron, USN, were active north of Iceland in late October-early November 1942. Lieutenant R. C. Millard and his crew in Catalina 'H' sank *U-409* just to the north of Iceland on 5

ARCTIC INTERLUDE

November. The last two ships of Operation FB to sail, SS *Daldorch* and *Briarwood* must have been quite close to the position in which *U-409* met her end at around the same time. Perhaps that was the reason for recall, though it will be remembered that *Northern Spray*'s encounter with *U-212* on 31 October near Jan Mayen did not affect other sailing plans in any way whatever.

Seaman Gunner Albert Wray, RN, was a 20-year-old DEMS gunner on board *Daldorch* at that time. Fortunately for us he kept a diary of events. After the aborted voyage, while the ship was back in the Clyde, he sent this diary back home by registered mail for safe keeping. He was rather unfortunate in that his letter was intercepted by censor No. 1921 at Gourock. Nothing happened immediately. The ship sailed and made the round voyage to north Russia in convoy and duly docked at Middlesbrough. Civilian police CID officers came on board and interviewed Gunner Wray. He was interrogated about the diary for a few hours and then he was handed over to the Royal Navy. He served ten days detention in Hartlepool police cells for the offense and then forgot about the incident completely. In March 1946, out of the blue, the original envelope, complete with diary, dropped through his letterbox. There was no accompanying letter at all. From this diary, however, we can confirm the following facts on the aborted independent voyage.

The crew were first informed of the impending voyage on 24 October and some of *Daldorch*'s crew opted out. The gunners, both RN and RMA were given no such option. Those opting out were informed that they would be kept on board the troopship *Cameronian*, then at anchor in Hvalfjord, until the operation was complete. Replacement firemen, a steward and some ABs joined the ship on 31 October. More men opted out and were replaced on 1 November. *Daldorch* sailed at 4:30 p.m. on 3 November. While at sea news was received of ships ahead being attacked on 4 November. At 7:45 that evening, some twenty-seven hours after sailing, the vessel was turned round and headed back to Hvalfjord at full speed, on orders received by radio. Reykjavik was sighted at 11:30 p.m. on 5 November and the vessel anchored during the early hours of the 6th.

News was received that *Chulmleigh* was on the rocks at Spitzbergen. The diary entry on 16 November obviously refers to SS *John H. B. Latrobe*. The diary also throws more light on the events prior to sailing.

Rumors flourished on board *Daldorch*: 'ladies' were coming on board!... the ship was sailing to Russia alone!... the ship would be at anchor for several more weeks until escorts were available! Speculation was running wild when the 2nd Mate informed everyone that a naval officer would be coming on board the next day to address the whole crew, meanwhile clean up and muster in the mess at 1100.

The naval officer arrived and his address went along these lines, says Gunner Wray.

> 'I am sorry that no one has been to visit your ship. I am here to put that right. Please tell me what you are short of... socks, gramophone records, soap, books, magazines or perhaps a dartboard? Come on, lads, fire away.'
>
> One Liverpool lad shouted, 'Our tea, sugar, cocoa, butter and tinned milk rations are not too good.'
>
> The Navy man replied that he would personally see to it that these rations were increased by fifty percent, and indeed they were.
>
> He went on to say, 'Now listen carefully. On Sunday you will be visited by a very important person and also by your port commander. Please clean out your mess in readiness for them.'

Gunner Wray states that all the things requested by the crew were delivered to the ship by a tender the next day.

Sunday arrived and the port commander, his aide, a lieutenant and a very well dressed civilian came on board. The civilian was introduced as Mr. Bullimore and he addressed the men. He began in an easy style. Gunner Way said,

> One point I distinctly remember is him telling us just how expensive it was to have a shirt laundered in Iceland. He soon got down to the real purpose of his visit and informed us that he had been tasked with getting our cargo to Russia in a simple and easy way. We, and other ships, were to sail solo. One small ship in a vast ocean. No one would find us. It was the safest way to Murmansk.
>
> The DEMS ratings were told it was their duty to sail and there was not really any need for this address. He went on, 'However, I am paying a £50 bonus for this trip and *all* who sail for me get my bonus.' He then opened his briefcase and gave each one of the DEMS ratings a large white £5 note saying, 'Have a drink on me lads. You'll be home by Christmas.'

This was followed by a few more jokes. He then left with the high ranking RN officer and went to the saloon to address the merchant navy personnel. The officers were to get £100 for the trip.

After the brass had left our mess the lieutenant took over and gave us all a post office will form and a few other papers for us to sign. The lieutenant then told us that Mr. Bullimore had run his ship through the Franco blockade on several occasions during the Spanish Civil War of the 1930s. He had earned the nickname of Captain Potato Jones because a large part of his cargo had been potatoes. He was well experienced in such voyages.

We certainly know that *Daldorch* left Hvalfjord after the 4 December and that on or before 16 December 1942, returned to Greenock where the old articles were closed and fresh articles opened. Seventeen of her crew from the previous voyage, mainly key personnel, resigned articles for the next voyage. She sailed from Greenock on 21 December and arrived in Loch Ewe the following day. She sailed in convoy JW51-B with her American friend *John H.B. Latrobe* and twelve other merchantmen. The convoy suffered no losses in merchant ships despite being attacked by German surface forces, *Hipper*, *Lützow* and six destroyers. Two British escorts and one German destroyer were sunk in the battle.

Among the escorts were two trawlers. The first, HMT *Northern Gem*, a German-built vessel, prior to her being requisitioned by the Admiralty had been based at Grimsby though she carried a London registry. She had fished these waters constantly, summer and winter in pre-war days with only the weather to contend and she would do so again after the war when she would then be a true Grimsby vessel, fully registered in the port. The other trawler escort in JW-51B, HMT *Vizalma*, however, had not yet been on a single fishing voyage. When war came in 1939 she was under construction for the Atlas Steam Fishing Company of Grimsby. She was taken over by the Admiralty while still on the stocks and was fitted out as an anti-submarine trawler. She survived the war and was finally handed over to her Grimsby owners and made her first fishing trip to the waters she had patrolled during the six years of war.

For this second voyage of *Daldorch* there were only the usual minor misdemeanors such as five men failing to join the ship at Greenock, one man being discharged for misconduct. The most interesting feature of the articles is an entry for one of the engineering officers. He was a British national but held an Indian certificate of competence, issued in Bombay. He had sailed with *Daldorch* from Liverpool to Loch Ewe and Iceland and back to Greenock on her earlier voyage. When he re-signed articles for the second voyage the entry was annotated 'to be discharged before the vessel leaves the UK,' and indeed he was. One wonders again by choice or otherwise?

During *Daldorch*'s stay in Murmansk the Russians gave a big dinner party for the merchant ship masters, escort captains and other high ranking officials. The venue was the Arctic Hotel but unfortunately on the night of the party, 17 January 1943, there was a widespread blanket of heavy fog. The ships were spread over a twenty square mile area and so due to the inclement weather quite a large number of the guests could not attend. Captain Thomson of *Daldorch*, however, was fortunate in that his vessel was still alongside the wharf at Murmansk. The dinner was a marathon meal set out in three separate rooms. The guests (and the meal) progressed from one room to the next. The food was magnificent and was liberally interlaced with the best Russian vodka, white wines from the Caucasus, champagne from Georgia and brandy from the Balkans. Not surprisingly, very few of the guests remember much more than this! Captain Thomson remained with Paddy Henderson's and became Commodore of their fleet in the 1950s.

Daldorch returned from Murmansk in convoy RA-52 with *Briarwood*. She brought home a cargo of Russian timber and cotton for discharge at Middlesbrough, arriving safely on 14 February 1943. The only other entry in official records for *Briarwood* shows that she rescued Indian Greaser Jabed Ulla and four other Indian seamen from a raft in the Indian Ocean after their ship, the 7,119 gross ton *Garoet* (Captain P. de Raadt), on a voyage from Mormagoa to Durban in June 1944, had been sunk by *U-181* (Korvette-Kapitän Freiwald), the most successful of the long range U-cruisers, type IXD-2.

Chapter 10

Operation FB in Retrospect

THE first casualty of war is the truth they say, and this has been proven to be so, however, the next few hypothetical casualties are not quite so easily defined. Strong contenders for inclusion in the first three must be common sense and logic. How many brave men have been sacrificed for a hopeless cause or for propaganda advantage?

Did we really think we could have stopped the Germans from overrunning and consolidating Norway in 1940 for instance; Lt. Cdr. Eugene Edmonds, VC, and his flight of very vulnerable Swordfish aircraft were thrown against the might of the German capital ships in a desperate but unsuccessful attempt to stop these ships breaking through the Channel from France to Germany. Most of the Swordfish crews paid the ultimate price for their gallant efforts.

All these actions were carried out by brave and courageous men, that is not in question, but did the planners ever give thought to the cost in human life? Did the politicians have any sleepless nights, knowing that their pre-war policies had found our Armed Services and the civilian support services, so ill-equipped when the inevitable war arrived? I wonder.

We can only hope, albeit without too much conviction, that the present day defense planners and politicians will not allow us to be caught with our trousers around our ankles as we have been so many times in the past. Even more hopefully they will not be called upon to prove their point in the future and even more hopefully than that, Tommy Atkins and his co-service equivalents will not have to pay the ultimate price for any possible mistakes of the 'top brass' as he has so often had to do in the past.

No belligerent was immune from these situations. Did the French Defense Department, for instance, honestly believe that Hitler would batter his head against the Maginot Line when all he had to do to completely nullify this expensive structure was to invade Belgium and pop 'round the end! His track record, after all, at this time for respecting national boundaries was not too good. Did General Tojo and Admiral Yamamoto honestly believe that they could take on the might of the

United States and win? Even by taking the action at Pearl Harbor? They were no doubt influenced by the revelation of the true weakness of the British and Dutch in the Far East when the Germans handed them "Top Secret" documents to this effect, captured by the surface raider *Atlantis* from the m.v. *Automedon* on 11 November 1940. But despite these enormous and disastrous initial setbacks, the final outcome was not really in doubt.

Did Hitler think that he could succeed against Russia where Napoleon had failed? No, they had all let their heart's rule their heads. Logic had been brushed aside to allow day dreams to take over, and millions of innocent victims paid the price for their misused power.

Operation FB was certainly not mounted for propaganda purposes because there was no following large-scale publicity. There was, however, some publicity and to say the least it was deliberately and highly misleading, to the general public as well as to the enemy. Examination of the newspaper article, which is obviously an official press release, together with the relevant crew lists and log books for the British ships involved shows the following discrepancies and unquestionable facts.

The article names Captain James Shaw as being in command of the vessel which is unnamed in the article. Captain Shaw was in command of SS *Briarwood*. Captain W. H. Lawrence, CBE, had indeed previously been in command of the same vessel but then for at least the duration of Operation FB he seems to have held an entirely different appointment—something akin to Commodore of the operation. SS *Briarwood* did not sail independently to North Russia—during Operation FB she was one of the two British ships that returned to Iceland. *Briarwood* had sailed to North Russia in earlier convoys, but never independently. After her aborted attempt she sailed to Russia in the next convoy, returning in convoy, too. As we have already seen *Briarwood* had been in action with the enemy on a number of previous occasions, each time with distinction.

The two British ships that did sail independently and reached Russia safely, both returned in convoy. Neither of these two ships were even built when the *Jervis Bay* convoy referred to in the newspaper article (HX-84, 5 November 1940) was attacked, but as we have seen, *Briarwood* was one of the ships in this convoy. The two successful British ships were both wartime-built ships and neither was attacked to the degree that the article suggests, neither do they claim shooting down any aircraft on this voyage. The article is actually a propaganda version of the whole operation rolled into one, with more than a dash of Hollywood thrown in for good measure. Dr. Goebbels would have wished he had the writer on his own staff.

Convoys to North Russia were resumed early in December, only a month later, so surely there was no operational urgency. It seems more likely that it was an operation of convenience. Joe Stalin was pressing the Allies for more supplies, ships for PQ-19 were already in various stages of readiness and since no escorts were to be provided for the independents then no great extra planning effort was needed on that score. Some experience of sailing independent merchant ships through heavily defended enemy waters had already been gained on the Gibraltar to Malta route and to a lesser degree on the route now being proposed. A second wave of independents, planned for the next moonless period was canceled on 25 November when it was decided that there would be no further trickle movements of merchant ships to North Russia. It is not revealed if this decision was because of the high price paid by the men and ships of Operation FB or that the decision to resume convoys to North Russia in December 1942 instead of as previously planned, January 1943, had already been made, thus negating the need for further independent sailings.

Lieutenant Commander Gough of the DEMS organization submitted a report to his Commander in Chief, dated 1 November 1942, suggesting that the second wave of independents be sailed for North Russia 'as soon as possible' for the following reasons.

1. The enemy would not be expecting a second wave!
2. The morale of the merchant crews was high.
3. Because before losses became generally known it could truthfully be said that the operation 'appeared to have been successful.'

He suggested 29 November as the most suitable date stating that two British ships were already to sail (*Briarwood* and *Daldorch*), two other British ships then at Hvalfjord still had incomplete crews, and would need men from the United Kingdom. *Empire Meteor* was not due in Iceland until 15 November due to repairs at present being carried out in the United Kingdom. Six American ships were already at anchor in Hvalfjord but they had no HF wireless installation and this would take about two or three days to be fitted.

We can see by the date of the memoranda by Lt. Cdr. Gough that up to this date no ships had yet been attacked or lost. *Empire Gilbert* was detected by aircraft on that date.

It seems that Operation FB was run as a stop-gap measure on the direct orders of Churchill and Roosevelt. Part of the operation that has not so far been mentioned was to sail a number of ships from North Russia to Iceland. Eight ships were sailed, all were Russian. The sailings were spread over a longer period from 29 October to 25 November— this period extended well beyond the moonless period deemed so necessary for the eastbound sailings! Only one of these ships was lost, the 7,000 ton Russian tanker *Donbass*, found on 7 November by the German destroyer *Z-27*.

There were other independent westbound sailings during the second half of December, fifteen Russian ships and all arrived safely. These ships, however, were not part of Operation FB.

Whether or not the operation could be called successful is open to question. The Russians probably thought it was, after all they had received five cargoes that otherwise they would not have had, and in addition they had only lost one ship, but that represented their total effort in the eastbound part of the operation. The Americans fared a little better, they had lost one ship and one had been damaged but sixty percent of their effort reached Russia safely. The British suffered hardest, only two of their ships reached Russia, three were lost with nearly all their crews and two returned to Iceland. If one calculates that a total of twenty-two ships were involved and that six of these were lost, then the material loss amounted to over twenty-five percent. Approximately 1,325 Allied merchant seamen and gunners sailed in the twenty-two ships and 332 of this number lost their lives, again a statistical loss of twenty-five percent. The heavy losses to convoy PQ-17, twenty-three merchant ships from a total of thirty-six amounts to a staggering sixty percent, materially speaking, but when the figures for all sailings to North Russia (over 850 ships) are considered, then the figures come out at between six and seven per-cent materially. Some 829 merchant navy personnel were lost on this route together with more than 1,000 Royal Navy men. The numbers who survived but were left with terrible injuries to body, mind or both is not known. The cost in RN ships was two cruisers, six destroyers, three sloops, two frigates, three corvettes and three fleet minesweepers.

PQ-18, the last convoy to sail before Operation FB, lost thirteen merchant ships from a total of forty, thirty-three percent, despite being escorted by a formidable number of RN ships from mighty battleship to humble armed trawler.

The reader may well have noticed that one anomaly remains unanswered. I refer of course to HM Submarine *Tuna* and the upturned hull she saw near to the position of *Chulmleigh*'s grounding. *Chulmleigh*'s master and crew abandoned the vessel, leaving her upright. She was then attacked without a great deal of success by five German aircraft. *U-625* then found her still upright and in the 'lagoon.' *Tuna* had meanwhile found an upturned wreck also in a 'lagoon.'

In June 1943 the Luftwaffe photographed a snow-covered merchant ship aground near the South Cape of Spitzbergen, though the exact position is not quoted. Close examination of the photograph shows it to be a steamer of the same class as *Chulmleigh*. Detailed examination of the funnel shows two horizontal bands which in peacetime would have contained Tatem's broad red band. They had been overpainted with wartime standard gray of course, but the dimensions are compatible with those of the pre-war red band. Other features of the ship also closely resemble those of *Chulmleigh*.

If my assumption is correct, that the photograph is indeed that of the grounded *Chulmleigh*, then what ship did *Tuna* see? It is very doubtful if it could have been *Empire Sky*, according to the log of *U-625* she was not sunk until the late evening of that day.

Captain W. S. Lewis of Gwent served his apprenticeship with Tatem's, owners of *Chulmleigh* and expressed the following opinion when contacted on the subject. "Having painted the funnel of *Chulmleigh* and one of her sister ships, on many occasions, I am convinced that the photograph is indeed that of SS *Chulmleigh*."

The question remains, however, was it justifiable to send civilians, including boys of sixteen and men of over sixty, volunteers though they were, to almost certain death should their vessel be sunk. That is another issue.

Seldom in the past have politicians, the military and the populations of Europe had such an opportunity to 'get things right' by peaceful negotiations. All sides appear to want a genuine peace in the future. Of course there will be problems, big ones, but the rewards for future generations are enormous. East and west have both failed miserably in the past. Let us hope that for the sake of all those people who gave their lives in World War II that the various governments will make the most of this golden opportunity to ensure that never again will men and women have to endure needless hardships such as those described in these pages. We owe it to them to make it work.

Appendix 1

Allied Merchant Navy, Armed Guard and DEMS Casualty, Survivor and Crew Lists

SS *Empire Gilbert* (British)

Name	Rank	Age	Home
Adamson, Swainston	L/Bdr.	38	County Mayo
Aisthorpe, Eric	RN Gunner	21	Grimsby
Anderson, William	Fireman/Trimmer	30	Glasgow
Avison, James Sydney	Chief Officer	35	Birmingham
Barrow, Alexander	Able Seaman	19	Aberdeen
Beard, Thomas William	3rd Radio Officer	19	Liverpool
Birch, Ronald	Deck Boy	17	Walsall
Blackley, Charles Dawson	3rd Engineering Officer	48	Glasgow
Brigham, Leonard	RN Gunner	25	Hull
Burgess, Harold	RN Gunner	28	Derby
Burns, Henry	Assistant Steward	21	S. Shields
Burt, Sydney R.	Gunner	40	Northampton
Butt, William Robert	Chief Engineering Officer	44	Weymouth
Carey, George	Deck Boy	17	Brentford
Carter, Dennis	Gunner	20	Gainsborough
Clark, Robert	Assistant Cook	21	S. Shields
Cooper, L.	RN Gunner	?	unknown; joined at Loch Ewe
Craig, Donald	Fireman/Trimmer	33	Aberdeen
Cummings, Ralph Thomas	Messroom Boy	20	N. Shields
Currie, Hugh	Fireman/Trimmer	24	Belfast
Day, Stanley Bertram	Able Seaman	22	London
Dickinson, Harold	RN Gunner	20	Rossendale
Fisher, Ronald Samual	2nd Officer	25	Newcastle
Girvan, Charles T.	RN Gunner	45	London
Gleghorn, Edward Sutherland	Chief Steward	33	N. Shields
Hall, James Keean	Fireman/Trimmer	36	S. Shields

Name	Rank	Age	Home
Herrington, Joseph Stevenson	Steward	25	N. Shields
Hopkins, Arthur***	Gunner	23	Manchester
Hunter, Robert	RN Gunner	21	Loch Gelly
James, Richard Caddick	Chief Radio Officer	52	London
Jones, Stanley T.	RN Gunner	20	London
Jones, Thomas Walter	Fireman/Trimmer	20	Llandilo
Kelman, Geoffrey*	Able Seaman	22	Mill Hill, Middlesex
Lisher, Ambrose Toward	Greaser	41	S. Shields
McCabe, Peter	Baker	37	Linwood, Renfrewshire
McLean, Daniel	2nd Engineering Officer	39	Glasgow
Meadows, Douglas D.***	Gunner	20	Gloucester
Milburn, Theodore	Cook	63	S. Shields
Mohan, William Jas. Mathieson	4th Engineering Officer	22	Glasgow
Oliveira, Antonio D. R.	Fireman/Trimmer	32	Portugal
Peters, Maurice	W/Sgt.	25	Cornwall
Potts, Thomas	Assistant Steward	19	Monkseaton, Northumberland
Prentice, F.	Gunner	20	Glasgow
Preston, George T.	RN Gunner	34	Brierley
Purdy, Alfred	Able Seaman	37	Lambeth, London
Ritchie, David Christie	Fireman/Trimmer	36	Aberdeen
Sandiford, Wilfred	2nd Radio Officer	21	Manchester
Scott, James Dalgleish**	Bosun	37	Galashiels
Shields, William	Donkeyman	34	Sunderland
Smith, Charles Leonard	Assistant Steward	17	S. Shields
Souter, Alex	Able Seaman	19	Lossiemouth, Moray
Stewart, John	Sailor	20	Lossiemouth
Stobbs, Thomas	Cabin Boy	17	S. Shields
Stockdale, William Alfred	Fireman/Trimmer	21	Workington
Thompson, Joseph Castle	Sailor	19	Durham
Thraves, Ronald William	Fireman/Trimmer	20	London
Todd, George	Fireman/Trimmer	28	Whitehaven
Traynor, Joseph	Greaser	55	Jarrow
Urwin, Ralph***	Deck Boy	17	S. Shields
Wall, Bernard	L/Bdr.	32	Eton

Name	Rank	Age	Home
Watson, Alexander	Assistant Steward	20	S. Shields
Weldon, J. T.	Gunner	24	Glasgow
Williams, William	Master	54	Pwelheli
Wilson, John Wesley	3rd Officer	29	Hebburn
Younger, William Henry**	Carpenter	28	Southwick

Total casualties 47 Merchant Navy plus 16 DEMS Gunners.
* Royal Humane Society Testimonial
** Kings Commendation for Brave Conduct
*** Prisoner of War

SS *EMPIRE SKY* (BRITISH)

Name	Rank	Age	Home
Appleby, Eric	3rd Officer	21	Scarborough
Browne, Thomas	Gunner	26	Wexford, Eire
Burgess, Stanley Frederick	RN Gunner	20	Bedminster
Bushen, William Edger, MBE	Chief Officer	27	Llandaff
Butler, Arthur	Sailor	31	Hornsea
Butler, John George	Donkeyman	32	Hornsea
Carr, James	Fireman	39	Greenock, Renfrew
Chatfield, Ernest	Galley Boy	16	Hull
Conn, Terence	Steward	27	Hull
Donner, Charles Henry	Donkeyman	63	Hull
Ellams, Douglas Francis	Gunner	23	Liverpool
Emeny, H.	RN Gunner	20	Suffolk
Finckle, Charles Henry	2nd Radio Officer	23	Sunderland
Foster, Leonard**	Bosun	43	Hull
Gant, Gordon William	Baker	22	Hull
Girdley, Herbert	Able Seaman	33	Hull
Glossop, Reginald David	RN Gunner	19	Bristol
Gowshall, Jas. Henry	Able Seaman	28	Barton on Humber
Gravell, Clifford Newton	2nd Officer	27	Goole
Green, Edward Leslie	Able Seaman	42	Hull
Hales, Phillip	Messroom Boy	16	Hull
Hall, Robert	Fireman	46	Leith
Hayes, John	Gunner	29	Manchester

Name	Rank	Age	Home
Hinchcliffe, Leonard William	RN Gunner	27	Burton-on-Trent
Hodges, Percy Viv. Chas.	Fireman/Trimmer	31	Sydney
Jarvis, Robert Frank	RN Gunner	19	Banbury
Jones, Alexander	Ordinary Seaman	39	Sowerby Bridge
Jones, William McConnell	2nd Engineering Officer	53	Glasgow
Leneghan, Daniel	W/Bdr.	32	Douglas I.O.M.
Mariner, Alfred	RN Gunner	21	London
Mason, Alan	Cabin Boy	16	Hedon, Hull
McInally, Charles	RN Gunner	25	Glasgow
McNeil, Ignatius	Fireman/Trimmer	34	Nova Scotia
Moat, Roy	Ordinary Seaman	39	Hull
Morley, Thomas	Master	51	Northampton
Murray, John	Fireman	24	Aberdeen
Newman, Leslie	Carpenter	33	Hull
O'Neill, Patrick	RN Gunner	21	Glasgow
Osborne, Arthur Stanley	Gunner	26	London
Parkinson, Walter Overton**	Donkeyman	64	Hull
Phillips, George William	Chief Cook	32	Hull
Read, George Fulcher	Steward	33	Hull
Redgrave, Eddie	Fireman/Trimmer	28	Hull
Redshaw, Tom	3rd Engineering Officer	27	Hull
Rhodes, George	Cabin Boy	17	Grimsby
Rushton, John Hartley	3rd Radio Officer	21	Colne, Lancs.
Russell, John	Gunner	24	Coatbridge
Sheppard, Jack Donald	Fireman/Trimmer	24	Harwich
Stevenson, Gibbon Wm. Gordon	—	34	Watford
Stoackley, Edward Edgar	W/Sgt.	39	Co. Durham
Taylor, Charles Brown	Fireman/Trimmer	31	S. Shields
Trott, Charles Henry	Able Seaman	34	Hull
Turner, John Snowdon	Chief Radio Officer	24	Gourock
Vaughan, Stephen	Able Seaman	51	Hull
Wear, Edward	Fireman/Trimmer	33	London
White, Albert**	Chief Engineering Officer	49	Sunderland
Whyles, Edward	Able Seaman	28	Worksop
Wilcock, Henry Charles	L/Bdr.	21	Liverpool

Name	Rank	Age	Home
Williams, William	Gunner	42	Wallasey
Willis, Sydney Daimon	Gunner	20	Sheffield

Total of 42 Merchant Navy casualties. The vessel carried 18 DEMS gunners, ten from the 4th Regiment Maritime Royal Artillery and eight from the Royal Navy.

SS *WILLIAM CLARK* (USA)

CASUALTIES

Name	Rank	Age	Home
Allison, Jay Cruz	Messman	32	Philippines
Anderson, John*	2nd Mate	33	Hungary
Anderson, Randall B., Jr.	A.B.	22	Pennsylvania
Brown, Harry Waldo	Oiler	45	Massachusetts
Domingo, Francesco**	Utility	33	Philippines
Elian, Walter E.	Master	?	?
Espejo, Maxi Serrino	Steward	36	Philippines
Everhart, Robert Ray	Deck Cadet	20	Pennsylvania
Fowler, Len George	Oiler	33	Galveston
Garritzen, Herman Gerad	Engineer Cadet	20	New Jersey
Grein, Maynard Leslie	Fireman/WT	20	Minnesota
Hayden, Edward Emmett	Bosun	39	New York
Kenigsburgh, John	3rd Assistant Engineer	50	Latvia
Martinez, Frank	Chief Engineer	50	Spain
Mosley, Joseph James	Ordinary Seaman	21	Georgia
Poblacion, Eugene P.	Carpenter	38	Puerto Rico
Smith, Peter Joseph	Engineer Cadet	21	Massachusetts
Whaley, Vincent Emerson	Radio Operator	24	New York

* Died before rescue.
** Died in hospital, Akureyri, 5 December 1942.

SURVIVORS RESCUED BY HMT *ST. ELSTAN*

Name	Rank	Age	Home
Alvarez, Manuel*	Chief Cook	39	Spain

ARCTIC INTERLUDE

Name	Rank	Age	Home
Ambrosio, Vincent J.	FWT	29	New York
Barber, Willard J.*	Clerk/Typist	24	New York
Butterick, Walter T.	Wiper	17	New York
Castro, Simeon de	Messman	41	Philadelphia
Christopher, Theodore	A.B.	26	New Jersey
Erck, Carl B.	A.B.	23	New York
Goldsmith, William F.	Chief Mate	35	Massachusetts
Holland, Richard E.*	Deck Cadet	19	Philippines
Howard, Lawrence	Third Mate	28	Connecticut
Peck, Joseph F.	First Assistant Engineer	49	Michigan
Rodriguez, Manuel	Oiler	48	Spain
Szewczuk, John	Ordinary Seaman	21	Rhode Island

* Repatriated on USS *Chateau Thierry*, 7 December 1942.

Chief Mate William F. Goldsmith was appointed Master of SS *Mana* and took home to the U.S. some survivors from *William Clark* about a week after arriving in Iceland.

Survivors Rescued by HMT *Cape Palliser*

Name	Rank	Age	Home
Antonio, Guadalupe	Utility	38	Philippines
Bush, Charles Roby, Jr.*	A.B.	38	Mississippi
Gholston, Arley C.	Oiler	29	?
Guerra, Ramon	2nd Cook/Baker	48	Spain
Larson, Alfred E.**	Ordinary Seaman	21	North Carolina
Librada, Emiliano	Messman	32	Philippines
Lindblom, Ernest M.	A.B.	57	Sweden
Manning, John Wallace*	A.B.	21	Ohio
McCormick, Michael***	2nd Assistant Engineer	36	Michigan
Stevens, Murl A.	FWT	22	Texas

* Repatriated to the U.S.A. on SS *Seminole*, 26 December 1942.
** Repatriated to the U.S.A. on SS *West Gotomska*, 15 April 1943.
*** Very seriously ill.

Armed Guard List (Incomplete)

Name	Rank	Note
Allison, W. Erwin	Seaman 1c	Survived, landed Reykjavik

Name	Rank	Note
Bivins, James Glenon	Seaman 1c	Survived, landed Reykjavik**
Dougherty, Paul T.	Seaman 2c	Survived
Harris, John D.	Lieutenant (commanding)	Lost in Masters boat
Leary, Robert G.	Seaman 2c	Survived, landed Reykjavik
Mignus, Paul E.	Seaman 1c	Survived, landed Akureyri
Morrison, Leo Earl	Seaman 2c	Survived, landed Reykjavik
Price, Donald Everett	Seaman 2c	Survived, landed Reykjavik
Priore, Frank Paul	Seaman 2c	Survived, landed Reykjavik
Scott, Raymond Clifford	Seaman 1c	Survived, landed Reykjavik
Seeley, James Lowell	Seaman 2c	Survived, landed Reykjavik
Simpson, Austin Edward	Seaman 1c	Survived, landed Reykjavik**
Solomon, Milton Sydney	Seaman 2c	Survived, landed Reykjavik
Spinazola, Anthony N.	Seaman 2c	Survived, landed Reykjavik**
Sylvester, Leonard	Seaman 1c	Survived, landed Akureyri
Taylor, Ranza E.	Seaman 2c	Survived, landed Reykjavik
Thomas, William Elmus	Seaman 2c	Died in 2nd Mates boat*
Trotter, Clifford A.	Seaman 2c	Survived, seriously ill, landed Akureyri
Underwood, Arthur Lee	Seaman 1c	Survived, landed Reykjavik**

*   Buried Akureyri
** Commended for meritorious conduct

The three lifeboats that left *William Clark* were as follows: Masters Motorboat: 23 men including 12 Armed Guard; Chief Mates: 26 men including 13 Armed Guard; Second Mates: 17 men including 5 Armed Guard

ARMED GUARDS LOST IN MASTERS BOAT

Name	Rank
Carr, James	?
Phillips, Calvin David	Seaman 2c
Price, Robert	Seaman 2c
Rodriguez, Jose	Seaman 2c
Ryan, James L.	Seaman 1c
Seifert, Joseph Hugh	Seaman 1c
Suto, Eugene George	Seaman 2c
Tervo, Leslie Sylvester	Seaman 2c
Trammell, Elmo	Seaman 2c
Truman, Marvin N. R.	Seaman 2c
Turner, Arron Elwood	Seaman 2c

SS *Chulmleigh* (British)

Survivors

Name	Rank	Age	Home	Notes
Burnett, T.	Gunner	20	Liverpool	BEM 30 November 1943
Callan, F.	RN Gunner	30	Oldham	
Clark, David Firth	3rd Officer	34	Newton Abbot	
Hardy, Andrew Thomas	Able Seaman	27	Shetland	
Paterson, Robert Beatty	Chief Radio Officer	25	Dunoon	
Peyer, R. A.	L/Sgt.	23	Norbury	BEM 30 November 1943
Swainston, J.	Gunner	38	Co. Durham	
Whiteside, R.	Gunner	20	Liverpool	BEM 30 November 1943
Williams, Daniel Morley	Master	35	Cardegan	

Casualties

Name	Rank	Age	Home
Alexander, George	Fireman/Trimmer	28	Kelty
Colvin, Richard Stanley	Chief Engineering Officer	47	N. Shields
Davies, John Islwyn	Chief Steward	30	Trefine, Pem.
Dennison, Donald Edward	Messroom Boy	18	London
Fenn, Ernest James, OBE*	Chief Officer	45	Sunderland
Franklin, Clive Russell	Cook	22	Highgate, Middlesex
Gordon, Dennis	Sailor	18	Aberdeen
Graham, Alexander	Sailor	19	Aberdeen
Graham, Mitchell	Fireman/Trimmer	21	Kirkcaldy
Herd, Alexander Pearson	Fireman/Trimmer	28	Leven
Hill, Andrew Campbell	4th Engineering Officer	23	Dundee
Jackson, George	Fireman/Trimmer	26	Methil
Jeans, John Douglass Frank	Apprentice	19	Pennington
Johnston, William Lawrence	Able Seaman	44	Shetland
Larkin, Ernest George William	3rd Radio Officer	19	Hanwell, Middlesex
Lowe, Byron F.	Fireman/Trimmer	20	Harrow, Middlesex

Name	Rank	Age	Home
Maclennan, Finlay	Bosun	33	Nairn
Marritt, Peter William	Apprentice	16	Hornsea
Marshall, William Morris	Fireman/Trimmer	31	Methil
McDonald, Herbert	Galley Boy	18	Edinburgh
McVicker, Harry James	2nd Radio Officer	22	Llanelly
Middlemiss, Richard Alexander	2nd Engineering Officer	37	Edinburgh
Nicholson, James Francis	Able Seaman	32	Shetland
Owens, Soloman	Carpenter	55	Carnarvon
Painter, Stanley	Steward	20	Islington
Pounder, William	Apprentice	16	Hull
Reid, Alfred	Greaser	44	Grangemouth
Russell, John	Fireman/Trimmer	45	Sunderland
Scollay, Magnus William	Able Seaman	27	Shetland
Smith, John	Fireman/Trimmer	19	Methil, Fyfe
Sneddon, Alex Nicholson	Cabin Boy	17	Edinburgh
Starkey, James	2nd Officer	34	Edinburgh
Suttie, John	Donkeyman	34	Methil
Watson, William	Fireman/Trimmer	29	Penarth, Glam.
White, Alexander George	Assistant Cook	19	Stratford
Wood, James	3rd Engineering Officer	34	Runcorn

*   Lloyds War Medal for Bravery at Sea

Service Casualties

Name	Rank	Age	Home
Bentley, J. W.	Gunner	32	Rochdale
Calvert, B.	RN Gunner	26	London
Gow, C.	W/Sgt.	32	Glasgow
Herlock, J. E.	RN Gunner	27	London
Hulme, J. P.	RN Gunner	19	Edinburgh
Matton, K.	RCN Gunner	20	Canada
Penny, F.	RN Gunner	19	Liverpool
Pepper, S.	Gunner	38	Hebburn
Proctor, T.	Gunner	30	Burnley
Pryer, H. A.	RN Gunner	25	Chatham
Robinson, W.	RN Gunner	33	Sunderland
Warren, G. S.	Gunner	22	Manchester
Willoughby, F.	RN Gunner	43	Eastbourne

All the military gunners were from the 4th Regiment Royal Maritime Artillery.

John Islwyn Davies was the first man to die from exposure, on 10 November. Two more men, John Suttie and John Russell died on the 11th. George Jackson and Mitchell Graham both died on the 12th. It was four days before Chief Engineer Richard Stanley Colvin succumbed and a further four days before 19-year-old Alexander George White died. Men began to go quite quickly then, Apprentice Marritt on the 22nd, Alfred Reid on the 23rd. Royal Navy gunner Robinson was next on the 24th, Carpenter Owens on the 25th, 18-year-old Donald Edward Dennison and 19-year-old Royal Navy gunner Hulme fell victim to their circumstances on the 26th. Apprentice William Pounder on the 28th, Gunner G. S. Warren and 3rd Engineer James Wood departed this world on the 29th day of that fateful November. Andrew Campbell Hill, the 4th Engineer, passed away on the 30th. Thirty-one-year-old William Morris Marshall clung to life for a further two weeks before he lost the battle on 13 December. The last man from those who had managed to reach the shore, 28-year-old fireman George Alexander died on Christmas Eve despite the careful attention of the relatively fit survivors.

SS *Dekabrist* (USSR)

Name	Rank	Age	Notes
Alexebich, Michael Philipovich	Fireman	26	Died
Alshyerski, Dmetri Arisamovich	Seaman	25	Died
Andronov, Michael Fedorovich	Cleaner		Died
Belyev, Stephan Polukarpovic	Master		
Borodin, Vasiley Nichalovich	Seaman		
Byrenkov, Philip Arisomovich	3rd Engineer	45	Died
Chanine, Nichola Ivanovich	Fireman	26	Died
Colin, Vasiley Pavlovich	Seaman	29	Died
Delyok	Fireman		Died
Dolgalyev, Ivan Syergyevich	Electrician	30	Died
Dryechenski, Vasiley Fedorovich	Seaman		Died Hope Island
Fadylaev, Michael Petrovic	Fireman	31	Died
Fomin, Pavel Ivanovich	Seaman	30	Died
Fomin, Vasiley Ivanovich	Seaman	30	Died
Gianovski, Fedor Gregorovich	2nd Engineer		Died Hope Island
Grebenik, Vladimir Alexseevich	Machinist Operator	19	Died
Gyerasinov, Ivan Dmetrovich	Fireman	28	Died

Name	Rank	Age	Notes
Ivanov, Nicholas Fyedorovich	Senior Fireman	38	Died Hope Island
Kamenski	USSR Navy		Died
Karkov, Boris Antonovich	Fireman		Died Hope Island
Klemov, Ivan Metrovanovich	Fireman	29	Died
Klyevsor, Ivan Michaelovich	Chief Engineer	38	Died Hope Island
Kondrashkin, Alexi Michaelovich	Fireman	25	Died
Kopshevski, Anatolu Alexandrovich	Fireman	24	Died
Korsyetov, Peter Ellich	1st Mate		Died Hope Island
Kruvoshei, Sergei Yakovlyevich	Machinist Operator	28	Died
Lobanov	USSR Navy		Died on submarine
Madveldev, Karp Trofimovich	Senior Cook	45	Died
Mascalensko, Pantyely Polykarpovich	Seaman		Died
Matvyechyk, Maxine Akimovich	Fitter	22	Died
Melenchyk, Philip Vasilovich	Fireman	31	Died
Michealenski, France Ivanovich	Fireman	27	Died
Moosalyev, Ivan Vasilovich	Fireman	28	Died
Moospenkey, Vasiley Dmetrovich	Fireman		Died
Natilich, Nadejda Matvevna	Doctor	29	Female
Nicolin, Stepan Alexandrovich	Fireman	34	Died
Novekov, Vlac Arkipovich	Baker	29	Died Hope Island
Omyelchenko, Nichola Gyravich	Fireman	19	Died
Pasdnyakov, Vasiley Dmetruyevich	Fireman	28	Died
Petroshenko, George Koosmich	Machinist Operator	29	Died
Petrov, Styrokovich Alexandra Ignatevich	Bosun	33	Died Hope Island
Petrysha, Gregory Pumenovich	Fireman	27	Died
Pimovsky, Vladimir Nicholovich	Fireman	26	Died
Popov, Andre Gregorevich	Cook	26	Died
Popov, Peter Dyerovich	Fireman	27	Died

Name	Rank	Age	Notes
Prytokov	USSR Navy		Died Hope Island
Rybalsky, Dmeatry Dmetrovich	Machinist Operator	27	Died
Rysyev, Alexandra Ivanovich	Machinist Operator	32	Died
Scherbakov, Boris Metrovanovich	Radio Operator	27	Died Hope Island
Schyerbakov, Prokovy Fyedosovich	Fireman	29	Died
Shevchenko, Vasiley Petrovich	Fireman	33	Died
Shyrovski, Anabolye Koosmich	Machinist Operator	33	Died
Skborsov, Constantin Geographic	Seaman	26	Died
Slyosar, Stepan Petrovich	Senior A.B.	33	Died
Smirnoff, Constantinovich Gregory	Seaman	27	Died
Soshnikov, Innokente Sergevich	Seaman	42	Died
Strykov, Alex Vasilovich	Seaman	33	Died
Swanyock, Alexi Pavlovich	Fireman		Died
Tanasov, Maxim Philipvich	Fireman		Died Hope Island
Taraev, Nichola Avanaseivich	Fireman	29	Died Hope Island
Tedyev, Vladimir Illi	2nd Mate		Died
Terentev, Peter Nicholovich	Fireman	29	Died
Tkachenko, Vladimir Dennisovich	Machinist Operator	24	Died
Trepeson	3rd Mate		Died
Tretyakov	USSR Navy		Died Hope Island
Tryfanov, Michael Yakoblevich	Dutyman		Died
Vyedovor, Alexandra Semenovich	Seaman	29	Died Hope Island
Yebeling, Nicholavich Vladimir	Chief Officer		Died
Yefumov, Nichola Andrevik	Fireman		Died Hope Island
Yefyemenko, Vladimir Vasilovich	Machinist Operator	31	Died
Zobnin, Vasiley Stepanovich	4th Engineer		Died

Eight other crewmen, all firemen and unnamed also died. Total complement 80 persons. The reader will no doubt notice that some persons mentioned in the text do not appear in the crew list above. The author is unable to explain this anomaly.

SS *Briarwood* (British)

Name	Rank	Age	Home
Abraham, C.	DEMS	20	Northampton
Aitchison, G. W.	DEMS	20	Sunderland
Aldwin, R.	Ordinary Seaman	19	London
Anderson, J. L.	F/T	40	S. Shields
Batty, G.	DEMS	35	Newcastle
Bilsdon, E.	DEMS	25	London
Blenkey, E. M.	3rd Engineer	23	Stockton
Boyne, J.	F/T	29	Nova Scotia
Brown, G. W.	DEMS	33	London
Butler, J.	F/T	25	London
Carter, T.	DEMS	24	London
Chapman, R.	1st Mate	29	Bristol
Connor, G.	DEMS	38	Plymouth
Cox, F. E.	Ship's Cook	26	Middlesboro
Crofts, J. E.	DEMS	29	Larch
Downe, L.	Sprnry DEMS	22	Normanton
Fater, G. S.	DEMS	22	Bourne
Forbes, W.	A. B.	30	Belfast
Goodison, S.	Ordinary Seaman	21	Middlesboro
Gowan, J. M.	F/T	19	Barrow
Greenwood, H.	DEMS	22	Oldham
Hardy, J.	2nd Mate	26	Hull
Harefield, J.	DEMS	30	Croydon
Harrison, W.	Chief Engineer	52	Middlesboro
Hay, A. F.	DEMS	23	London
Hetherington, J. R.	Chief Steward	29	S. Shields
Hutchinson, E. S.	Donkeyman	42	Hull
Jollands, F. W.	A. B.	23	Glasgow
King, G.	DEMS	19	Cardiff
Larson, M.	F/T	46	Denmark
Laurie, W. L.	2nd Engineer	36	West Hartlepool
Lawrence, W. H.	Master	36	London
Liddle, R.	Assistant Cook	19	S. Shields
Lightfoot, F. T.	Assistant Steward	18	Scarboro
Lucy, E.	DEMS	27	Cork
Lunn, D. A.	DEMS	20	Essex
Mackie, H.	DEMS	31	Dunfirmline
McGarvey, P.	Bosun	38	Co. Donegal
Mitchell, S.	M. R. Steward	17	Middlesboro
Mitchell, W.	Ordinary Seaman	17	Middlesboro
Palfreyman, N. E.	3rd Radio Officer	26	Bollington
Pearson, W.	F/T	45	Hull
Poole, F.	DEMS	25	Glamorgan
Priestley, G. N.	DEMS	32	Halifax
Proctor, D. R. S.	1st Radio Officer	18	Manchester
Roberts, F.	A. B.	22	West Hartlepool
Roscalf, P.	Senior Assistant Steward	21	Middlesboro
Shadlock, E.	DEMS	23	Grimsby
Shaw, J.*	Staff Captain	34	West Hartlepool

Name	Rank	Age	Home
Simons, R. E.	3rd Mate	20	Hull
Smith, J. P.	A. B.	30	Middlesboro
Spencer, J. W.	4th Engineer	21	Washington
Still, W.	Greaser	43	Australia
Sutherland, J.	A. B.	27	Darlington
Townsend, C. G.	Greaser	39	Whitby
Turnbull, G.	2nd Radio Officer	31	Sunderland
Wells, R.	Ordinary Seaman	21	Middlesboro
Williams, R. T.	DEMS	27	Ledbury
Wright, F.	F/T	22	Portsmouth

Mr. Shaw was Master of the vessel until 14 September 1942 and was then superseded by Mr. Lawrence, but became Staff Captain on 3 November 1942.

SS *JOHN H. B. LATROBE* (UNITED STATES)

Name	Rank
Bell, Oree Jerome	Able Seaman
Carey, William J.	Radio Operator
Clarke, James A.	Messboy
Colket, Edward W.	Bosun
Drinkwater, James M.	Engineering Cadet
Dunean, Y. W.	Able Seaman
Elmore, Theodore	Utility
Foskey, Leon Ernest	Carpenter
Gavin, Patrick	Wiper
Gomm, Alfred E.	Able Seaman
Gubeira, Linardo	Wiper
Ham, Russell W.	Able Seaman
Hand, Wallace A.	Ordinary Seaman
Harris, J.	Messman
Hodgdon, Alonzo L.	Master
Hodgetts, William S.	Deck Cadet
Johnson, David	Messman
Kettles, George	Messman
Keyes, Lawrence	Messboy
Kinnaird, James S.	Second Assistant Engineer
Larsen, Martin B.	First Mate
Ledwick, Mitchell A.	Deck Engineer
Leetz, Irving C.	Second Mate
Lewis, Isham	Messboy
Lewis, Ivan G.	Steward
Mann, Frank J.	Fireman/Watertender
Mann, Harold E.	Fireman
Marshall, Roland L. J.	Able Seaman
Morris, William	Chief Cook
Parish, William G.	Ordinary Seaman
Patterson, Robert	Utility
Perritt, Edward J.	Oiler
Pomianek, Joseph S.	Fireman/Watertender
Rector, Curtis L.	Oiler
Reeves, Jean Miles	Third Mate

Name	Rank
Robertson, James T.	Third Assistant Engineer
Samardjic, John J.	Able Seaman
Shaw, John T.	Ordinary Seaman
Shepard, Robert S.	Oiler
Shope, Allen T.	First Assistant Engineer
Stewart, Fred W.	Second Cook
Strange, J. E.	Wiper
Tessaromatis, Menchios	Fireman/Watertender
Thrush, John H.	Chief Engineer

During the long time between U.S. ports there were several changes among the crew as follows: Daniel E. Young, Alexander Chapelonis, Mariano Arroyo, John G. Jarvis, Justin O'Keefe, Warren Buckman, Joseph M. Carista, Willard Watson, Elliott N. Mufflin, Hanston K. Vanterpool.

Age and U.S. state of birth had been deliberately obliterated on the crew list copy by the U.S. National Archives because of the privacy acts.

Armed Guard

Name	Rank
Davis, Everett E., Jr.	Able Seaman, USN (Joined at New York)
Folk, William L.	Seaman Second Class, USNR
Gaines, Raymond D.	Seaman Second Class, USNR
Glenn, Warren N., Jr.	Seaman Second Class, USNR
Mathias, Arthur R., Jr.	Seaman Second Class, USNR
Maxwell, Charles M.	Seaman Second Class, USNR
McAuley, Jack F.	Seaman Second Class, USN
McKinney, Donald R.	Seaman Second Class, USNR (Ashore at New York)
McSparron, John P.	Seaman Second Class, USNR
Menzies, William B.	Seaman Second Class, USN
Meyer, Paul W.	Seaman Second Class, USNR
Miller, Andrew P.	Seaman Second Class, USNR
Miller, George	Seaman Second Class, USNR
Miller, William L.	Seaman Second Class, USNR
Monica, Rudolph J.	Seaman Second Class, USNR
Murphy, Henry W.	Seaman Second Class, USNR
Murray, Joseph F.	Seaman Second Class, USN
Parks, William E.	Seaman Second Class Signalman (Joined at Philadelphia)
Perkins, Harold C.	Seaman Second Class, USNR
Pulitano, Anthony	Seaman Second Class, USNR
Reynolds, Charles H.	Lt. (j.g.), USNR
Rokolin, Karl E.	Seaman Second Class, USNR
Scheynayder, Claude L.	Seaman Second Class, USNR
Scott, Robert	Seaman Second Class, USNR
Shelton, Richard L.	Seaman Second Class, USN
Stockwell, Hosea D.	Able Seaman, USN (Joined at New York)

SS *Daldorch* (British)

Name	Rank	Age	Home
Allan, J. H.	2nd Mate	31	London

Name	Rank	Age	Home
Atherden, W.**	DEMS	27	Liverpool
Attard, A.	F/T	32	Cardiff
Bennett, C.	DEMS	22	Abesford
Beswick, F.**	DEMS	32	Stockport
Betts, S.	Messroom Boy	16	Liverpool
Bishop, H. S.	Carpenter	34	Tem G'tng
Borg, E.*	F/T	32	Cardiff
Borg, J.	F/T	22	Cardiff
Bugaria, U.	F/T	46	Cardiff
Carpenter, S.	DEMS	24	Watford
Carslaw, W. McN.	Cadet	20	Glasgow
Chatterton, W. J.**	3rd Radio Officer	18	Liverpool
College, W.	DEMS	35	Chester le Street
Court, P. J.	A. B.	21	London
Gilliat-Hammerson, T.	DEMS	37	Rotherham
Greenhall, J.	5th Engineer	20	Glasgow
Harlingham, P. J.	DEMS	30	London
Harrington, W.	Ordinary Seaman	27	London
Harvey, D. O.**	1st Mate	32	Hamilton
Innes, J.	A. B.	24	Dublin
Johnston, G.	Assistant Steward	16	Liverpool
Langton, H.	Cabin Boy	16	Liverpool
Lewis, M.	A. B.	25	Holyhead
Ley, G. A.	2nd Cook and Baker	30	Glasgow
Lindsay, J.	DEMS	21	Blantyre
Macleod, J.**	Bosun	46	Barra
Mann, J.	A. B.	48	Pontypridd
Marshall, R. W.**	1st Radio Officer	21	Hull
McDonald, J.	A. B.	21	Glasgow
Milos, A. K.	F/T	29	Cardiff
Mizzi, A.	Donkeyman/Greaser	55	Cardiff
Mizzi, P.	F/T	28	Cardiff
Morgan, D. T.**	Chief Steward	38	Barry
Newport, J.	DEMS	21	Oldham
Pavloff, T.	Donkeyman/Greaser	49	Cardiff
Porter, S.	DEMS	23	Greenock
Potter, H.	DEMS	35	Todmorden
Preedy, F. W.	DEMS	32	Bedworth
Pritchard, O.	A. B.	26	Holyhead
Rattray, N.	4th Engineer	22	London
Rimmer, G.**	Ship's Cook	43	Liverpool
Robinson, J.	DEMS	27	St. Neots
Scortoni, C.	F/T	55	Cardiff
Shaw, W.	A. B.	33	Liverpool
Smith, D. M.**	Cadet	19	Glasgow
Stewart, R.	Assistant Cook	21	Dundee
Sykes, H.**	Chief Engineer	45	Crewe
Symaciary, S. Z.	F/T	37	Glasgow
Tarry, J. R.	3rd Engineer	21	Crewe
Thomas, W.	DEMS	31	Liverpool

Name	Rank	Age	Home
Thomas, W.	F/T	27	Glasgow
Thomson, W.**	Master	44	Ormskirk
Townshead, R. V. K.**	2nd Radio Officer	24	London
Turner, J.	Assistant Steward	18	Liverpool
Vassello, J. B.	F/T	24	Cardiff
Watson, J.	DEMS	31	London
Watts, R. S.**	Cadet	17	Glasgow
Wilkinson, W.**	DEMS	20	Liverpool
Wilson, F.**	DEMS	19	Preston
Wilson, J. S.**	3rd Mate	21	Dunoon
Woodward, A. E.	2nd Engineer	37	Harwich
Woolley, A.	2nd Steward	22	Liverpool
Wray, A.**	DEMS	20	Manchester

SS *JOHN WALKER* (U.S.A.)

Name	Rank	Age	Home
Adams, Thomas J.	Fireman/Water Tender	48	Kansas
Baker, James H., Jr.	Wiper	20	Maryland
Baril, Joseph G.*	Second Mate	30	Connecticut
Beardsley, Edwin L.	Purser	22	Indiana
Beebe, Kenneth R.	Second Cook/Baker	35	Ohio
Blanchard, Edward F.	Wiper	18	New York
Boeltner, William R.	Utilityman	51	?
Brocklander, John J.	Junior Engineer	29	Maryland
Brown, Augustus	Able Seaman	37	New York
Bulla, Ralph W.	Able Seaman	27	North Carolina
Dorsey, Joseph	Deck Maintenance++	32	Ohio
Duwell, Charles C.	Chief Cook	30	Michigan
Epstein, Morey	Messman	21	California
Fennessy, John T.	Third Assistant Engineer	21	Ireland
Flood, Mayland D.	Ordinary Seaman+	21	Philadelphia
Garcia, Jose	Wiper	46	Spain
Ginley, Edward P.	Fireman/Water Tender	36	Massachusetts
Hales, Walter	Oiler	36	Mississippi
Hernandez, Guillerino	Messman	26	Puerto Rico
Jenssen, John E.	Master	?	?
Kennell, Louis G.	Ordinary Seaman	22	Massachusetts
Kritzman, George	Engineer Cadet	19	Spain
Larsson, George Trevor****	Third Mate	25	Australia

Name	Rank	Age	Home
McNaught, Franklyn C.	Third Mate**	34	Massachusetts
Meador, Leroy V.	Radio Operator	21	Texas
Miller, George N.	Oiler	47	North Dakota
Motte, Charles de la	Chief Steward	40	Germany
Nakonechny, Bobdon	Able Seaman	26	Pennsylvania
Perogini, Joseph R.	Ordinary Seaman	21	Ohio
Posada, Fernando	Utilityman	20	Puerto Rico
Rafferty, Frederick J.	Able Seaman***	37	Kansas
Rawding, Bruce B.	First Mate	37	New York
Reed, Marvin C.	Able Seaman	27	Montana
Saferight, Bert	Oiler	39	Virginia
Solivan, Joaquin	Assistant Cook	35	Puerto Rico
Thomas, Stanley L.	Able Seaman	24	Pennsylvania
Tilton, William	Messman	36	Massachusetts
Travis, Harrison O., Jr.	First Assistant Engineer	24	New York
Vladesco, Nicolai	Second Assistant Engineer	57	Rumania
White, Frank	Chief Engineer	43	British
Wild, William	Fireman/Water Tender	44	New York
Williams, Nelson M.	Deck Cadet	18	Connecticut

*   Killed in action 26 December 1942. Buried Imperial War Cemetery, Lynness.
**   Promoted to Second Mate, 27 December 1942.
*** Later Bosun.
**** Signed on in Loch Ewe, U.K., 15 January 1943.
\+   Promoted to Able Seaman, 13 September 1942.
++ Promoted to Ordinary Seaman.

Lieutenant (j.g.) Milton A. Stein was in command of the Armed Guard. Members of the Armed Guard were: Bernard Hugh, Seaman 2nd Class, Paul Hyde, Thomas L. Jackson, Rudolph J. Langston, Robert Martin, Seaman 2nd Class F. Miller, Seaman 2nd Class J. Pawluk, and Raymond W. Williams.

SS *Empire Scott* (British)

Name	Rank	Age	Home
Anderson, P.	A. B.	29	Shetland
Armitage, A.	F/T	29	Hull
Ballard, R.	Galley Boy	16	London
Beveridge, J. A.	DEMS	22	Dundee
Boarde, W.	F/T	52	Hull
Brettle, F.	Baker	24	Liverpool
Cameron, H.	Assistant Steward	19	Paisley
Campbell, E.	2nd Steward	33	Barrhead
Cheyne, A. G.	Carpenter	42	Shetland
Costine, C.	4th Engineer	33	Ayr
Crabtree, C.*	F/T	25	Paisley
Devitt, G.	DEMS	32	Liverpool

ARCTIC INTERLUDE

Name	Rank	Age	Home
Docherty, J.	F/T	39	Coatbridge
Donald, W.	3rd Engineer	28	Glasgow
Duff, W.	Greaser	54	Edinburgh
Dunlop, D.	Assistant Steward	22	Airdrie
Dunn, J.	DEMS	32	Bury
Evans, W.	Assistant Steward	20	Glasgow
Ferguson, J.	Chief Engineer	37	South Shields
Fosbrooke, N.	2nd Radio Officer	31	Stockport
Fraser, W.	Donkeyman/Greaser	46	Aberdeen
Futter, D. J.	DEMS	22	Docking
Galt, W.	Deck Boy	17	Glasgow
Glendinning, F.	F/T	30	Glasgow
Greer, J.	DEMS	27	?
Hair, J. D.	Master	35	South Shields
Harvey, B.	Donkeyman/Greaser	37	Glasgow
Heaton, A.	DEMS	30	Bury
Hendrie, G. E.	2nd Engineer	49	Glasgow
Hitchman, L.	Ordinary Seaman	18	London
Hodgson, J.	F/T	43	Hull
Holdstick, F. T.	DEMS	27	Hull
Hope, A. A.	Ordinary Seaman	18	Glasgow
Jackson, A. H.	DEMS	32	Plymouth
Johnson, J. D.	DEMS	35	Lancaster
Jones, D. C.	DEMS	31	?
Kay, J.	A. B.	29	Shetland
Kennedy, R.	Assistant Cook and Baker	38	Glasgow
Kirnnet, W.	Ship's Cook	38	Glasgow
Lang, D.	1st Mate	29	I of Arran
Laurie, W. J.	Chief Steward	40	Glasgow
Lawson, D.	DEMS	21	Holmfirth
Long, G. W.	Cabin Boy	17	Broomfield
Macdonald, J.	2nd Mate	27	Loch Maddy
MacDougal, D. A.	Assistant Steward	17	Nova Scotia
Macpherson, R.	3rd Radio Officer	19	Bangor
McArthur, S.	F/T	44	Glasgow
McLean, J.	Assistant Cook	26	Stornoway
Meacon, A.	DEMS	28	Manchester
Miller, J.	DEMS	31	Sutton in Ashfield
O'Brien, J.	F/T	31	Ireland
Oldham, J.	DEMS	29	Birkenhead
Pest, W.	DEMS	25	Ferryden
Price, W. G.	DEMS	35	Exeter
Ramsay, A.	A. B.	31	South Shields
Sillin, J. (non British national)	A. B.	45	Riga
Smith, F.	1st Radio Officer	29	Blackburn
Thomas, D.	DEMS	20	Harden City
Thomason, R. A.	A. B.	39	Shetlands
Turner, R.	DEMS	27	Middlesboro
Urquhart, J. W.	3rd Mate	20	Clydebank
Vance, D.	DEMS	20	Glasgow

Name	Rank	Age	Home
Walker, A.	DEMS	26	Linthwaite
Watson, J.	DEMS	27	S'land
Watson, T.	DEMS	39	York
Whalen, W.	DEMS	29	Liverpool
Will, E.	DEMS	30	London
Williams, F.	Cabin Boy	18	London
Wishart, R.	Bosun	27	Shetland
Woolhouse, J.	Deck Boy	17	New Zealand
Yorke, J.	F/T	25	Fifeshire

* Fireman Crabtree was hospitalized in Murmansk due to illness. His pay and allowances were withheld until repatriation.

The vessel had Arab firemen until reaching Altbea on the outward journey, when they were replaced.

SS *Hugh Williamson* (U.S.A.)

Name	Rank
Amarel, Archibald	Utility
Beattie, Howard	Able Seaman
Brzezinski, Stanislaus	Oiler
Byrne, Edward M.	Chief Engineer
Cousins, R. A.	Master
Erickson, Arthur	Second Assistant Engineer
Fulford, Fred	Second Cook
Gomez, Joaquin	Wiper
Gruz, Juan, Jr.	Able Seaman
Habura, Gregory	Deck Engineer
Helmstrom, Wilhelm	Carpenter
Hirons, Maurice L.	Able Seaman
Horne, William G.	Chief Steward
Johannsen, Erick	Bosun
Johnson, Harold	Chief Mate
Jorgensen, Jorgen	Second Mate
Knapp, William D.	Third Assistant Engineer
Kramer, Paul	Ordinary Seaman
Kumbat, Anthony	Able Seaman
Larivee, Ernest L.	Ordinary Seaman
Larson, Wilford	Able Seaman
Lipscombe, Lee	Ordinary Seaman
Lourido, Manuel	Utility
Martin, Galvin	Chief Cook
McKay, Jerome S.	Third Mate
Miller, Peter	Fireman/Watertender
Montgomery, Herbert E.	First Assistant Engineer
Muir, Philip	Messman
Parker, Stephan E., Jr.	Deck Cadet
Piorkowski, Walter	Oiler
Senter, Sydney	Messman
Sexton, Leo F.	Crew Messman
Sheddan, Arthur	Radio Operator
Siren, Richard	Fireman/Watertender

Name	Rank
Stebelski, Theodore	Oiler
Suelnis, Frank	Fireman/Watertender
Villianos, Nicholas	Wiper
Wilkins, Fernando D.	Able Seaman
Williams, Paul R.	Engineering Cadet

ARMED GUARD

Name	Rank
Cartabona, Vincent Ralph	Seaman 1st Class, USN
Douglas, Elrie Henry, Jr.	Seaman 1st Class, USNR
Fairbanks, Charles Simon	Seaman 1st Class, USN
Hecht, Joseph Edward	Signalman 3rd Class, USNR
Megason, Buel Harding	Seaman 1st Class, USN
Morris, David Conrad	Seaman 1st Class, USNR
Peterson, Clifford Odin	Seaman 1st Class, USN
Schmidt, Anton Gustav	Seaman 1st Class, USNR
Smith, Herbert Franklin, Jr.	Seaman 1st Class, USNR
Thomas, Arthur Carlus	Seaman 1st Class, USNR
Thomas, Custis William	Seaman 1st Class, USNR
Thomas, Roy Eugene	Seaman 1st Class, USNR
Turner, Doyle Mead	Seaman 1st Class, USN
Vacca, Richard, Jr.	Seaman 1st Class, USN
Valent, Anthony Joseph	Seaman 1st Class, USNR
Van Horn, Harry Gustav	Seaman 1st Class, USNR
Vandenberg, John Joseph	Seaman 1st Class, USN
Vanderloo, Edward Joseph	Seaman 1st Class, USNR
Vanderman, Marion Leon	Seaman 1st Class, USNR
Vaughn, Vincent Burdette	Seaman 1st Class, USN
Versak, Michael	Seaman 1st Class, USNR
Williams, Charles Harding	Seaman 1st Class, USN
Wise, Roger Philip	Ensign (commander)

Further information restricted or unavailable due to U.S. Privacy Act as previously mentioned.

SS *Empire Galliard* (British)

Name	Rank	Age	Home
Akers, R. D.	1st Radio Officer	39	Hereford
Broadley, H.	F/T	21	Glasgow
Brown, J.	2nd Radio Officer	19	Sunderland
Burdis, W.	Assistant Steward	21	Sunderland
Butcher, J. A.	Chief Engineer	41	Hebburn
Canner, W.	DEMS	19	Burton-on-Trent
Charleston, J.	DEMS	19	Broxburn
Cook, B.	F/T	19	Clydach
Cooper, W.	DEMS	26	Erith
Coulson, S.	DEMS	19	Chapwell
Crabtree, E.	DEMS	19	Bradford
Davey, K. W.	DEMS	21	Brotton
Davies, J. A.	DEMS	21	Leadbury

Name	Rank	Age	Home
Duncan, R.	Carpenter	52	Sunderland
Easton, J. B.	DEMS	19	Torquay
Edmundson, A.	O. S.	23	South Shields
Garraghan, T.	Cabin Boy	16	Sunderland
Gencovski, F.	Donkeyman/Greaser	58	Riga
Gibson, H.	Ship's Cook	22	Belfast
Green, H. E. N.	F/T	40	South Shields
Henderson, H. M.	O. S.	18	Heathfield
Hill, A.	A. B.	64	London
Hobson, A.	F/T	45	Sunderland
Hodgson, R. C.	3rd Engineer	27	Sunderland
Howe, R.	2nd Mate	25	Tees-side
Jenkins, R.	F/T	18	Sunderland
Joyce, H.	A. B.	34	Jarrow
Laythorpe, A.	1st Mate	29	Sunderland
Liddle, J. G.	F/T	29	South Shields
Lisle, J.	Assistant Steward	23	Sunderland
Mathews, E. A.	DEMS	24	Kettering
May, R.	Bosun	50	South Shields
McAlister, S.	F/T	31	South Shields
McBayne, G.	F/T	27	South Shields
McClony, E.	F/T	41	Glasgow
McLean, M. J.	A. B.	25	Plymouth
Mellars, H.	Assistant Steward	19	Sunderland
Miller, J.	O. S.	19	West Hartlepool
Milne, J.	A. B.	26	Jarrow
Mitchell, J.	Master	51	Whitby
Montgomery, J.	Assistant Cook	18	Dundee
Morgan, J.	Donkeyman/Greaser	36	Carlisle
Musgave, J. C.	A. B.	19	South Shields
Nicholson, P.	4th Engineer	25	Sunderland
Pope, W. J.	2nd Cook and Baker	22	South Shields
Purvis, G.	DEMS	20	Berwick
Raeburn, H.	F/T	52	South Shields
Robertson, A. B.	DEMS	20	Kircaldy
Rogers, J. N.	2nd Engineer	47	Lynemouth
Rose, R.	3rd Radio Officer	19	Bayford
Sargent, G. L.	DEMS	27	Ramsay
Scarfield, A.	F/T	28	South Shields
Smith, W. F.	DEMS	42	Durham
Sorensen, J. (non-British national)	A. B.	39	Denmark
Sproxton, A. J. W.	Cabin Boy	17	Sunderland
Stoves, R.	3rd Mate	26	Newcastle
Strult, R.	Chief Steward	54	Sunderland
Thomas, L.	Donkeyman/Greaser	29	London
Willis, A.	F/T	18	Porthcawl
Wooliams, D. L.	O. S.	18	Kent

Note: "Galliard" is of Celtic origin and signifies valor, strength and prowess.

SS *RICHARD H. ALVEY* (U.S.A.)

Despite the most intensive research at the U.S. National Archives, Washington, D.C., and all the regional branches, it has been impossible to unearth a crew list for this vessel on this particular voyage. The name of the Master was Captain C. E. Forisland and the Merchant Navy crew totaled thirty-nine.

ARMED GUARD

Name	Rank
Denning, Matthew Haywood	Seaman 1st Class, USN
Goad, Albert Lee	Seaman 2nd Class, USNR
Hughes, George Davis	Seaman 2nd Class, USNR
La Vack, Dewey Devere	Seaman 2nd Class, USNR
La Vack, Roland Edward	Seaman 2nd Class, USNR
La Vack, Valmore Deupray	Seaman 2nd Class, USNR
Larson, Miles Eugen	Seaman 2nd Class, USN
Laux, Raymond Harold	Seaman 2nd Class, USN
Law, Kenneth William	Seaman 2nd Class, USNR
Lester, Edgel Celsus	Seaman 2nd Class, USNR
Levercom, Michael Eugene	Seaman 2nd Class, USN
Lewis, Ted Barron	Seaman 2nd Class, USNR
Lien, Selvin Milton	Seaman 2nd Class, USNR
Melillo, Dominic	Seaman 2nd Class, USNR
Meyer, Siegfried William	Seaman 2nd Class, USN
Mulhern, Frederick Francis	Seaman 2nd Class, USNR
Nelson, Elmer John	Seaman 2nd Class, USNR
O'Konski, Carl John	Seaman 2nd Class, USN
Papini, Harold	Seaman 1st Class, USNR
Platt, Robert B.	Ensign, USNR
Pritika, Herman Abraham	Seaman 2nd Class, USNR
Smith, Edgar	Seaman 2nd Class, USN
Thomas, Robert Alvis	Seaman 2nd Class, USN

Appendix 2

Ship Details

SS *Empire Gilbert*

British. Port of registry: Sunderland. Owned by Ministry of War Transport, managed for them by Turner Brightman and Company. Built in 1941 by Bartram and Sons, Sunderland. 6,640 gross register tons. 432 feet overall, 417 feet between perpendiculars, 56 foot beam. Triple expansion engines. Dry cargo. Fitted with D/F. Radio call sign BCNS.

SS *Empire Sky*

British. Port of registry: Sunderland. Owned by Ministry of War Transport, managed for them by Claymore Shipping Company Ltd. Built in 1941 by J. Thompson and Sons Ltd., of Sunderland. 7,455 gross register tons. 439 feet overall, 424 feet between perpendiculars, 60 foot beam. Triple expansion engines. Dry cargo. Radio call sign BCKJ.

SS *Chulmleigh*

British. Port of registry: London. Owned by the Dulverston Steamship Company and managed for them by W. J. Tatem. Built in 1938 by William Pickersgill and Son, Sunderland. 5,445 gross register tons, 430 feet by 56 feet with a molded depth of 26 feet. Cruiser stern. Triple expansion engines. Radio call sign GJGM.

SS *Dekabrist*

USSR. Port of registry: Odessa. Built in 1903 by Vickers and Maxim Ltd., Barrow. Originally named *Anadyr* she was sold by her British owners and re-named *Franche Comte* and finally passed into Russian hands. She was a twin-screw vessel of 7,363 gross tons, 478 feet by 56 by 32 feet. Owned by Government, Black and Azov Steamship Company. Radio call sign UOML.

SS WILLIAM CLARK

United States. Port of registry: Portland, Oregon. Owned by the United States Maritime Commission and managed for them by the Isthmian Steamship Company. She was built in February 1942 by the Oregon Shipbuilding Corporation as yard number 172. 7,176 gross register tons. 441 feet by 57 feet by 37 feet. She was a standard dry cargo 'Liberty' ship. *William Clark* was sponsored by Mrs. A. Shea. The ship was named after William Clark (1770-1838); born near Charlottesville, Virginia; in 1802 to 1804 he and Merriweather Lewis made an overland expedition from St. Louis, Missouri, to the mouth of the Columbia River; the expedition was directed by President Jefferson; William Clark later served as Governor of the State of Missouri. Radio call sign KVXI.

SS JOHN H. B. LATROBE

United States. Built by the Bethlehem Steel Corporation as yard number 2039 in July 1942. Standard dry cargo 'Liberty' ship. Scrapped 1969. Calmar Steamship Corporation were managers of this vessel in 1942. The vessel was sponsored by Miss D. Frances Almond and was named after H. B. Latrobe (1803-1891); he was born in Philadelphia, was educated as a lawyer and became counsel for the Baltimore and Ohio Railroad in 1828 until his death; he was a founder member of the Maryland Institute for the promotion of Mechanical Arts and the inventor of the stove known as 'The Baltimore Heater'; he was also a founder member of the American Colonization Society and was elected president of this society in 1853. Radio call sign KGBL.

SS JOHN WALKER

United States. Built by the Bethlehem Steel Corporation as yard number 2055 in July 1942. Standard dry cargo 'Liberty' type ship. Scrapped 1961. United Fruit Company were the manages of this vessel in 1942. *John Walker* was sponsored by Mrs. Arthur J. Williams and the vessel was named after John Walker (1744-1809); born at Castle Hill, Virginia, he served as U.S. Senator for Virginia in 1790. Radio call sign KFJH.

SS *Richard H. Alvey*

United States. Built by the Bethlehem Steel Corporation as yard number 2040 in July 1942. Standard dry cargo 'Liberty' type ship. Scrapped 1961. A. H. Bull and Company were the managers of this vessel during 1942. This vessel was sponsored by Miss Polly Patterson Bradley and was named after Richard H. Alvey (1826-1926); he was born in St. Mary's County, Maryland, and educated as a lawyer; he served as a judge and was imprisoned during the Civil War for advocating extreme state rights; he was appointed chief justice of Federal Courts of Appeals for the district of Columbia by President Cleveland in 1893. Radio call sign KGIM.

SS *Hugh Williamson*

United States. Built by the North Carolina Shipbuilding Company in July 1942. Standard dry cargo 'Liberty' type ship. Ran ashore at Pernambuco on 18 June 1946, while on a voyage Mobile to Buenos Aires. Refloated on 27 June and taken to Rio de Janeiro and then Santos. Laid up as damaged until scrapped in June 1948. American South African Lines were the managers of this ship in 1942. This vessel was sponsored by Mrs. Richard D. Dixon and was named after Hugh Williamson (1735-1819); he was born at West Nottingham, Pennsylvania, and was educated as a physician; he served a s a surgeon in the North Carolina Militia, 1780-82 and as a Congressman from 1784 until 1793. Radio call sign KFGS.

SS *Empire Scott*

British. Port of registry: South Shields. Owned by Ministry of War Transport and managed for them by A. Crawford and Company Ltd., Glasgow. Built in 1941 by Redhead and Sons, South Shields. 6,150 gross register tons. 421 feet by 54 feet. Triple expansion engines. Became *Walter Scott* in 1946, *Zafiro* in 1960, *Oriental* in 1961. Scrapped Hong Kong 1963. Radio call sign BCNK.

SS *Empire Galliard*

British. Port of registry: Sunderland. Owned by Ministry of War Transport and managed for them by Common Brothers Ltd., Newcastle. Built 1942 by J. L. Thompson and Sons Ltd., at Sunderland. 7,170 gross register tons. 424 feet by 57 feet. Triple expansion engines. Became *Aert van der Neer* in 1943, *Maasland* in 1946, *M. Bingul* in 1959. Scrapped 1966. Fitted with D/F and echo sounding device. Radio call sign BCVX.

SS *SPREE*

German. Port of registry: Bremen. Built 1936 by A. G. Weser, Bremen. Owned by Nordeutscher Lloyd. Originally named *Agira*, name changed in 1936 to *Spree*. 2,867 gross register tons. 295.4 feet by 46.1 feet by 23.4 feet. Cruiser stern, two decks. Triple expansion engine with LP turbine. Mined in March 1944 off Denmark but salvaged and towed to Stavanger unrepaired. Taken over by Allies after the war and allocated to the Netherlands. Several changes of ownership/name until scrapped in the UK in the 1960s. Radio call sign DOCF.

SS *DALDORCH*

British. Port of registry: Glasgow. Owned initially by Steamship Daldorch Company Ltd., and managed by J. M. Campbell and Son. Sold to Paddy Hendersons early in the war. Survived the war. Built 1930 by W. Beardmore and Company Ltd., Dalmuir. 5,571 gross register tons. 407.8 feet by 55.2 feet by 28.7 feet. Triple expansion engines with LP turbine. Fitted with D/F. Radio call sign GRMK.

SS *BRIARWOOD*

British. Port of registry: Middlesboro. Owned by Joseph Contantine S.S. Line Ltd. Built in 1922 by Northumberland Shipbuilding Company at Newcastle. 4,019 gross register tons. 364.8 feet by 51 feet by 24.9 feet. Triple expansion engines. Fitted with gyro compass, ESD and D/F. Had been damaged by bombing in the English Channel before this episode. Survived the war. Radio call sign GQYR.

LIST OF WESTBOUND SHIPS OF OPERATION FB

All these vessels were Russian, they all sailed from the Kola Inlet on the day shown and arrived at Akureyri, Iceland.

Name	Date Sailed	Date Arrived
Mussoviet	29 October 1942	7 November 1942

Azerbaijan	31 October 1942	9 November 1942
Chernyshevsky	2 November 1942	11 November 1942
Donbass	4 November 1942	7 November 1942 (sunk)
Komsomoletz	14 November 1942	24 November 1942
Dvina	24 November 1942	5 December 1942
Mironich	25 November 1942	5 December 1942
Yelina	25 November 1942	5 December 1942

Appendix 3

Letters to Next of Kin

THE
CLAYMORE SHIPPING CO., LIMITED.

DIRECTORS
S. P. RICHARD.   J. C. CLAY.
F. T. DEWEY.

TELEGRAPHIC ADDRESS: "CLAYMORE, CARDIFF."
TELEPHONE: CARDIFF 6527 & 6528
"SCOTTS" CODE.

60, Mount Stuart Square,
Cardiff

12th February, 1946.

Mrs. E. Rhodes,
34 Harold Street,
<u>Grimsby</u>.

Dear Madam,

    We regret having to write you again in connection with the tragic loss of the s.s. "EMPIRE SKY", but feel you would like to know that we have now received a communication from the Admiralty.

    They state that information has been received from German sources that the vessel was sunk by U-boat in the vicinity of Bear Island. It is reported that no trace of the vessel or life-boats was seen afterwards.

    We are sorry we have no further details to give you, but would like to again express to you our deepest sympathy in the loss you sustained.

            Yours faithfully,

         FOR AND ON BEHALF OF
         THE CLAYMORE SHIPPING Co. Ltd.

                DIRECTOR

TURNER, BRIGHTMAN & Co.
C F BRIGHTMAN
E F LONG
A A MILLS

SHIP BROKERS   CFB/EP

THE Z STEAMSHIP Co LTD
THE ZINAL STEAMSHIP Co. LTD.

TELEGRAPHIC ADDRESS
ZEUS - AVE - LONDON (INLAND)
ZEUS - LONDON (FOREIGN)

TELEPHONE No BISHOPSGATE 7377

Stone House,
134, Bishopsgate,
London, 18th December, 1942.
E.C.2.

CODES USED
SCOTTS 1906 & APPENDIX
BOE & THE NEW BOE

Mrs. H. Urwin,
5, Charles Street,
Whitburn Colliery,
Near SUNDERLAND.

Dear Madam,

      It is with deep regret that we have to convey to you the very sad information that the steamship in which your son, Mr. R. Urwin, was serving, is now gravely overdue, and she must be presumed lost, and we are informed that it cannot be hoped that there are any survivors.

      The Admiralty report that there is a possibility that the ship has been sunk by enemy action, and, whilst the cause of loss is thus uncertain, we are authorised to inform the next-of-kin that they will be treated in all respects as that members of the crew have lost their lives by enemy action.

      We wish to extend to you our sense of profound sympathy in the sorrow which this sad message must occasion you.

      We share in mourning the loss, with a gallant Ship's Company, of one who served faithfully and well, our hope being that you will derive strength from the knowledge that he served nobly in his Country's time of peril.

Yours faithfully,

TURNER BRIGHTMAN & CO

C F BRIGHTMAN
E F LONG
A A MILLS

SHIP BROKERS

THE Z STEAMSHIP CO LTD
THE ZINAL STEAMSHIP CO LTD

TELEGRAPHIC ADDRESS
ZEUS - AVE - LONDON INLAND
ZEUS - LONDON (FOREIGN)

TELEPHONE No BISHOPSGATE 7377

CFB/EP

Stone House,
134, Bishopsgate,
London, 30th December, 1942.
E.C.2.

CODES USED
SCOTT'S 1906 & APPENDIX
BOE & THE NEW BOE

Mrs. H. Urwin,
5, Charles Street,
Whitburn Colliery,
SUNDERLAND.

Dear Madam,

In reply to your letter of enquiry, we regret that there is no news of any survivors from the ship on which your son was serving, nor can there now be any hope of further news.

We are kindly permitted by the Admiralty to inform relatives desirous of further information that the ship was bound for North Russia, and sailed from her last port on the 1st November, this being the last that was certainly known. As far as can be estimated, it is most likely that her loss would have occurred about the 5th November.

With regard to the Allotment Note, we regret that we cannot make any further payments, the authority given by it having ceased immediately on official notification of the Loss.

If you suffer from pecuniary need, due to any unavoidable adverse conditions, you may rank for a Pension, in which case you should apply for a Form of Application to the Ministry of Pensions, Norcross, Blackpool.

With kindest thoughts,

Yours faithfully,

TURNER, BRIGHTMAN & Co

C F BRIGHTMAN
E F LUNG
H A MILLS

SHIP BROKERS   CFB/EP

THE Z... STEAMSHIP CO LTD
THE ZINAL STEAMSHIP CO LTD

TELEGRAPHIC ADDRESS
ZEUS - AVE - LONDON (INLAND)
ZEUS LONDON (FOREIGN)

TELEPHONE NO BISHOPSGATE 7377

Stone House,
134, Bishopsgate,
London, 9th February, 1943.
E.C.2.

CODES USED
SCOTTS 1906 & APPENDIX
BOE & THE NEW BOE

Mrs. H. Urwin,
5, Charles Street,
Whitburn Colliery,
Near Sunderland.

Dear Madam,

      Replying to your letter of enquiry, it is indeed sad that, due to effluxion of time, it is not possible to hold out hope of any more news of the crew of the vessel in which your son was serving.

      It is true, on the information which reached us after the loss, that your son volunteered, in common with all the rest of the gallant Ship's Company, for this particular service, which presented hazards in whatever form undertaken, and we deeply regret that this ship failed to reach her destination.

      We appreciate that your Insurance Company must await official notification before dealing with claims, and we regret that the formalities necessarily take some time to complete. We can assure you, however, that matters are being dealt with as quickly as possible, and we hope that you will be able to obtain a Certificate of Death on application, say in about three weeks time, to:-

          The Registrar General of Shipping and Seamen,
            Llantrisant Road,
              Llandaff,
                CARDIFF.

                    Yours faithfully,

TURNER BRIGHTMAN & Co

SHIP BROKERS

CFB/EP

Stone House,
134, Bishopsgate,
London,   15th March, 1943.
E.C.2

Mrs. H. Urwin,
 , Charles Street,
Whitburn Colliery,
Near SUNDERLAND.

Dear Madam,

   We are indeed gladdened on learning from your letter received this morning that your son is a survivor. Please allow us to hasten in offering you and your family our kind congratulations, and to say that we appreciate how the very hard load which you have had to bear has now so happily been lifted.

   Very naturally we regret that your son could not send forward any news about his shipmates, to answer the hope which one may now feel regarding the possibility that there may be other survivors. It would seem almost certain that he is not permitted to send such information, but should any later communication convey further news, may we ask you to be so good as to forward it to us immediately.

   With kind thoughts,

          Yours faithfully,

ARCTIC INTERLUDE

BUCKINGHAM PALACE

The Queen and I offer you our heartfelt sympathy in your great sorrow.

We pray that your country's gratitude for a life so nobly given in its service may bring you some measure of consolation.

George R.I.

This scroll commemorates

Serjeant E. E. Stoackley
Royal Regiment of Artillery

held in honour as one who served King and Country in the world war of 1939-1945 and gave his life to save mankind from tyranny. May his sacrifice help to bring the peace and freedom for which he died.

MARITIME

PROTECTION OF DEFENSIVELY EQUIPPED MERCHANT SHIPS

1664

1st Maritime Regiment of Foot.

LATER TO BE CALLED

The Royal Marines

1940

Ack Ack Gunners for D.E.M.S.

LATER TO BECOME

The Maritime Royal Artillery

You E.E. Stockley *served in this Famous Unit from* Early 1941 *to* 14 Nov. 1942 *(lost at sea) and have worthily carried on the Traditions of your Forefathers in keeping the sea lanes open to Merchant Ships for the carrying of products vital to the needs of a Country at War.*

This is given you as a memento and appreciation of the valuable services you personally have rendered.

Wm. Stephenson, Lieut. Colonel
MARITIME ROYAL ARTILLERY.

Appendix 4

U-Boat Log Book Entries and Insignia

U-625 Kriegstagebuch Entries for 6 November 1942

Selected excerpts translated from the KTB of *U-625*. Note: First ship is SS *Chulmleigh*; second ship is SS *Empire Sky*.

- 00.00 h Position grid AB 6226, wind NE 2, sea 1, cloudy, atm. Pressure 1015 mb
- 04.00 h Arrived in patrol area
- 10.25 h Radio received: "British steamer grounded on South Cape of Spitzbergen."
Set course 25 degrees at 14 knots.
- 10.30 h Three Junkers 88 bombers sighted in true 170 degrees course 330 degrees. Seem to fly to Spitzbergen.
- 11.35 h Ahead aircraft approaching. General quarters, crash dive down to A-10. Going up to periscope depth, aircraft out of sight.
- 11.45 h Surfaced.
- 13.00 h Ahead land sighted, the South Cape. Patrolling Junkers 88 reports a freighter in (Luftwaffe) grid 17 East 6747 with three life boats.
- 14.00 h On surface mast top of ship sighted and submerged for a close observation of the ship. Ship looks rather normal, no damage visible. Stern about one meter deeper. Light smoke from the funnel, ship seems to be live. Two guns. Boats are lowered, but no more visible. Estimate tonnage 4000 tons.
- 16.00 h Grid AB 3281, wind NE 1, sea 1, clear air, cloudy, atm. Pressure 1015 mb.
Dusk coming up, therefore surfaced for a coup de grace torpedo. The ship seems to be not heavily damaged and could be salvaged presumably. It ran aground in a rocky area, that it entered through a small channel from south, now blocked by drift ice. I fire a torpedo from tube III

through a gap between two cliffs.
Hit after 116 sec. A second torpedo fired from tube I fails without detonation, although rocks everywhere. Ship sank deeper by bow, until deck awash. Stern rises. Seems to be aground by stern, and now is listing to starboard.
Give order to fire 20 rounds incendiary ammunition, but it cannot be set afire. A fine gunnery training.

16.30 h	Return to the patrol area.
17.37 h	Dived for reloading torpedo tubes.
18.30 h	Propeller noises in true 150 degrees.
18.40 h	Surfaced and set course 150 degrees true at high speed.
19.00 h	Port ahead a shadow, a large ship, general course 90 degrees, speed 8 knots. Passed to reach a position ahead.
20.00 h	Approach for attack.
20.14 h	Fire two torpedoes from tube I and II, but fail the target. Ship looks like increasing its speed. Follow and pass again for a favorable attack position from ahead. Ship is zigging at 12 knots.

Fire a salvo from tubes III and IV, again failed.
Ship turns off soon after I had fired. Once again I follow and proceed on parallel course with the aid of my radar. That is a fine method and more exact, if dead reckoning simultaneously, and it's quicker. Ship runs now 10 knots. Pass it and proceed on same course ahead of it.
Ship runs now more calmly with less zaggs at constant 10 knots. I wait another half hour, now light is brighter due to Aurora Borealis. I intend to fire at short distance to prevent any escape maneuver.
I assume it had listened my first torpedoes and turned off in time to avoid a hit.

22.24 h	Attacked, fire two torpedoes from tubes I and II. Hit on bow and behind superstructure. Ship is listing at first to starboard, then to port, bow sinks deeper. Transmits radio message. Name of ship not recognized. Boats are lowered. Astern an aircraft on a catapult. On deck aircraft lashed and large boxes. On bow and stern guns. Ship has six holds. Estimate 6500 tons. Ship now stopped.

Fire a torpedo from tube V, hit after 35 sec.
Ship explodes in a great detonation, night is brightened to daylight, a fire column rises in the sky, wreck parts splash around in the water that seems to boil. Many splinters hit

our boat.

A short time later smoke only marks the scene of disaster. The life boats have also disappeared.

Return to the patrol area.

U-212 KRIEGSTAGEBUCH ENTRIES

Selected excerpts translated from the KTB of *U-212* (Vogler) by Otto Giese.

30 October 1942

0400	Grid AA.9527. Wind SW force 3, sea force 1-2, overcast visibility about 4 sea miles.
0800	Grid AA.9519.
1200	Grid AA.9517 distance covered; surfaced 110.5 sea miles.
1443	AA.9525 submerged for test dive.
1530	Surfaced.
1600	AA.9526 FT from Adm. Nordmeer: "Vogler check into ice border from AE.1150 to AA.8530 via AA.56. Then return to Narvik Andfjord. Report results after passing 5 degrees west." Befehlshaber Nordmeer.
1700	Proceed on course to AE.11. Am proceeding at economical speed. The boat has to struggle against the heavy seas.

31 October 1942

0400	AA.9465. Visibility 5 sea miles, seas force 3-4.
0800	AA.9482.
0910	AA.9482 (near Jan Mayen Island). Smoke clouds in sight to port bearing 225 degrees, distance 3½ sea miles. I am veering away in order to gain a favorable forward attack position. Since I have the bright horizon behind me and since it's twilight I will attempt a dawn attack, however, I must hurry. For this reason I must proceed at the highest speed. I can very clearly see the black smoke and estimate the speed of the vessel to be 12 knots steering a northeast course. As the visibility is excellent and there is nothing else in sight I assume that she is sailing alone.
1103	As I am getting closer to attack position I see through the periscope that the vessel is a modern trawler converted into a

	subchaser (U-Bootsjäger), her armament consisting of one gun on the poop deck and three anti-aircraft guns midships. In spite of this I am determined to attack. She is maneuvering very suspiciously. A British Liberator making wide sweeps of about 3,000 meters flies out of sight bearing 60 degrees to starboard.
1203	I turn towards the vessel to begin my attack. At the same moment the trawler turns towards me with high speed. I immediately dive to A+60 [140 meters] heading 250 degrees. When we are only 60 meters down a depth charge explodes with a loud roar approximately 20 meters below us! We suffer no damage only a "shaking up"! I order "Rig for silent running!"
1225	Above us the trawler makes two passes and drops a series of 5 to 6 depth charges. Only faint ASDIC impulses can be detected and soon he no longer can be heard with hydrophones.
1425	Surface. The Bewacher is in sight about 6 sea miles to our starboard stern. I disengage at high speed on the surface (making a "run for it"!). We are seen and the enemy comes after us at full speed. At about 7 miles distance artillery is fired and we can see the spray and smoke clouds from the shells hitting the water at about 1,000 meters aft.
1511	I quickly signal: (FT.1423) "Grid AA.9450 Bewacher and aircraft!" U. Vogler.
1512	We finally outdistance the enemy. He is last seen on a bearing of 60 degrees. I continue on to the ice reconnaissance mission.
1600	AA.8666. Wind northwest, calm seas.

1 November 1942

0400	AB.1249.
0430	We reach the ice border and now are running slow ahead with both engines along it at a distance of 9 miles.
0800	AE.1225.
1200	AA.8833. Distance traveled: surfaced 260 sea miles, submerged 6 sea miles.
1600	AA.8833. The ice border to the south is very irregular with a wide ice field running about 15 miles into the open sea. Any convoy or single vessel must keep clear of this area.

The ice borders to the north are much more defined and vessels can maneuver more safely. These conditions were probably caused by the frequent northeast storms we have endured for the past few days. I have mapped the ice fields. See drawing (Skizze) #2.

Geheim-Kommandosache

Stellungnahme des Admiral Nordmeer zum KTB U.212
für die Zeit vom 27 Sept-5 Nov 1942

The attack on subchasers has little or no chance of success as the target is too small and maneuverable. Otherwise, no comment.

Author's Note

The "trawler" was HMT *Northern Spray*.

U-586 KRIEGSTAGEBUCH

Uhrzeit	Angabe des Ortes, Wind, Wetter, Seegang, Beleuchtung, Sichtigkeit der Luft, Mondschein usw.	Vorkommnisse
2.11.	**Nordmeer.**	
		Vorbei? Es ist kaum zu fassen.
0020		Sofort wieder rangedreht. Dampfer hat anscheinend nichts gemerkt. Eigener Kurs 60° H.P.
0034		Jetzt erst mal Fahrt ausgedampft.
		Dampfer peilt quer auf ca. 2000 m. Peilung steht fast bei 9 sm. Beide G.P.
		An seiner Bb.-Seite aufgedampft.
0042		auf 50° gegangen.
0100		Qu. A.A. 9467.
		Standort Qu. A.A. 9467
		Auf 70° gegangen.
0117		Dampfer peilt rw. 250°. Anlauf beginnt! Will es nochmal mit einem 2-er Fächer versuchen.
		Beide L.P. Hart Bb. Auf Hundekurve vangelaufen. Eingestellte Werte: γ = 80°
		v_g = 9 sm.
		v_t = 30 sm.
		T. = 4 m.
		E. = 800 m.
		f. = 110 m.
		ψ = 6,5'.
0118		Fächer - los!
		Schußkurs 175°. E. = ca 600 m.
		Qu. A.A. 9467.
		Hart Stb. mit L.P. nach achtern abgedreht.
		Ein Blinder müßte die Nähe des Bootes fühlen, so wird drüben gefilzt.
		Von der Hälfte des Weges an durchbrechen die beiden Aale mehrfach die Oberfläche; unmittelbar vor dem Ziel das letzte Mal.
0119		Nach 31 sec, = 450 m. Treffer Mitte und 10 m. hinter dem Bug. Etwa 100m. hohe erst schwarze, dann grauweiße Detonationswolke, die den Dampfer der Sicht für ca 2 Min. entzieht. Danach nichts mehr von ihm zu sehen. Nach einer weiteren Min. eine starke Unterwasserdetonation. Auf dem Wasser eine weißes Bojenlicht und fünf weitere,

- 29 -

Datum und Uhrzeit	Angabe des Ortes, Wind, Wetter, Seegang, Beleuchtung, Sichtigkeit der Luft, Mondschein usw.	Vorkommnisse
2.11.	Nordmeer.	
		an- und ausgehende weiße Lichter.
		Auf 600-m. Welle nichts gehört, obwohl ein
		deutscher Sender um 0140 Uhr offen gefragt:
		"Wer gab um 0130 h. t.t.t......?" mehr konnte
		wegen Fremdstörer nicht aufgenommen werden.
		Es ist kaum anzunehmen, daß nach einem Treffer
		Mitte die F.T.-Station noch klar war.
0140		Einen Haken geschlagen und zu den Lichtern an
		der Versenkungsstelle gelaufen.
		2 auf einem Balken schwimmende Tommies und ein
		von einem mit 6 Mann besetzten Floß aus dem
		Wasser gezogen.
		Die beiden ersten waren nach diesem halbstün-
		digem Bade bei 1° C plus, völlig erstarrt und
		jeder Bewegung unfähig.
		Die Namen:
		1.) Douglas Meadows Nr. 5186087.
		Gunner beim Maritime Antiaircraftcorps.
		20 Jahre.
		2.) Artur Hopkins Nr. 1496856 Bombardier
		(Korporal) 24 Jahre.
		3.) Ralph Urwin Seemann, bei der Merchant Navy
		19 Jahre.
		Die Aussagen der Gefangenen ergaben: S.S. "Em-
		pire Gilbert" ca. 7500 Brt. seit 1941 in Dienst
		von Sunderland über Reikjavik nach Rußland
		(Hafen unbekannt) unterwegs mit Kriegsmaterial
		(Lebensmittel, Munition 25 Tanks usw.)
		Schwesterschiffe: Empire Sunrise 7459 Brt.
		Empire Mist 7250 Brt.
		Am 30.10. Reikjavik aus. 66 Mann Besatzung.
		Bewaffnung: 1 U-Bootskanone achtern, Kaliber
		nicht zugegeben, und 4 - 2 cm Flak in Einzel-
		lafette. Beim Abdrehen nach dem ersten Anlauf
		will der Ausguck Boot undeutlich gesehen haben
		zu. A.A. 9468.
0200		
0210		Beide L.F. Kurs 180°. Nachgeladen.

U-Boat Insignia

U-212

U-354

U-354

U-435

U-586

U-625

U-703   U-703

Appendix 5

Official Signals and Documents for Operation FB

SECRET

WARNING: This is an unparaphrased version of a secret cypher or confidential code message and the text must first be paraphrased* It it is essential to communicate it to persons outside British or Allied Government Services.
(*Note: Messages shown as having been sent in a One-Time Pad: "O.T.P." are excepted from this rule.)

```
                                      0625Z/3 January.
SECRET              MESSAGE                                 IN.

From GEAR BOX.                        Date 3.1.43.
                                      Recd. 1418.

           BRITISH CYPHER 5 O.T.P. BY W/T.   CORRECTION.

Addressed Admiralty.

IMPORTANT.

A reconnaissance party found yesterday 2nd January 9 survivors
from s.s. CHULMLEIGH in a hut at Cape Fine which they had
reached in one life boat.(?)   3 of the men brought to
Barentsburgh.   The others will get preliminary attention
at (?Cape Line).   Names of survivors
Captain D. M. Williams
3rd Mate D.F. Clark
Radio Officer R.B. Paterson
A/B A.J. Hardy
L/Sergeant R.A. Peyer
Gunner J.B. Burnett
Gunner R.R. Whiteside
Gunner J.W. Swainston.
A.B/R.N.F. Cullan.

                                      0625 Z/3.

1st Lord.
1st S.L.(2).
V.C.N.S.
A.C.N.S.(H).
A.C.N.S.(U.T.)
N.A. 1st S.L.
Ops.(3).
O.D.(5).
O.I.C.(3).
D.N.I.(5).
D. of P.(3).
D. of P.(Q).
D.S.D.(2).
M.(13) for W.O. and A.M.
Admiral Blake.
Capt. Larking, L.O.N.N.
D.T.D.(4) and to inform R.G.S.S. Cardiff.
D. of S.T.(2).
Cdr. Holbrook.
```

ARCTIC INTERLUDE   271

MOST SECRET

WARNING: This is an unparaphrased version of a secret cypher or confidential code message, and the text must first be paraphrased if it is essential to communicate to persons outside MI5...

To: TUNA
   Dutch S/m O.15,
Repeated. F.O.(S) 661
   GEARBOX.

Date 6.11.42.

From: Admiralty

IMPORTANT.

begins: —   Following intercepted at 0318Z on 500 Kc/s

(CHULMLEIGH) S.O.S. de GJGM struck reef south of south Cape Spitzbergen making water rapidly.

Ends.

0732A/6.
Duty Signal Officer.

1st Lord.
1st S.L.(2)
D.F.S.L.
V.C.N.S.
A.C.N.S.(H)
N.A. 1st S.L.
D.O.D.(H) (2)
D.O.D.(F) (2)
D of P (2)
D of P (Q)
D.N.I.(4)
D.D.I.C.(2)
Duty Capt.
D.S.D.
Hd of M (13) for
   W.O. & A.M.,
Ad. Blake,
Capt Larking (L.O.N.N.)
         (Personal)

272   ARCTIC INTERLUDE

HUSH-MOST SECRET   OUT

HUSH MOST SECRET   MESSAGE   2030A/2nd November
                                               OUT
                                  Date   2.11.42

To A.C.I.C., 702
    Repeated C. in C. Home Fleet, 254
    F.O.(S) 621.

<u>   Naval Cypher Flag Out by W/T & T/P   </u>

From   Admiralty

<u>HUSH MOST SECRET</u>

<u>IMMEDIATE</u>

            Operation F B.

            Your 2101/31/10 (not to C.in C. H.F.
or F.O.(S)). Two repeat two additional British
ships now ready are to be sailed in continuation of
the sailings given in your 0057/28/10.

2.   It has been decided that the remainder
of the 2nd Group shall wait until after the return
of Q P 15.

                    2030A/2

                        for D.T.D. (172)

V.C.N.S.
A.C.N.S.(H)
A.C.N.S.(T)
N.A.1st S.L.
D.T.D.(2) T.D.002163/42
D.T.D.(M)
D.O.D.(H)
D.O.D.(F)
Duty Capt.
D. of P.(2)
D.M.S.

SECRET

October 9, 1942

SECRET
PRIORITY

FROM: OPNAV
TO : ALUSNA LONDON

FOR HARRIMAN FROM HOPKINS.

PRESIDENT HAS REFERRED YOUR 082214 TO ME. AFTER CONSULTATION WITH DOUGLAS, WHO APPROVES THIS WIRE, THE DECISION HERE IS AS FOLLOWS:

YOU ARE AUTHORIZED TO ARRANGE IMMEDIATELY FOR FIVE SHIPS TO GO IN THE FIRST PERIOD AND TO MAKE SUCH ARRANGEMENTS AS YOU THINK BEST IN REFERENCE TO CARGO, SHIPS, MASTERS, CREWS, ARMAMENT AND SAFETY EQUIPMENT. DOUGLAS WILL BE IN TOUCH WITH YOU LATER IN REFERENCE TO DISPOSITION OF THE BALANCE OF SHIPS AND CARGOES.

HARRY HOPKINS

SECRET

COMINCH FILE

UNITED STATES FLEET
HEADQUARTERS OF THE COMMANDER IN CHIEF
NAVY DEPARTMENT, WASHINGTON, D. C.

~~SECRET~~

October 7, 1942

DECLASSIFIED
E.O. 11652, Sec. 3(E) and 5(D) or (E)
OSD letter, May 3, 1972
By _____ NARS Date 5-29-77

MEMORANDUM FOR: Admiral Land – War Shipping Administration.
Mr. Harry Hopkins – Munitions Allocation Board.

Subject: Shipments to North Russia during remainder of Calendar Year 1942.

1. The running of PQ 18 was accomplished last month with the expenditure of about one-third of the total number of ships in the convoy – and that with the employment of some 77 combatant type ships in the escort and covering forces.

2. No such strength of escort and covering forces will be available during the remainder of the current calendar year so that regularly constituted convoys to North Russia will not be resumed before January 1943.

3. In the meantime, the British are undertaking to sail ten selected ships, with **volunteer** crews, singly and at about 200-mile intervals to North Russia in order to employ evasion and dispersion as an alternative to the non-availability of escort and covering forces. The last of the British ships committed to this enterprise is to sail about November 9th.

4. The British invite the United States to "tail on" from November 10th with similar commitments as to suitable ships sailing, singly for North Russia. I convey herewith the President's concurrence in the invitation of the British – and this memorandum may be taken as a directive to the addressees to take steps to supplement the British effort in getting shipping into North Russia.

E. J. KING

Copy to:
Admiral Leahy
General Marshall
Vice Chief of Naval Operations
ACoS (P)
 Via
CoS;
DCoS; CinC
President's Aide

NAVY DEPARTMENT Op-23L-JH
WASHINGTON (SC)S76-3
Serial 097923

March 30, 1942   CONFIDENTIAL

CONFIDENTIAL

From: The Secretary of the Navy.
To: Master M.S./S.S. **JOHN H. B. LATROBE**   7191 Gross Tons.
SUBJECT: Instructions for Scuttling Merchant Ships.

    1.   It is the policy of the United States Government that no U. S. Flag merchant ship be permitted to fall into the hands of the enemy.

    2.   The ship shall be defended by her armament, by maneuver, and by every available means as long as possible. When, in the judgment of the Master, capture is inevitable, he shall scuttle the ship. Provision should be made to open sea valves, and to flood holds and compartments adjacent to machinery spaces, start numerous fires and employ any additional measures available to insure certain scuttling of the vessel.

    3.   In case the Master is relieved of command of his ship, he shall transfer this letter to his successor, and obtain a receipt for it.

FRANK KNOX.

D. N. TREGO / for
Port Director

PHILADELPHIA, PA.
Port

August 18, 1942
Date

A. L. HODGDON
Received by   Master

                                Master

RECEIVED by
Room 165
AUG 19 1942

Copy to: C.N.O.
          BuOrd.
          BuShips.

ROUTE TO:-
File No. (SC)
Ser. No.
Copy No. 4
RCN 444732

NB100/QS-1
Serial - 0432   November 20, 1942.
CONFIDENTIAL
- -

    (k) This paragraph as well as several others indicates lack of familiarity with orders which were issued to the Master. These orders contained safe routes adjacent to mine fields, alternate routes near the destination, and listed localities where help (such as food and warmth) might be expected.

    (l) The following is an extract from the Radio Instructions contained in the orders which were issued to the Master:

> RADIO WATCH.
>
> > Reference - C.A.M.S.I. 145 as amended by C.A.M.S.I. 171. BAMS Lettered Message "JN".
> > BAMS Area concerned is - Area One A.
> > Zone and Area Broadcasts-See C.A.M.S.I. 145, Table 13A.
> > Hours of Radio Watch - Schedule of broadcasts shown in C.A.M.S.I. 145, Table 13A are to be copied irrespective of the number of Radio Operators on board. Guard Z 500 Kc/s (600M) between BAMS broadcasts as far as the number of Radio Operators on board will permit. Ships with 3 Radio Operators are to keep watch continuously, ships with 2 Radio Operators for not less than 16 hours per day, ships with one Radio Operator for not less than 8 hours per day. When in the White Sea guard 500 Kc/s instead of Portishead between the following times:- 0400 to 0600, 0800 to 1000, 1200 to 1400, 1600 to 1800, all times are G.M.T. (G.C.T.). Expect messages from Radio Archangel (RIR2) and Radio Mezen (KIK2).

    (m) Not concurred in.

    (n) No comment.

    (o) No comment.

B. B. Berry
D. B. BERRY.

CONFIDENTIAL

FROM: COMMANDING OFFICER, H.M.S "ST ELSTAN".

DATE: 14th, November. 1942.

TO: ADMIRAL COMMANDING ICELAND (C).

SUBJECT: Report of Proceedings. 1st to 14th November.

Sir,

I have the honour to submit the following Report of Proceedings from 1st to 14th November.

At 0815z/1 "St Elstan" weighed, passing Hvalfjord boom at 0900z/1.
Passage proceeded without incident until p.m. the 3rd. Weather was calm and visibility extreme, Greenland being sighted at over 100 miles. At 1830z/3 H.D No 435 was received addressed to "St Elstan", "Cape Palliser", "Northern Pride" and an unknown shore authority. As it was re-coded by "T" Tables it could not be decoded. I considered that this might be discovered, but at 0300z/4 no correction had been made, so my 0400a/4 was made to A.C.I.C. Reply was not received until 1130z/4 when "St Elstan" was in position 73 degs 42' North & 8 degs 40' West.
At 1236z/4 an S.O.S was received from s.s. "William Clark" in position 71 degs 2' North & 13 degs 5' West. "St Elstan" proceeded at best speed to this position. Visibility was poor, remaining at ¼ mile except for occasional clear patches. From 1400z to 1630 z/5 weather was clear but I was not contacted by the Catalina who reported boats in positions referred to in your 1801a/5 and 1845a/5.
I proceeded to this position and searched in the area until 0800z/6 when a star fix was obtained. Ship had been navigated by Dead Reckoning for the last 48 hours and position was 30 miles to South and East'd of D.R. Working back from this position I found that I was within 2 miles of the reported position of the boats at 1600 and 1900/5. As Catalina had not been sighted I concluded that his position was an error & proceeded to the position of the wreck.
At 0915z/6 a Fock-Wulf Kurier approached from the Westward and flew round outside effective gun range for half an hour. Enemy report was made at 0915z/6 and acknowledged by Whitehall .
When in position 71 degs North & 12 degs 25' West a large oil patch was seen but no wreckage; oil seemed to be still coming to the surface. As darkness was setting in and visibility decreasing I continued slowly to Northward intending to search the area round the oil at daybreak. At midnight wind increased to force 7 from the East with a very rough sea, short steep swell, and continuous rain with a visibility of about ½ to 3 miles. At 0413z/7 the after look-out reported

and a search was carried out until 0755 when a dark object was sighted at Green 20 degs, distance ½ mile, showing a dim white light. Surface action stations were ordered and target illuminated by searchlight. It was identified as a boat and ship was manoeuvered to bring boat alongside Port side at 0808. Oil bags on the lee bow were most useful. The survivors were taken below and boat cast off at 0818 (see attached list of survivors). Wind force 7 with a high sea.

The survivors were in good health except for several minor cases of 'immersion foot'. These were treated accordingly and two of the men who complained of severe pain in their feet due to returning circulation were given Morphia.

It is considered that the general state of the boat's crew reflects great credit on the Chief Officer, Mr Goldsmith, who was in charge of the boat.

Mr Goldsmith informed me that a second boat, less crowded and with an experienced sailing ship man on board was probably making to the southward; and that a third boat equipped with a motor was attempting to make Iceland. This was reported in my 0900a/7.

Search was continued without result. Weather of gale force was experienced a.m /8th with a temperature of 27 degrees. At 1908z/8 a steady white light lasting 15 secs was reported bearing 200 degs. Action stations were ordered, starshell fired on bearing and a square search carried out until 0400z/9. Nothing further was seen or Asdic contact obtained. Search was continued to the Southward until 2000 z/12. Frequent winds of gale force with high seas were encountered, and from 0800z to 2000z/12 vessel remained hove-to, icing up heavily and shipping heavy seas.

At 2000z/12 I considered we had only sufficient coal to return to Reykjavik.

I have the honour to be, Sir
Your Obedient Servant.

R. M. Roberts.

LIEUTENANT – IN – COMMAND.

H.M.S. "ST ELSTAN"

RECORD OF SURVIVORS (ex-s.s "WILLIAM CLARK")

Name.		Rank.	Registered Number.
OLDSMITH,	William.F,	Chief Officer.	Z 102736.
OWARD.	Lawrence.H.	3rd Officer.	011672.
ECK.	Joseph.F.	1st Engineer.	008922.
OLLAND.	Richard.E.	Deck Cadet.	027844.
ARBER.	Willard.	Clerk.	-
HRISTOPHER.	Theodore.F.	A.B.	Z 269500.
OCK.	Carl. B.	A.B.	008038.
EWCZUK.	John.	Ord.Seaman.	Z 273833.
ODRIGUEZ.	Manuel.	Oiler.	Z 160728.
BROSIO.	Vincent.	Fireman.	Z 78971.
TTERICK.	Walter T.	Wiper.	Z 269768.
VAREZ.	Manuel.	Chief Cook.	Z 146621 -D1.
CASTRO.	Simon.	Messman.	Z 159189.

All the above are American Citizens and employed by the
ISTHMIAN STEAMSHIP CO: 71, Broadway, NEW YORK CITY. U.S.A.
* * * * *

All below are U.S Naval and Naval Reserve Ratings.

LEY.	James. L.	Seaman 2nd Class. U.S.N.R.	648 06 51.
MPSON.	Austin. E.	Seaman 1st Class. U.S.N.R.	615 03 16.
NDERWOOD.	Arthur.L.	Apprentice Sea. U.S.N.	272 87 31.
OTT.	Clifford R.	Seaman 1st Class. U.S.N.	342 52 20.
PIRAZZOLA.	Anthony.	Seaman 2nd Class. U.S.N.	202 30 42.
AYLOR.	Ramza E.	Apprentice Sea. U.S.N.	287 67 40.
ICE.	Donald E.	Seaman 2nd Class. U.S.N.	212 78 80.
ISON.	William.E.	Seaman 1st Class. U.S.N.	256 38 98.
RRISON.	Leo.E.	Seaman 2nd Class. U.S.N.R.	612 17 64.
OMON.	Milton. S.	Apprentice Sea. U.S.N.R.	652 28 64.
S.	James G.	Seaman 2nd Class. U.S.N.R.	669 02 6:.
Y.	Robert G.	Seaman 1st Class. U.S.N.	224 80 28.
RE.	Frank P.	Seaman 2nd Class. U.S.N.	647 40 86.

Extracts from the Patrol Report, HM Sub *Tuna*, November 1942

4 November 1942

1100 Received SOS from Russian merchant ship 7530N 3130E and another SOS from a ship in 7440N 20E.
1230 Received SOS from American ship to the westward.

6 November 1942

0045 Received SOS, very close, within 10 miles, followed by mumbo-jumbo.
0154 Hydrophone effect received, possibly a merchant ship, 60 revolutions. Saw a U-boat and attacked—missed.
0318 Received SOS from Chulmleigh direct, made for position. Found upturned hull in lagoon. Searched for boats, nothing found. Returned to wreck—position 762640N 164030E. Survivors may have landed on Sptizbergen.

List of Distress Calls Received Direct by *Tuna*

4 November 1942

1011 Russian WKPQ AAA 7530N 3130E. [The Russian trawler?]
1017 Same call repeated.
1041 J. H. B. Latrobe KGBL AAA 7447N 2000E.
1143 Russian YZIM 7530N 2710E AAASS.
1150 Same call repeated, took D/F bearing, 72 degrees.
1151 Same again and AAA 1 torpedo 75N 27E.

6 November 1942

0045 ? SOS SOS SOS. Very close, within 10 miles, bearing by D/F 50 degrees. SOS was followed by mumbo jumbo.
0318 Received SOS from SS *Chulmleigh*.
0423 Received further SOS from SS *Chulmleigh*.

Received signal from Admiralty later repeating distress calls from *Chulmleigh* and *William Clark*.

Author's Note

Comparing the above distress calls received by *Tuna* with those received by *John H. B. Latrobe* on 4 November, one can see that there are discrepancies as well as similarities.

Appendix 6

German Aircraft Involved

Note: Drawings are not shown in scale to each other.

Blohm and Voss Bv 138 flying boat
Maritime reconnaissance aircraft
Three Junkers Jumo engines
Wing span: 88 feet 7 inches
Length: 65 feet 4 inches

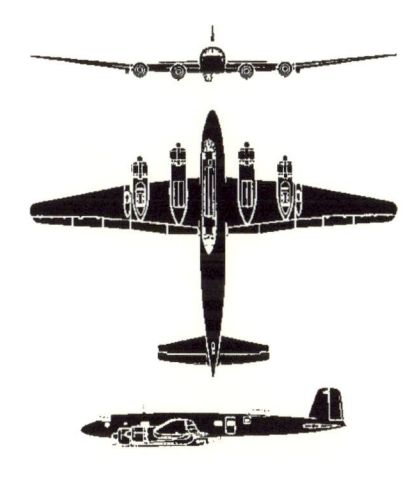

Focke-Wulf Fw 200C
Maritime reconnaissance bomber
Four BMW or Bramo engines
Wing span: 108 feet
Length: 78 feet

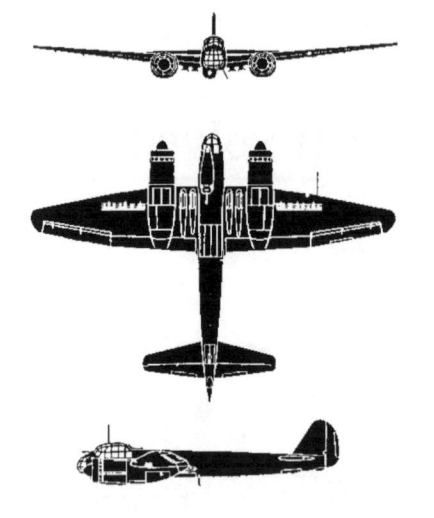

Junkers Ju 88
Bomber
Two Jumo engines
Wing span: 65 feet 6 inches
Length: 47 feet 2 inches

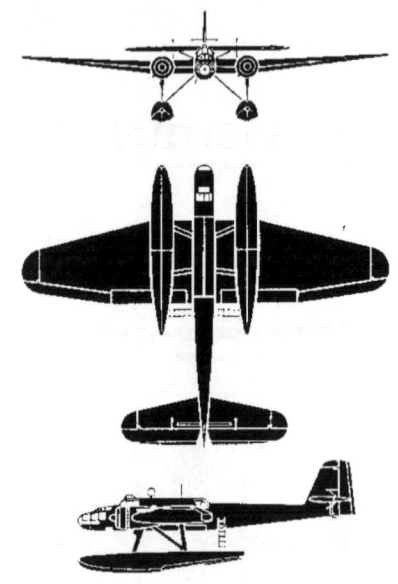

Heinkel He 115
Torpedo bomber
Two BMW engines
Wing span: 75 feet 9 inches
Length 57 feet 1 inch

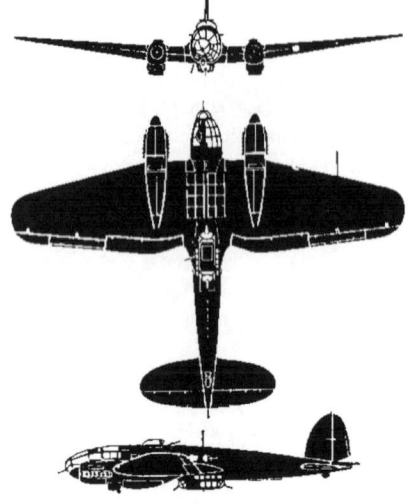

Heinkel He 111
Bomber
Two Jumo engines
Wing span: 73 feet 6 inches
Length: 53 feet 7 inches

Appendix 7

Allied Crew Documents and News Accounts

Excerpts from Diary of Clifford O. Peterson, USNR, SS Hugh Williamson

1942

17 August	Left Philadelphia. Bound for N.Y.
19	Arrived Pier 9 Staten Island.
23	Left Staten Is. & docked Cravens Pt. NJ.
25	Left NJ bound for Boston.
28	Left Boston bound for Halifax.
30	Arrived Halifax.
5 September	Left Halifax for Iceland.
17	Dropped anchor in Iceland.
8 October	First snow.
17	Left ship for Falcon Point.
1 November	Set sail for Russia (alone).
6	Empire Sky sunk a few miles astern.
7	My first taste of war and didn't like it.
11	Arrived Molotovsk, Russia. 11 ships started out and five of us there.
10 December	Left Molotovsk for Murmansk.
12	Arrived Murmansk.
25	A convoy came in from Iceland.
30	Left Murmansk bound for Scotland.

1943

10 January	Arrived Lockhue [sic], Scotland, safe & sound.
23	Left Scotland bound for the States.
31	Sighted Greenland.
10 February	Arrived New York.
12	Left New York for Philadelphia.
13	Docked Philadelphia.

Extract from L/Tel. Ian Fraser's Diary, October-December 1942, HM Trawler Cape Argona

25 October	Coaled from SS Empire Baffin and Empire Morn. Finished coaling from a Russian collier.
29	Under steam for immediate sailing.
30	Still at No. 19 Sawmill Berth.
31	Captain to very secret conference at Archangel.
1 November	Moved ship to Dvina Bar and anchored.
2	Captain informed crew that they would patrol North Arctic waters, then go to Murmansk. They would not be home for Christmas. Sailed—with orders to pick up and escort merchant ships that had been sailed independently from Iceland to North Russia.
4	Challenged a Ju 88, it answered correctly!
5	Sighted [HMT] Cape Mariato, hull down. Chipping ice. Received SOS from Empire Clarke [sic; no such named ship in Empire records, however, the American SS William Clarke sent a distress the previous day; no other explanation; SS Chulmleigh was the only ship to send an SOS on the 5th] passed to Cape Mariato by R/T.
6	Received signal informing us that three of the independent ships had been recalled to Iceland.
7	Challenged a Ju 88, received the correct reply but it then dropped two bombs, one was quite close. Course set to return to Iokanka.
8	Attacked by aircraft again.
9	Arrived Iokanka. Began coaling from lorries, Russian women doing the work.
11	Ordered to sail and pick up SS Empire Scott and Empire Sky.
12	Sailed. Weather very bad. Forward companionway carried away.
14	Sighted Cape Mariato.
15	Dodging to the weather—icing up.
16	Still dodging, still icing up.
17	Chipping ice—have developed a 30 degree list.
18	Saw a small convoy.
19	Arrived Iokanka.
5 December	Sailed with Cape Mariato to pick up SS Empire Galliard and Campfire from the White Sea and take themn to

	Murmansk. Received a message that SS Goolistan had been sunk.
9	Sailed to pick up SS Hugh Williamson and Richard H. Alvey from White Sea.
10	Met them, took them to Murmansk then we went to Polyarnoe, arriving 12th Dec.
17	Tied up alongside SS John Walker.
18	Coaling from SS John Walker. [John Walker was an oil burner, she must have carried coal as of her part cargo!]
21	Took on 75 tons of coal from SS Empire Scott.
22	Still coaling from Empire Scott.
25	Had a meal on board Empire Scott—ham, peas and spuds!

THE SHIP THEY CAN'T STOP SAILED TO RUSSIA AND BACK ALONE

[Date and source unknown]

A North-east port, Monday—A ship recently completed one of the most remarkable voyages of this war—a solo run to North Russia and back—and stepped up her bag of enemy aircraft from five to seven while doing it.

Weather-tanned, 36-year-old Captain James Shaw, whose home is in West Hartlepool, was met on the bridge by Captain W. H. Lawrence, CBE, of Glasgow, former captain of the ship.

Said Captain Lawrence: "Nice work, Jim."

The ship sailed through a hive of U-boats, Heinkels, and dive-bombers. She was repeatedly attacked, but hit back in such a way that U-boat commanders and airplane crews did not press home their attacks.

Two Heinkels attempted to do so. They were brought down in flames by the ace soldier-gunners, who chalked up their seventh kill. Their bag includes a four-engined Focke-Wulf which had a crew of 12 on board.

Five Journeys

Five times she has been on the North Russia run. And the only damage she has sustained was slightly dented bows when she struck a small iceberg.

Her crew of 37, nine of whom have been decorated, volunteered to go to North Russia out of convoy and without escort. Throughout the outward and return voyage every officer and man stood by. There was little sleep for any of them. The guns were manned day and night.

The "alert" sounded more times than the crew can remember.

The captain's logbook records there was hardly a day when the ship was not attacked by U-boat or airplane. Sometimes it was both. But every attack was beaten off.

Finally, to the surprise of Russian officials at the dockside, the lone British ship, heavily laden with war materials, drew alongside.

Special Post

Captain Lawrence, hero of the Russian convoys, handed over command of the ship to Captain Shaw when he took up a special Admiralty appointment two months ago.

Said Captain Lawrence: "The old ship has been through the worst that you can get at sea these days. But she has stood up to every bit of it.

"She was in the *Jervis Bay* and other heavily attacked convoys, has been on the North Russia run four times, and to top everything she has made a lone voyage to North Russia and back, got through without a scratch, and brought down two enemy bombers while doing so. That's nice work."

Ran Arctic Blockade

[Date and source unknown]

Two British naval officers who saw service in Russia's Arctic regions during the war reached Brisbane today in the British India freighter *Charles Dickens*.

They are Captain A. T. G. Burge (master of the *Charles Dickens*) and Chief Engineer G. E. Hendrie.

Mr. Hendrie served in ships which took £2millions worth of machinery and munitions via the Arctic route to Murmansk, in Northern Russia.

He made an unescorted trip in the *Empire Scott* (now the *Walter Scott*) from Iceland to Murmansk at the end of 1942.

Because of the lack of escort vessels at the time, it was decided to send 10 ships at 12-hourly intervals without naval protection. Only three ships got through—the others were never heard of again.

Mr. Hendrie's ship was under almost continuous attack from submarines and planes during the 12-day trip. She managed to arrive safely by dodging behind icebergs and hiding in the fog.

For his part in this trip Mr. Hendire received the DSC.

In Murmansk, Mr. Hendrie met Captain Burge, who was British sea transport officer there.

The *Charles Dickens*, which came from Calcutta via Torres Strait and Townsville, brought 1,200 tons of sacks, paraffin wax, tea, and hessian for Brisbane.

The vessel, together with others of the company, are named after famous British literary giants.

Aid-Russia Ship Carried Danger Cargo; Cabin Boys Win DSM in Lone Voyage

[*Daily Express*, Thursday, 1 April 1943]

Express Staff Reporter: Sunderland, Wednesday

Two Sunderland cabin boys—one so tiny that their shipmates called them Mutt and Jeff—who sailed in a ship making a lone and hazardous voyage to Russia with a vital and dangerous cargo have been awarded the Distinguished Service Medal.

The awards, says the *London Gazette*, are "for great bravery."

The boys, Terence Patrick Carraghan, of Guildford Street, and Arthur Sproxton, of Hutton Street, were 16 when they sailed.

A fortnight ago, on the same day, they passed their 17th birthday.

Terence, just 5 feet tall and only six stone, made up his mind early to go to sea.

Time after time shipping pool officials chased him away. "You're too small," they told him.

He returned so often that they sent for his mother and asked her: "has he really left school?"

Then Terence pestered his mother till she signed his papers.

All Volunteered

Arthur, son of a policeman, had an easier time getting a ship. His policeman father had run away to sea at 16, and his grandfather did the same thing at the same age.

It was from his grandfather that he got the great stories of the old sailing ship days.

And to make it easier at the docks, 16-year-old Arthur was nearly 6 feet tall and sturdily built.

When Terry returned to his Sunderland home tonight he told me that he and Arthur had a good time in Russia during the time they were there. He said:

"An important chap from the Russian Government came on board and said he had to thank us for the Russian people for getting the cargo through. Before we left for Russia we were asked if we were willing to go out of convoy, and everybody volunteered.

"Since I left that ship I have been on coasters. But I did not like it. There's not enough adventure on those ships. I want to be out to sea again, and now I have just been fixed up with another ship.

"I hope I shall be going to Russia again. Arthur is now in another ship and away to sea. Perhaps I shall meet him again soon."

Mrs. Sproxton said that Arthur had been serving his time as an engineer at a local shipyard. Every day for months he had asked his mother and father if he could go to sea. They tried to persuade him to give up the idea.

She said: "That only seemed to make him more determined to go. We could not stop him, and eventually, to get a little peace, we signed his papers."

His 81-year-old grandfather, Mr. James Adamson, now an invalid, is proud of young Arthur. He told me: "The sea is in that boy's blood. I knew he would make good."

THE LAST WISH OF A GREENOCK WIDOW

[? *Sunday Post*, 13 September 1987]

It was a bitter night in November 1942. The SS *Empire Sky* was sailing off Bear Island in the Arctic Ocean, her holds packed with ammunition, heavy tanks lining her decks, when she was hit by a torpedo from a German U-boat.

The crew rushed to the lowered lifeboats and were rowing away when a second torpedo struck and a massive explosion lit the night sky. There were no survivors among the lifeboats and even the U-boat was damaged in the blast and had to limp home.

Among the sailors who perished that night was James Carr. Back home in Smith Street, Greenock, his sorrowing widow Kate was left with three bairns to bring up. Many a time she went hungry herself to make sure the children were fed.

She made a good job of raising the three and instilled into them the difference between right and wrong and the importance of keeping promises. Several times she told them something else. That when her time came, she wanted to be beside her man.

Sadly, Kate passed away in July and her daughter began the task of fulfilling her mother's dying wish. So, some weeks later, from the Hull-based *Arctic Corsair*, the captain and crew reverently scattered the ashes on the cold waters off Bear Island.

After 45 years, Kate was united again with her husband.

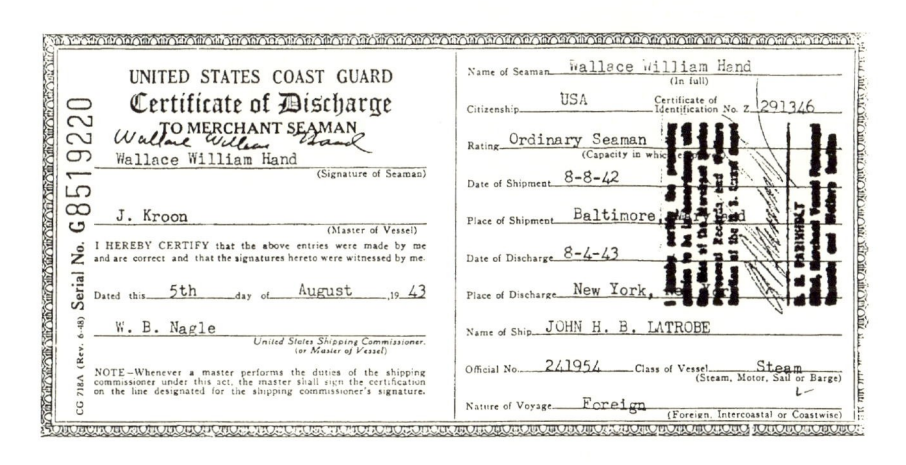

Above: Certificate of Discharge for Ordinary Seaman Wally Hand.

SEVENTEEN: DIED IN ACTION
Former Harold Street Schoolboy

Seventeen year old Victor James Jennings, son of Mrs. Jennings, of 87, Guildford-street, Grimsby, is reported to have been killed in action at sea.

An old boy of Harold - street School, and later of Little Coates School, he worked for Kemps, cycle dealers, Cleethorpe - road, before joining the Merchant Navy in 1941.

Jas. Jennings

9

Name LANGSTON, Rudolph John
(Name in full, surname to the left.)

No. 329 11 75 Rate S1c USN { A.A.
                                  P.A.

Date reported July 31, 1942

Ship U.S.N., AGC., BROOKLYN, N.Y.
or
Station ~~AGS., SEC. BASE, LITTLE CREEK, VA.~~
From

2-19-43 Detached duty completed as armed guard on board U.S. Armed Merchant Vessel *S.S. John Walker*

1 MAR 1943
Appointed Gunner's Mate Third Class this date. Authority: BuPers. ltr. Pers-635-owc-P27- MM (4021) of May 29, 1942.

WM. J. COAKLEY,
Comdr., U.S.N.R.,
Commanding.

Date transferred _____
To _____

_____
Signature and rank of Commanding Officer.

Date received _____
Ship
or _____
Station
From _____

_____
Signature and rank of Commanding Officer.

NRB—33967—10-22-42—100M.

This and next four pages: Rudi Langston's service record.

Name: **LANGSTON, Rudolph John**
(Name in Full, Surname to the Left)

329 11 75   Rate **GM3c, USN**
(Service No.)

Date Reported Aboard: **April 24, 1943**

LION THREE
(Present Ship or Station)

RS, NOB, NORFOLK, VIRGINIA
(Ship or Station Received From)

July 2, 1943

From: The Chief of Naval Personnel
To: LANGSTON, Rudolph John, Gunner's Mate Third Class, USN.
Via: Commanding Officer, "LION THREE".
Subject: Commendation.

1. The Chief of Naval Personnel takes pleasure in commending you for your outstanding bravery and skill as a member of the Navy Gun Crew aboard an American merchant ship which was repeatedly subjected to vicious aerial bombardment during a recent voyage through the war zone.

2. Reports of the occurrences indicate that on one occasion eight separate attacks were made upon the vessel by a large number of enemy bombers which, for two and a half hours, doggedly persisted in their

Date Transferred _____

To _____

_____
Signature and Rank of Commanding Officer.

Date Received Aboard: _____

_____
(New Ship or Station)

_____
(Last Ship or Station)

Signature and Rank of Commanding Officer.

ORIGINAL
FOR SERVICE RECORD

Name **LANGSTON, Rudolph John**
(Name in Full, Surname to the Left)

Service No. **329 11 75** Rate **GM3c, USN**

Date Reported Aboard: **April 24, 1943**

LION THREE
(Present Ship or Station)

RS, NOB, NORFOLK, VIRGINIA
(Ship or Station Received From)

---

determination to sink her. Yet the Armed Guard Crew, who had never been in an air raid before, met the planes with such a terrific barrage of deadly fire that not only were all the bombers driven off, but two of them were forced to flee in a blazing and badly damaged condition. When a third attacker suddenly swooped out from behind a snowbank dead ahead, the Navy crew, with all guns blazing, instantly pumped a mighty volley of accurate shellfire into him, compelling the plane to turn tail and drop behind the bank, immediately after which a tremendous splash in the sea was observed. During this and the many other battles throughout the long, cold voyage, the men of the Armed Guard Unit, by their competence, endurance, and cooperation with the other personnel aboard, saved their ship and her vital cargo from destruction.

Date Transferred _____

To _____

_____
Signature and Rank of Commanding Officer.

Date Received Aboard: _____

_____
(New Ship or Station)

_____
(Last Ship or Station)

_____
Signature and Rank of Commanding Officer.

ORIGINAL
FOR SERVICE RECORD

Name: **LANGSTON, Rudolph John**
(Name in Full, Surname to the Left)

329 11 75 Rate **GM3c, USN**
(Service No.)

Date Reported Aboard: **April 24, 1943**

LION THREE
(Present Ship or Station)

RS, NOB, NORFOLK, VIRGINIA
(Ship or Station Received From)

---

3. Your courageous conduct on the above occasions was in keeping with the best traditions of the Naval service.

4. A copy of this letter has been made an official part of your record in the Bureau.

/s/ RANDALL JACOBS

- - - - - - - - - - - - - - - - - - -

LION THREE   July 5, 1943

Above commendation delivered to man at Captain's Inspection, Saturday, June 10, 1943, with congratulations.

/s/ J.E.REINBURG,Jr.,

Date Transferred _____

To _____

_____
Signature and Rank of Commanding Officer.

Date Received Aboard: _____

_____
(New Ship or Station)

_____
(Last Ship or Station)

_____
Signature and Rank of Commanding Officer.

ORIGINAL
FOR SERVICE RECORD

Name __LANGSTON, Rudolph John__
(Name in full, surname to the left.)
No. _329 11 75_ Rate _Sea2/c USN_ {A.A. / P.A.

Date reported **31 JUL 1942**

Ship or Station __AGC., REC. STA. SO. BROCKLYN, N. Y.__

From ~~AGS., SEC. BASE, LITTLE CREEK, VA.~~

AUG 6 1942
Detached duty as armed guard on board U.S. Armed Merchant Vessel.

27 JAN 1943
Rating changed this date from S2. to S1c. Authority: BuPers.ltr.Pers.67-Mt-P17-2/MM (3937) of Nov. 5, 1942.

WM. J. COAKLEY,
Comdr., U.S.N.R.,
Commanding.

Date transferred ____
To ____

Signature and rank of Commanding Officer.

Date received
Ship or Station
From ____

Signature and rank of Commanding Officer.

Appendix 8

List of Merchant Ships That Sailed to North Russia Between August 1941 and the End of the War in Europe

THE list is not necessarily complete. It lists all vessels that sailed; some were of course sunk before reaching Russia, others returned to port with damage or defects. Some of the vessels sailed to Russia more than once, but are listed only once, though where possible the different convoy numbers are given. Some 347 U.S. merchant ships sailed to North Russia, the remainder were British, Russian, Panamanian, Dutch and Norwegian. Nationality is given where known. Eight hundred eleven vessels were escorted to Russia, 720 arrived safely, 715 were escorted back, 680 arrived in UK ports. Eighty-seven vessels were lost by enemy action, seven by other causes and thirty-two vessels returned to their departure ports. It will be seen from the list that in numerous instances ships are listed in return convoys without showing the outward convoy, this is because I have so far been unable to establish the number of the convoy in which the outward journey was made. Over 611 vessels are listed.

Notes
(B) Bombed and sunk while in Russian port.
(R) Returned to harbor.
(S) Sunk.
*   Ironclad became *Marina Raskova*.

Name	Country	Convoys
Abner Nash	USA	JW-56B, RA-57, JW-61, RA-62
Adolph S. Ochs	USA	JW-60, RA-61, JW-64, RA-65, JW 67, JW 63
Aert Van Der Neer	Dutch	JW-56A, RA-57
Afrikander (S)	Panamanian	PQ-18
Alamar (S)	USA	PQ-16
Alanson B. Houghton	USA	JW-63, RA-64, JW-67
Albert C. Ritchie	USA	JW-56B, RA-57, JW-66, RA-67
Alchiba	Dutch	Dervish, QP-1
Alcoa Banner	USA	PQ-16, QP-14
Alcoa Cadet	USA	PQ-15

Name	Country	Convoys
Alcoa Rambler	USA	PQ-15, QP-12
Alcoa Ranger (S)	USA	PQ-17
Aldan	USSR	Independent
Alexander White	USA	JW-57, RA-58
Almamata	USSR	PQ-6, QP-13, QP-1, PQ-4
Amasa Delano	USA	JW-62, RA-63
American Press	USA	QP-13, PQ-16
American Robin	USA	PQ-16, QP-13
Andre Marti	USSR	PQ-14 (R), PQ-18, QP-15, RA-53 (R), QP-3
Andrew Carnegie	USA	JW-58, RA-59
Andrew G. Curtin (S)	USA	JW-56A
Andrew Moore	USA	JW-52
Andrew Turnbull	USA	JW-62, RA-63
Andrew W. Preston	USA	JW-61, RA-62
Aneroid	British	PQ-7B, QP-6
Archangelsk	USSR	QP-13
Arcos	USSR	QP-5, PQ-14 (R), QP-3, PQ-16
Arthur L. Perry	USA	JW-54-B, RA-55A
Artigas	Panamanian	PQ-12, QP-10, JW-53, RA-54B
Arunah S. Abell	USA	JW-58, RA-59, JW-60, RA-61, JW-64, RA-65
Ashkhabad	USSR	QP-9, PQ-11
Atheltemplar (S)	British	PQ-14, QP-11, PQ-18
Atlantic	British	PQ-5, PQ-16, RA-54B, QP-13, QP-8, JW-53, QP-2, PQ-1, PQ-9/10
August Belmont	USA	JW-62, RA-63, JW-66, RA-67
Azerbaijan	USSR	PQ-17, Independent
Ballot	Panamanian	PQ-13, QP-11, JW-51B
Banderos	Norwegian	JW-54A (R)
Barbara Frietchie	USA	JW-58, RA-59A, JW-62, RA-63, JW-67
Barrwhin	British	QP-9, PQ-11
Bateaux (S)	Panamanian	PQ-13, PQ-11
Bayou Chico	Panamanian	PQ-15, QP-12
Beaconhill	Panamanian	JW-53, RA-54
Beaconstreet	British	QP-10, PQ-12
Beau Regard	USA	JW-51A, RA-52
Bellingham (S)	British	PQ-17, QP-14
Bello-Russia	USSR	RA-51
Belomorkanal	USSR	QP-10, PQ-12, QP-15
Ben F. Dixon	USA	JW-64, RA-65
Benjamin Harrison	USA	PQ-17, QP-14
Benjamin H. Hill	USA	RA-64, JW-66, RA-67
Benjamin H. Latrobe	USA	JW-58, RA-59
Benjamin Schlesinger	USA	JW-58, RA-59, JW-61, JW-65, RA-66
Bering	USA	JW-53, RA-54B
Bernard N. Baker	USA	JW-55B, JW-63, RA-64, RA-67, JW-67
Blair Nevis	British	PQ-1, QP-2
Bolton Castle (S)	British	PQ-17
Botavon (S)	British	PQ-15, QP-7, PQ-7B
Briarwood	British	PQ-3, PQ-11, PQ-14, Independent, JW-51A, QP-11, RA-52, QP-4, PQ-5
British Corporal	British	PQ-14 (R)

Name	Country	Convoys
British Governor	British	JW-53, RA-54A
British Merit	British	RA-65
British Patience	British	JW-60, RA-61
British Pride	British	PQ-8, QP-8
British Promise	British	JW-59, RA-60, JW-63, RA-64, JW-67
British Respect	British	JW-62, RA-63, JW-66, RA-67
British Statesman	British	JW-55B, RA-56
British Valour	British	JW-57, RA-58
British Workman	British	PQ-8, QP-8
Brockhurst Livingston	USA	JW-55B, RA-56
Budenni	USSR	QP-13, PQ-4
Byron Darnton	USA	JW-57, RA-58, JW-64, RA-66
Caesar Rodney	USA	JW-57, RA-58, JW-63, RA-64, JW-67
Calobre	Panamanian	JW-51B, RA-53
Campfire	USA	PQ-18, QP-15 (R), RA-51
Cape Corso (S)	British	PQ-15, QP-4
Cape Race	British	PQ-15, QP-4, QP-12, PQ-3
Capira	Panamanian	PQ-15, QP-13, PQ-1, QP-2
Capulin	USA	PQ-12, QP-10
Cardinal Gibbons	USA	JW-55B, RA-56, JW-60, RA-61, JW-67
Carlton (S)	USA	PQ-16 (R), PQ-17
Cecil N. Bean	USA	JW-62, RA-63, JW-66, RA-67
Charles A. McAllister	USA	JW-56B, RA-57, JW-59, RA-60, JW-65, RA-66
Charles Bullfinch	USA	JW-56A (R), JW-57, RA-58, JW-67
Charles Dauray	USA	JW-59, RA-60
Charles G. Curtis	USA	JW-58
Charles M. Schwab	USA	JW-57, RA-58, JW-63, RA-64
Charles R. McCormick	USA	PQ-18, QP-15
Charles Scribner	USA	JW-56A, RA-57, JW-63, RA-64
Charles S. Henderson	USA	JW-58, RA-59
Cherniyshevsky	USSR	PQ-16, PQ-7B, QP-2, QP-6, Independent
Chester Valley	USA	JW-51B, RA-53
Christopher Newport (S)	USA	PQ-17
Chulmleigh (S)	British	PQ-5, QP-13, Independent
City of Flint	USA	PQ-11, QP-9
City of Joliet (S)	USA	PQ-14 (R), PQ-16
City of Omaha	USA	PQ-16, QP-13, JW-53, RA-54
Clark Howell	USA	JW-59, RA-60
Cocle		QP-4, PQ-3, PQ-7
Cold Harbor	Panamanian	QP-8, PQ-7A
Collis P. Huntingdon	USA	JW-55A, RA-56, JW-61
Copeland (Rescue)	British	JW-54A, RA-54B, JW-57, RA-58, JW-66, RA-66
Cornelius Harnett	USA	JW-52, RA-53
Crosby S. Noyes	USA	JW-63, RA-64
Daldorch	British	Independent, JW-51B, RA-52, PQ-11, QP-9, JW-54B, RA-55B
Daniel Drake	USA	JW-54A, RA-55A
Daniel Morgan (S)	USA	PQ-17

ARCTIC INTERLUDE 301

Name	Country	Convoys
Daniel Willard	USA	JW-55A, RA-56, JW-60, RA-61, JW-64, RA-65
Dan-Y-Bryn	British	PQ-14, QP-11, PQ-18, QP-15, JW-52, RA-53, QP-4, PQ-4
Daphnella	British	JW-57, RA-58
Dartford	British	QP-7, PQ-8
David B. Johnson	USA	JW-59, RA-60, JW-66, RA-67
David Stone	USA	JW-60, RA-61
Deerlodge	USA	PQ-15, QP-14
Dekabrist (S)	USSR	Independent, QP-5, PQ-6
Del Sud	USA	JW-52, RA-53
Dexter W. Fellows	USA	JW-60, RA-61
Dneprostroi	USSR	PQ-12, QP-10
Dolabella	British	JW-58, RA-59, JW-61, RA-62, JW-65, RA-66
Donald W. Bain	USA	JW-61, RA-62
Donbass (S)	USSR	PQ-17, Independent
Dover Hill	British	JW-51B (R), RA-54B, JW-53
Dunboyne	USA	QP-11, PQ-13
Dvina	USSR	Independent
Dynastic	Panamanian	JW-51A, RA-52
Earlston (S)	British	QP-9, QP-12, PQ-17
Edmund Fanning	USA	JW-54A, RA-55A, JW-63, RA-64
Edward A. Savoy	USA	JW-60, RA-61
Edward E. Spafford	USA	JW-60, RA-61
Edward H. Crockett	USA	JW-59, RA-60
Edward L. Grant	USA	JW-56B, RA-57, JW-59, RA-60
Edward N. Hurley	USA	JW-62, RA-63, JW-67
Edward P. Alexander	USA	JW-58, RA-59
Edward Sparrow	USA	JW-57, RA-58
Edwin L. Drake	USA	JW-56A, RA-57, JW-64, RA-65
Effingham (S)	USA	PQ-13
Egoro	Norwegian	JW-67, RA-67
El Almirante	Panamanian	QP-7, JW-51A, RA-52, PQ-8
El Capitan (S)	Panamanian	QP-4, PQ-17, PQ-3
El Costan	Panamanian	PQ-12, QP-10
Eldina	USA	PQ-13, QP-11
Eldorado	—	PQ-13
Eleanor Lord	USA	JW-61, JW-65, RA-66
Elijah Kellogg	USA	JW-59, RA-60
El Estero	Panamanian	PQ-13, QP-11
El Largo	Panamanian	QP-8, PQ-9/10
El Mirlo	Panamanian	PQ-6, PQ-14, QP-4, QP-10
Elna II	USSR	PQ-1
El Occidente (S)	Panamanian	PQ-10, QP-10, QP-12
El Oceano	Panamanian	JW-51A, RA-52, PQ-5 (R), PQ-6
Elona	British	QP-8, PQ-6
El Oriente	Panamanian	JW-52, RA-53
Eloy Alfaro	USA	JW-58 (R), JW-61, RA-62, JW-65, RA-66
Empire Activity	British	PQ-7B, QP-6
Empire Archer	British	JW-51B, RA-53, JW-55A, RA-56, JW-63, RA-64
Empire Baffin	British	PQ-16, PQ-18, QP-15, QP-9, QP-13, JW-52 (R), JW-53 (R), PQ-11, QP-3, PQ-2
Empire Bard	British	PQ-14 (R), PQ-15, RA-57, RA-59A

Name	Country	Convoys
Empire Beaumont (S)	British	PQ-18
Empire Buttress	British	JW-59
Empire Byron (S)	British	PQ-12, QP-9, PQ-17
Empire Carpenter	British	JW-54A, RA-55A, JW-57
Empire Celia	British	JW-54A, RA-55A, JW-57, RA-58, JW-60, RA-61, JW-63
Empire Clarion	British	JW-52, RA-53
Empire Cowper (S)	British	PQ-13, QP-10
Empire Elgar	British	PQ-16, RA-59A
Empire Emerald	British	JW-51B, RA-53, JW-64, JW-67
Empire Flint	British	JW-64, RA-65
Empire Fortune	British	JW-53, RA-54
Empire Galliard	British	Independent, JW-53, RA-51, RA-54
Empire Garrick	British	JW-62, RA-63, JW-66, RA-67
Empire Gilbert (S)	British	Independent
Empire Halley	British	QP-7, PQ-7B
Empire Howard (S)	British	PQ-14, PQ-7B, QP-6
Empire Kinsman	British	JW-53, RA-54
Empire Lawrence (S)	British	PQ-16
Empire Lionel	British	JW-54B, RA-56
Empire Magpie	British	QP-9, PQ-11
Empire Mavis	British	QP-13, PQ-6
Empire Merit	British	JW-64
Empire Meteor	British	JW-51A, RA-52, QP-13, PQ-4
Empire Morn	British	PQ-15, PQ-18, QP-12, QP-15
Empire Nigel	British	JW-54A, RA-55A, JW-57
Empire Pickwick	British	JW-55A, RA-56 (R), RA-57
Empire Ploughman	British	JW-56A, RA-57
Empire Portia	British	JW-52, RA-54
Empire Prowess	British	JW-58, RA-59A, JW-67
Empire Purcell (S)	British	PQ-16
Empire Ranger (S)	British	PQ-13
Empire Redshank	British	PQ-7B, QP-6
Empire Scott	British	Independent, JW-53, RA-54B, RA-51
Empire Selwyn	British	PQ-16, QP-8, QP-13, PQ-10
Empire Sky (S)	British	Independent
Empire Snow	British	PQ-18, QP-15, JW-52, RA-53
Empire Stalwart	British	JW-54B, RA-55B, JW-65, RA-63, JW-65
Empire Starlight (B)	British	PQ-13
Empire Stevenson (S)	British	PQ-18, QP-13, PQ-5
Empire Tide	British	PQ-17, QP-14
Empire Tourist (S)	British	JW-56B, RA-57
Empire Tristram	British	PQ-18, QP-15, JW-52, RA-53
Empress of Australia	British	JW-61A, RA-61A
Empress of Canada	British	Special to Spitzbergen
Esek Hopkins	USA	PQ-18, QP-15
Esneh	British	Dervish, QP-1
Eugine Field	USA	JW-54B, RA-56
Eulima	British	QP-5, PQ-4
Executive (S)	USA	JW-51B, RA-53

Name	Country	Convoys
Exford	USA	PQ-17, PQ-18, QP-15
Explorer	British	QP-8, JW-53 (R), PQ-6
Expositor	USA	PQ-15, QP-12
Exterminator	Panamanian	PQ-14 (R), PQ-16, QP-13
Fairfield City (S)	USA	PQ-17
Fisher Ames	USA	JW-54A (R)
Fort Astoria	British	JW-55A, RA-56
Fort Bellingham (S)	British	JW-56A
Fort Boise	British	JW-62, RA-63, JW-65, RA-66
Fort Brule	British	JW-57, RA-59
Fort Columbia	British	JW-54B, RA-55B, JW-58, RA-59
Fort Crevecoeur	British	JW-56B, RA-57, JW-58, RA-59, JW-61, RA-62, JW-64, RA-65
Fort Glenora	British	JW-59, RA-60
Fort Hall	British	JW-55A, RA-56, JW-58, RA-59
Fort Highfield	British	JW-62, RA-63, JW-67
Fort Island	British	JW-62, RA-63
Fort Kullyspell	British	JW-55B, RA-56, JW-58, RA-59
Fort Massac	British	JW-62, RA-63, JW-65, RA-66
Fort McMurray	British	JW-54B, RA-55A, JW-57, RA-58
Fort Missanabie	British	JW-55A, RA-56
Fort Nakasley	British	JW-55B, RA-56
Fort Norfolk	British	JW-56B, RA-57
Fort Poplar	British	JW-54B, RA-55B
Fort Romaine	British	JW-57, RA-58, JW-61, RA-62
Fort Slave	British	JW-56A, RA-57
Fort Thompson	British	JW-55A, RA-56
Fort Vercheres	British	JW-55B, RA-56, JW-58, RA-59A, JW-64, RA-65
Fort Yukon	British	JW-54A, RA-55A, JW-58, RA-59, JW-61, RA-62, JW-65, RA-66
Francis C. Harrington	USA	JW-63, RA-64
Francis Scott Key	USA	PQ-14 (R), PQ-15, QP-12, JW-53, RA-54, JW-58, RA-59, JW-60, RA-61, JW-64, RA-65
Francis Vigo	USA	JW-58, RA-59
Frank Gilbreth	USA	JW-59, RA-60
Frederick A. Kumner	USA	JW-60, RA-61
Frederick W. Taylor	USA	JW-60, RA-61
Frederick Engels	USSR	QP-8, QP-15, PQ-9/10
F. T. Frelinghusen	USA	JW-59, RA-60, JW-64, RA-65
Gallant Fox	Panamanian	PQ-13, QP-11
Gateway City	USA	JW-51A, RA-52
Gemstone	British	PQ-1, QP-2
George Gale	USA	JW-58, RA-59
George H. Pendleton	USA	JW-63, RA-64, JW-67
George M. Cohan	USA	JW-58, RA-59
George Steers	USA	JW-64, RA-65
George T. Angell	USA	JW-58, RA-59, JW-60, RA-61
George Weems	USA	JW-55A, RA-56, JW-67
Gilbert Stewart	USA	JW-54A, RA-55A, JW-58, RA-59
Goolisten (S)	British	PQ-18, QP-15

Name	Country	Convoys
Grace Abbott	USA	JW-58, RA-59, JW-65, RA-66
Greylock (S)	USA	JW-51A, RA-52
Gulfwing	USA	JW-52, RA-53
Harmatris	British	PQ-8, QP-14
Harmonic	British	PQ-1, QP-2
Harold L. Winslow	USA	JW-55B, RA-56, JW-61, RA-62, JW-64, RA-65
Harpalion (S)	British	PQ-13, QP-10, PQ-2, QP-3
Hartlebury (S)	British	PQ-17, QP-9, PQ-2, QP-3, PQ-11
Hawkins Fudske	USA	JW-58, RA-59, JW-60, RA-61, JW-64, RA-65
Heffron (S)	USA	PQ-16, QP-13
Hegira	USA	PQ-15, QP-13
Henry Adams	USA	JW-61, RA-62
Henry Bacon (S)	USA	JW-56B, RA-57, JW-63, RA-64
Henry B. Brown	USA	JW-57, RA-58
Henry Lomb	USA	JW-57, RA-58, JW-60, RA-61, JW-64, RA-66
Henry Villard	USA	JW-54A, RA-55A, JW-58, RA-59, JW-63, RA-64
Henry Wynkoop	USA	JW-56B, RA-57, JW-63, RA-64, JW-67
Herbrand	Norwegian	JW-59, RA-59A
Hollywood	USA	PQ-18, QP-15
Honomu (S)	USA	PQ-17
Hoosier (S)	USA	PQ-17
Hopemount	British	PQ-14, RA-51
Horace Grey (S)	USA	JW-54B, RA-56, JW-63
Horace S. Bushnall (S)	USA	JW-65
Hugh Williamson	USA	Independent, RA-51
Hybert (S)	USA	PQ-16, QP-13
Idefjord	Norwegian	JW-63, RA-64
Ilmen	USSR	QP-13
Induna (S)	British	PQ-13
Ironclad*	USA	PQ-14 (R), QP-15
Israel Putnam	USA	JW-53, RA-54
Ivaran	Norwegian	JW-67
Izora (S)	USSR	QP-8, PQ-9
James A. Farrell	USA	JW-55A, RA-56
James Bowie	USA	JW-53 (R)
James Gordon Bennett	USA	JW-54A, RA-55B
James Kerney	USA	JW-63, RA-64
James M. Gillis	USA	JW-61, RA-62, JW-65, RA-66
James Smith	USA	JW-54A, RA-55A, JW-58, RA-59
James Woodrow	USA	JW-55A, RA-56
Jefferson Davis	USA	JW-56A (R), JW-57, RA-58
Jefferson Myers	USA	JW-51B, RA-53
J. D. Yeager	USA	JW-63, RA-64
J. L. M. Curry	USA	JW-51A, RA-53
John A. Donald	USA	JW-57, RA-58
John A. Quitman	USA	JW-56A (R), JW-57, RA-58, JW-63, RA-64
John B. Lennon	USA	JW-58, RA-59
John Carver	USA	JW-58, RA-59
John Davenport	USA	JW-58, RA-59
John Fitch	USA	JW-54B, RA-56
John Gibbon	USA	JW-62, RA-63, JW-66, RA-67

Name	Country	Convoys
John H. B. Latrobe	USA	Independent, JW-51B, RA-53, JW-56B, RA-57
John Ireland	USA	JW-63, RA-64, JW-67
John J. Abel	USA	JW-55B, RA-56, JW-60, RA-61, JW-64, RA-65
John Lafarge	USA	JW-56B, RA-57, JW-59, RA-60, JW-63, RA-64
John Langdon	USA	JW-57
John Lawrence	USA	JW-53 (R)
John McDonogh	USA	JW-58, RA-59, JW-65, RA-66
John Penn (S)	USA	PQ-18
John Randolph (S)	USA	PQ-16, QP-13
John Rutledge	USA	JW-57, RA-58
John Sharp Williams	USA	JW-57, RA-58, JW-61, RA-62
John Stevenson	USA	JW-57, RA-58
John T. Holt	USA	JW-58, RA-59
John Vining	USA	JW-55B, RA-56, JW-60, RA-61
John Walker	USA	Independent, RA-51
John Wanamaker	USA	JW-55B, RA-56, JW-64, RA-65
John Witherspoon (S)	USA	PQ-17
John Woolman	USA	JW-57, RA-58, JW-60, RA-61
John W. Powell	USA	JW-57, RA-58
Joseph E. Johnson	USA	JW-53 (R)
Jose Marti	USA	JW-59, RA-60, JW-63, RA-64
Josephine Shaw Lowell	USA	JW-59, RA-60
Joseph N. Nicollet	USA	JW-56A (R), JW-58, RA-59
Joshua W. Alexander	USA	JW-57, RA-58, JW-63, RA-64, JW-67
Joshua Thomas	USA	JW-58, RA-59, JW-60, RA-61, JW-66, RA-67
Joyce Kilmer	USA	JW-58, RA-59, JW-61, RA-62, JW-64, RA-65
Julien Poydras	USA	JW-58, RA-59, JW-67
Julius Olsen	USA	JW-60, RA-61
Junecrest	British	JW-54A, RA-55A
Jutland (S)	British	PQ-15, QP-7, PQ-7B
Kara	USSR	Independent
Keith Palmer	USA	JW-61, RA-62, JW-66, RA-67
Kentucky (S)	USA	PQ-18
Kiev (S)	USSR	QP-10, PQ-12
Kingswood	British	PQ-11, QP-9
Komiles	USSR	PQ-18, QP-15, JW-53 (R), QP-13, PQ-5
Komsomoletz A-1	USSR	Independent
Kong Kaakon	Norwegian	JW-66, RA-67
Kotlin	—	RA-51
Krasnoe Znamaya	USSR	Independent
Krassin (Icebreaker)	USSR	PQ-15
Krazny Partizan (S)	USSR	Independent
Kronprinsen	Norwegian	JW-66, RA-67
Kusbass	USSR	QP-12, QP-3, Independent
Kuznets Lesov (S)	USSR	QP-15
Lacklan	British	JW-58, RA-59A, JW-63, RA-63, JW-65, RA-65
Lafayette	USA	PQ-18, QP-15
Lancaster	USA	PQ-15, QP-13
Lancaster Castle (B)	British	PQ-12

Name	Country	Convoys
Lancastrian Prince	British	Dervish, QP-1
Lapland	British	JW-55A, JW-59, RA-59, JW-61
Larranaga	USA	PQ-8, QP-8
Laurelwood	British	JW-61, RA-62, JW-62, RA-62, JW-66, RA-67
Lawrence J. Brengle	USA	JW-61, RA-62, JW-65, RA-66
Lebarron Russell Briggs	USA	JW-63, RA-64
Leo J. Duster	USA	JW-59, RA-60, JW-65, RA-66
Lewis Emery Jr.	USA	JW-55A, RA-56, JW-60, RA-61, JW-64, RA-65
Linn Boyd	USA	JW-62, RA-63, JW-66, RA-67
Llandaff	British	PQ-12, QP-9, JW-53, RA-54B
Llanstephan Castle	British	Dervish
Longwood	British	JW-62, RA-63
Lorca	British	PQ-1, QP-2
Lord Delaware	USA	JW-57, RA-58, JW-66, RA-67
Louis D. Brandeis	USA	JW-57, RA-58
Lowther Castle (S)	British	PQ-16, QP-9, PQ-11
Lucerna	British	JW-55A, RA-55B, JW-57, RA-58, JW-60, RA-61, JW-64, RA-65
Luculus	British	JW-59, RA-59A, JW-62, RA-62
Macbeth (S)	Panamanian	PQ-18
Makawao	Honduran	QP-9, PQ-11
Manna	Honduran	PQ-13, QP-10
Marathon	Norwegian	JW-51A, JW-53, RA-54B, JW-61, RA-62
Marie M. Meloney	USA	JW-57, RA-58, JW-64, RA-65
Marina Raskova	USSR	—
Marylyn	British	QP-9, PQ-11
Mary Luckenback (S)	USA	PQ-18
Massmar (S)	USA	PQ-16, QP-13
Mauna Kea	USA	PQ-16, QP-13
McKeesport	USA	—
Meanticut	USA	PQ-18, QP-15, RA-51
Michigan	Panamanian	PQ-16, QP-13
Mijdrecht	Dutch	JW-54A, RA-55B, JW-57, RA-58
Minotaur	USA	PQ-16, QP-14
Mirlo	—	PQ-6, QP-4
Mironich	USSR	Independent
Mobile City	USA	JW-53, RA-54
Montcalm (Icebreaker)	Canadian	PQ-15
Mora	—	PQ-15
Morris Hillquit	USA	JW-58, RA-59
Mormacmar	USA	PQ-13, QP-11
Mormacrey	USA	PQ-15, QP-13
Mormacrio	USA	PQ-14 (R), PQ-15, QP-12
Mormacsul (S)	USA	PQ-16
Mount Evans	Panamanian	QP-13, PQ-6
Msta	USSR	Independent
Mussoviet	USSR	RA-53, PQ-4, QP-1, Independent
Nacella	British	JW-59, RA-60, JW-63, RA-64
Nathaniel Alexander	USA	JW-57, RA-58, RA-61
Nathanael Greene	USA	PQ-18, QP-15

ARCTIC INTERLUDE

Name	Country	Convoys
Nathan Towson	USA	JW-57, RA-58, JW-64, RA-65
Navarino (S)	British	PQ-12, QP-10, PQ-17
Nelson W. Aldrich	USA	JW-62, RA-63, JW-66, RA-67
Nemaha	USA	PQ-16, QP-13
Neritina	British	JW-60, RA-61, JW-64, RA-65
New Westminster City (B)	British	Dervish, PQ-13, QP-1
Nicholas Biddle	USA	JW-58, RA-59, JW-61, RA-62, JW-65, RA-66
Nicholas Gilman	USA	JW-52, RA-53
Nordfjell (S)	Norwegian	JW-63, BK-3
Noreg	Norwegian	JW-56A, JW-58, RA-59, JW-60, RA-60, JW-61, RA-61, PQ-9/10
Norlys	Panamanian	JW-54A, RA-54B, JW-55B, RA-56
North King	USA	QP-9, PQ-11, PQ-1, QP-2
Oakley Wood	USA	JW-59, RA-60
Ob	USSR	Independent
Ocean Faith	British	PQ-18, QP-15, JW-52, RA-53
Ocean Freedom	British	PQ-17, QP-14, JW-53
Ocean Gypsy	British	JW-55B, RA-56
Ocean Messenger	British	JW-55B, RA-56
Ocean Pride	British	JW-55B, RA-56
Ocean Strength	British	JW-54B, RA-55A, JW-57, RA-58
Ocean Valour	British	JW-55B, RA-56
Ocean Vanity	British	JW-54A, RA-55A, JW-59
Ocean Verity	British	JW-54A, RA-55A
Ocean Viceroy	British	JW-55B, RA-56
Ocean Voice (S)	British	PQ-13, PQ-16, QP-14
Okhta	USSR	RA-51, Independent
Oligarch	British	JW-52, RA-51, RA-53
Oliver Ellsworth (S)	USA	PQ-18
Olopana (S)	USA	PQ-17
Oregonian (S)	USA	PQ-18
Oremar	USA	JW-51A, RA-53
Orient City	British	PQ-2, QP-3
Osmussar	USSR	Independent
Owen Wister	USA	JW-62, RA-63, JW-66, RA-67
Pan Atlantic	USA	PQ-17
Pankraft	Dutch	PQ-17
Park Benjamin	USA	JW-61, RA-62, JW-66, RA-67
Park Holland	USA	JW-54A, RA-55A
Patrick Henry	USA	PQ-18, QP-15
Paul Hamilton Hayne	USA	JW-56B, RA-57
Paul H. Harwood	USA	JW-63, RA-64
Paul Luckenback	USA	PQ-15, QP-12
Paulus Potter (S)	Dutch	PQ-17
Penelope Barker (S)	USA	JW-56A
Peter Kerr (S)	USA	PQ-17
Petrovsky	USSR	PQ-5, PQ-18, QP-15, QP-13, JW-53
Philip F. Thomas	USA	JW-57, RA-58, JW-63, RA-64, JW-67
Philip Livingston	USA	RA-56 (R), JW-55A, RA-57
Pierre S. Dupont	USA	JW-58, RA-59
Pieter de Hoogh	Dutch	PQ-14 (R), PQ-16, QP-13, JW-53, RA-54B
Pontfield	British	JW-51B, RA-54

Name	Country	Convoys
Pravda	USSR	QP-9
Puerto Rican (S)	USA	JW-51B, RA-53
Queen City	British	PQ-2, QP-3
Raceland (S)	Panamanian	PQ-13
Ralph Waldo Emerson	USA	JW-51B, RA-53
Rathlin (Rescue)	British	PQ-17, QP-14, JW-54B, RA-58, JW-58, RA-60, JW-59, RA-62, JW-62, JW-67, RA-67
Raymond B. Stevens	USA	JW-60, RA-61
Reigh Count	Panamanian	PQ-7B, QP-6
Renald Fernald	USA	JW-62, RA-63, JW-66, RA-67
Revolyusioner	USSR	QP-8, PQ-16, RA-51, QP-3, PQ-10
Richard Bassett	USA	JW-51A, RA-53
Richard Bland (S)	USA	PQ-17, JW-51A, RA-53
Richard H. Alvey	USA	Independent, RA-51, JW-56A, RA-57
Richard Henry Lee	USA	PQ-16, QP-13
Richard M. Johnson	USA	JW-57, RA-58, JW-60, A-61
River Afton (S)	British	PQ-13, QP-10, PQ-17, PQ-1, QP-2
R. Ney McNeely	USA	JW-63, RA-64
Roald Amundsen	Norwegian	JW-67
Robert Eden	USA	JW-57, RA-59
Robert J. Collier	USA	JW-57, RA-58, JW-67
Robert Lowry	USA	JW-56B, RA-57, JW-62, RA-63
Robert Weaver	USA	RA-59
Rodina (S)	USSR	QP-13, PQ-4, QP-1
Sahale	USA	PQ-18, QP-15
Saint Clears	British	PQ-5, QP-13
Sakko	USSR	Independent
Samannan	British	JW-59, RA-60
Samaritan	British	JW-60, RA-61, JW-63, RA-64, JW-66, RA-67
Samcalia	British	JW-59, RA-60
Samconstant	British	JW-59, RA-60
Samgara	British	JW-59, RA-60
Samidway	British	JW-59, RA-60
Samlyth	British	JW-59, RA-60
Samloyal	British	JW-59, RA-60
Samsuva (S)	British	JW-59, RA-60
Samtredy	British	JW-59, RA-60
Samual Chase	USA	PQ-17, QP-14
Samual McIntyre	USA	JW-56B, RA-57, JW-67
San Adolfo	British	JW-54B, RA-55A, JW-56A, RA-57
San Amada	British	
San Amrbosio	British	QP-5, JW-55A, RA-55B, JW-57, RA-57
San Cipriano	British	JW-51A, RA-53
San Cirilo	British	JW-56A, RA-57
San Venancio	British	JW-61, RA-62, JW-65, RA-66
Schoharie	USSR	PQ-18, QP-15
Schors	USSR	PQ-16
Scottish American	British	QP-12
Scythia	British	JW-61A, RA-61A
Seattle Spirit	USA	PQ-14 (R), PQ-15, QP-12
Sevzaples	USSR	PQ-12, QP-10, QP-1
Sheksna	USSR	Independent
Shelon	USSR	QP-9

Name	Country	Convoys
Shillka	USSR	Independent
Silas Weir Mitchell	USA	JW-59, RA-60, JW-63, RA-64
Silver Sword (S)	USA	PQ-17, QP-14
Skiensfjord	Norwegian	JW-55B, JW-64, RA-65
Soroka	USSR	Independent
South American		PQ-13
Southgate	British	PQ-7, QP-7, PQ-15, QP-12
Stage Door Canteen	USA	JW-55A, RA-56, JW-61, JW-65, RA-66
Stalingrad (S)	USSR	QP-7, PQ-18
Stanton H. King	USA	JW-62, RA-63
Star Bolshevik	USSR	QP-7, PQ-16, QP-13, QP-1, PQ-8
Steelworker	USA	PQ-16
Stepan Khaltourin	USSR	QP-9, QP-2, PQ-11
Stephen Leacock	USA	JW-62, RA-63
Stevenson Taylor	USA	JW-57, RA-58, JW-62, RA-63, JW-66, RA-67
St. Olaf	USA	PQ-18, QP-15
Stone Street	USA	PQ-12, QP-10 (R), QP-11
Stori	USSR	PQ-16
Sukhona (S)	USSR	QP-4, PQ-14 (R), PQ-18, Dervish return, QP-1, PQ-4
Syrian Prince	British	JW-61, RA-61
Syros (S)	USA	PQ-16
Tbilisi	USSR	QP-8, QP-15, JW-53, PQ-9/10
Temple Arch	British	PQ-12, QP-10, PQ-18, PQ-2, QP-15, JW-52, RA-53, QP-3
Texas	USA	PQ-15, QP-12
Thistledale	British	JW-55A, RA-56
Thitisi	USSR	PQ-18
Thomas Donaldson (S)	USA	JW-59, RA-60, JW-65
Thomas Hartley	USA	JW-53, RA-54, JW-57, RA-58
Thomas H. Sumner	USA	JW-59, RA-60
Thomas Kearns	USA	JW-54B, RA-55A (R), RA-55B
Thomas Scott (S)	USA	JW-55A, RA-56, JW-63, RA-64
Thomas Sims Lee	USA	JW-54A, RA-55A, JW-58, RA-59, JW-67
Thomas U. Walter	USA	JW-55B, RA-56, RA-61
Thorstein Veblen	USA	JW-56A, RA-57
Tobruk	Polish	PQ-13, QP-14, JW-53, RA-54
Topa Topa	USA	PQ-15, QP-12
Townsend Harris	USA	JW-58, RA-59, JW-64, RA-65
Trehata	British	Dervish, QP-4, PQ-14, QP-11, QP-1, PQ-5
Trekeive	British	QP-4, PQ-3
Trevorian	British	QP-9, PQ-10
Troubadour (B)	Panamanian	PQ-17, QP-14
Tshora	USSR	QP-2
Tsidlkovsky (S)	USSR	QP-11
Ufa	USSR	Independent
Uranakrayi	USSR	QP-10 (R)
Uritsky	USSR	Independent
U.S.O.	USA	JW-62, RA-63
Ussuri	USSR	RA-52
Vantzetti	USSR	Independent
Vermont	USA	JW-51B, RA-53

Name	Country	Convoys
Vetluga	USSR	Independent
Vill de Anvers	Belgian	PQ-1, QP-2
Virginia Dare	USA	PQ-18, QP-15
Vishera (S)	USSR	Independent
Vjatka	USSR	JW-63
Volga	USSR	RA-51
Wacosta (S)	USA	PQ-18
Wanstead	British	QP-4, PQ-3
Warren Delano	USA	JW-59, RA-60, RA-64
Washington (S)	USA	PQ-17
Wazaristan (S)	British	PQ-7A
West Cheswald	USA	PQ-14, QP-11
West Gotomska	USA	PQ-14 (R), JW-51A, RA-53
West Nilus	USA	PQ-16, QP-14
West Nohno	USA	QP-8, PQ-9/10
White Clover	Panamanian	PQ-18, QP-15
Willard Hall	USA	JW-56B, RA-57, JW-64, RA-66
William Clark (S)	USA	Independent
William D. Byron	USA	JW-58, RA-59, JW-66, RA-67
William Hooper (S)	USA	PQ-17
William H. Webb	USA	JW-57, RA-58
William H. Wilmer	USA	JW-62, RA-63
William L. Marcey	USA	JW-54B, RA-55A
William Matson	USA	JW-58, RA-59
William McKinley	USA	JW-58, RA-59
William Moultrie	USA	PQ-18, QP-15, JW-58, RA-59
William Pepper	USA	JW-58, RA-59, JW-61, RA-62, JW-65, RA-66
William R. Grace	USA	JW-58, RA-59A, JW-62, RA-63, JW-65, RA-66
Will Rogers	USA	JW-55B, RA-56
Willowdale	British	PQ-9 (R)
William S. Thayer (S)	USA	JW-58, RA-59
William Tyler Page	USA	JW-56A, RA-57, JW-62, RA-63, JW-66, RA-67
William Wheelwright	USA	JW-61, JW-65, RA-66
William Windom	USA	JW-54A, RA-55A
Windrush	USA	JW-51A, RA-52
Winifred L. Smith	USA	JW-56B, RA-57, JW-61, JW-65, RA-66
Winona	USA	PQ-14 (R)
Winston Salem	USA	PQ-17, QP-14
Woodbridge N. Ferris	USA	JW-56A, RA-57, JW-62, RA-63, JW-66, RA-67
Yaka	USSR	PQ-14
Yelna	USSR	
Yorkmar	USA	JW-51B, RA-53
Zaafaran (Rescue) (S)	British	PQ-17
Zamalek (Rescue)	British	QP-14, JW-60, RA-60
Zbokhta	USSR	Independent
Zebulon B. Vance	USA	PQ-15, QP-12

ARCTIC INTERLUDE 311

Appendix 9

Russian Convoy Details

EIGHT hundred eleven vessels were escorted to Russia by the Northern route. Seven hundred twenty of these arrived in Russia. Seven hundred fifteen were escorted back from Russia. Six hundred eighty of these arrived in UK/Iceland ports. Eighty-seven vessels were lost by enemy action. Seven lost by other causes. Thirty-two vessels returned to departure ports for various reasons.

Allied warship losses were: two cruisers, seven destroyers, three sloops, one frigate, three corvettes and four minesweepers. German losses were: one battleship, two destroyers, two auxiliaries and at least thirty U-boats.

THE CONVOYS

Dervish: Made up of seven merchant ships. Sailed Hvalfjord 21 August 1941. Arrived Archangel 31 August 1941. No losses. Captain J. C. K. Dowding, DSO, RD, RNR was Commodore.

PQ-1: Ten merchant ships. No losses. Captain D. Ridley was Commodore. Sailed Havlfjord 29 September 1941. Arrived Archangel 11 October 1941.

PQ-2: Six merchant ships. No losses. Commodore not known. Sailed from Scapa Flow 17 October 1941. Arrived Archangel 31 October 1941.

PQ-3: Eight merchant ships. One returned with ice damage. No losses. Commodore unknown. Sailed Hvalfjord 9 November 1941. Arrived Archangel 22 November 1941.

PQ-4: Eight merchant ships. No losses. Commodore unknown. Sailed Hvalfjord 17 November 1941. Arrived Archangel 28 November 1941.

PQ-5: Seven merchant ships. No losses. Commodore unknown. Sailed Hvalfjord 27 November 1941. Arrived Archangel 12 December 1941.

PQ-6: Seven merchant ships. No losses. Commodore unknown. Sailed Hvalfjord 8 December 1941. Arrived Murmansk 20 December 1941, Molotovsk 23 December 1941. Five of the merchant ships were ice-bound all winter.

PQ-7A: Two ships only. One ship lost. Commodore unknown. Sailed Hvalfjord 26 December 1941. Arrived Murmansk 21 January 1942. Two minesweepers of the escort failed to make contact with the convoy.

PQ-7B: Nine ships. No losses. Commodore unknown. Sailed Hvalfjord 31 December 1941. Arrived Murmansk 11 January 1942.

PQ-8: Eight ships. No losses. Commodore was Captain R. W. Brundle, Master of SS *Harmatris*. This vessel was damaged by the enemy but reached Russia safely. Sailed Hvalfjord 8 January 1942. Arrived Murmansk 17 January 1942. HMS *Matabele*, one of the escorts, was sunk. There were only two survivors.

PQ-9/-10: PQ-9 (seven ships) and PQ-10 (three ships) joined together at Reykjavik to make one convoy. Commodore unknown. Sailed Hvalfjord 1 February 1942. Arrived Murmansk 10 February 1942. No Losses. The sailing date was postponed initially because of the *Tirpitz* scare.

PQ-11: Thirteen ships. No Losses. Commodore unknown. Sailed Loch Ewe 6 February 1942. Left Kirkwall 14 February 1942. Arrived Murmansk 23 February 1942.

PQ-12: Sixteen ships. No Losses. Commodore was Captain H. T. Hudson, RD, RNR. This convoy had capital ship support. HMS *Shera* capsized and sank on passage. Sailed Reykjavik 1 March 1942. Arrived Murmansk 12 March 1942. PQ-12 had been located at noon 5 March 1942 and *Tirpitz* was sailed but did not find this convoy, nor did the British and German heavy units find each other. Together with QP-8 this was the first convoy to/from Russia to be covered by the Home Fleet.

PQ-13: Nineteen ships. Five ships sunk en route. Commodore was Captain D. A. Casey, CBE, DSO, RD, RNR. Sailed Reykjavik 20 March 1942. Arrived Murmansk 31 March to 1 April 1942. The convoy was scattered by bad weather. HMS *Trinidad* was torpedoed. The German destroyer *Z-26* was sunk in surface action. The convoy also contained three ex-Norwegian whalers that had been converted as magnetic minesweepers and were being delivered to Russia. The names were *Sull, Sumba,* and *Silja.*

PQ-14: Twenty-four ships. Sixteen returned to Iceland with weather damage. One ship sunk. Commodore was Captain E. Rees, DSC, RD, RNR. Sailed Reykjavik 8 April 1942. Arrived Murmansk 19 April 1942.

PQ-15: Twenty-five ships, including two icebreakers. Three ships lost. Commodore was Captain H. J. Anchor, OBE, RD, RNR. Yeoman of signals A. R. Marriott, DSM. HMT *Cape Palliser* rescued these two men (from *Botavon*). HMS *Punjabi* sunk in collision. Sailed Reykjavik 26 April 1942. Arrived Murmansk 5 May 1942. *P-551* Polish sub, sunk by our own forces in error.

PQ-16: Thirty-five ships. One returned with damage. Seven ships sunk. Commodore was Captain N. H. Gale, DSO, RD, RNR. Sailed Reykjavik 21 May 1942. Arrived Murmansk 30 May 1942 and Archangel 1 June 1942. SS *Carlton* was damaged by the enemy and towed back to Iceland by HMT *Northern Spray*. The anti-aircraft ship *Alynbank* accompanied this convoy.

Note: Two Russian ships sailed to Arctic ports from Iceland, sailing independently, in August 1942 and both got through after a long passage. On 20 July four destroyers sailed to Archangel with stores and arrived safely. The names of the merchantmen were, *Belomorcanal* and *Friedrich Engels*. The destroyers were HMS *Marne, Martin, Middleton* and *Blankney*. They refueled from the fleet oiler *Black Ranger* which was escorted by HMS *Wilton*.

PQ-17: Thirty-six ships. Two returned, twenty-three lost, eleven arrived. Figures do not include three rescue ships, one of which was sunk. Commodore was Captain J. C. K. Dowding, DSO, RD, RNR. Sailed Reykjavik 27 June 1942. Four ships arrived Archangel 11 July 1942. Six ships arrived Archangel 25 July 1942 and one ship arrived Molotovsk 28 July 1942. Two anti-aircraft ships were with this convoy, *Pozarica* and *Polmares*.

On 13 August 1942 the USS *Tuscaloosa* and the US destroyers *Rodman* and *Emmons* together with HMS *Onslaught* sailed from the Clyde with RAF ground crews and equipment together with a hospital and supplies for Allied sick and wounded in North Russia. They were met in the Barents Sea by HMS *Marne* and *Martin*. The medical unit was not allowed to land and returned in QP-14. *Tuscaloosa, Rodman, Emmons, Marne, Martin* and *Onslaught* returned to the UK, leaving Russia on 24 August and arriving in the UK on 28 August. They brought home survivors of Convoy PQ-17.

PQ-18: Forty ships. Thirteen lost. Commodore was Rear Admiral E. K. Boddam-Whetham, DSO. Rescue ship *Copeland* was with this convoy. Sailed from Loch Ewe 2 September 1942. Arrived Archangel 17 September 1942. Detected north of Iceland 8 September.

Between 13 and 28 October HM cruiser *Argonaut* and the destroyers HMS *Intrepid* and *Obdurate* took the medical unit that had not been allowed to land in Russia previously, back again to Archangel. The ships brought home the RAF ground crews and equipment together with some aircrews from the two Hampden squadrons that had been operating from North Russia. The aircraft had been handed over to the Russians.

Convoys to and from Russia were suspended for a time after these heavy losses. Operation 'FB' was launched. Thirteen merchant ships sailed independently for Russia, spaced at 200 mile intervals. Seven were British, five American, one Russian. Five were sunk or lost. Five reached Russia safely and three returned to Iceland. This was between 29 October and 2 November 1942.

Twenty-eight ships sailed independently in the opposite direction between 29 October 1942 and 24 January 1943 from various Russian ports. (The Russians claim forty ships made this passage and that at least ten were sunk, but this is unconfirmed in Allied sources). Only one ship was lost according to the Allies. Twenty-seven arrived safely in Akureyri, Iceland.

At this point convoys were renumbered beginning at JW-51A for the outward journey.

The following ships left for North Russia in convoy during January

1943; they all spent eight months in Russia before returning in convoy during September 1943. *Thomas Hartley, Francis Scott Key, Israel Putnam, John Lafarge, John Ireland.*

On 5 October 1943, the following ships sailed from the U.S. to North Russia via the Kara Sea; all were sunk en route. *Archangelsk*, 2480 grt; *Dikson*, 2900 grt; *Sergei Kirov*, 4146 grt; *Tbilisi*, 7169 grt.

JW-51A: Sixteen ships. No losses. Commodore was Rear Admiral C. E. Turle, DSO. Five ships of this convoy sunk by aircraft or mines after reaching Kola, says one report. Sailed Loch Ewe 15 December 1942. Arrived Kola 25 December 1942, Molotovsk 27 December 1942.
JW-51B: Fourteen ships. No Losses. Commodore was Captain R. A. Melhuish, RIN, Rtd. SS *Dover Hill* developed engine trouble and did not sail with this convoy. The convoy was attacked by German surface forces. HMS *Achates* and *Bramble* were sunk. The German destroyer *Friederich Eckholdt* was sunk. Sailed Loch Ewe 20 December 1942. Arrived Kola 3 January 1943; Archangel detachment arrived there on the 6th. Escort included six destroyers and five smaller escorts, under Capt. R. St. V. Sherbrooke in *Onslow*. Detected by U-boat on the 30th, south of Bear Island. *Hipper, Lützow* and six destroyers sailed to intercept. *Sheffield* and *Jamaica* left Kola to act as cover in Barents Sea.

JW-52: Fourteen ships. One returned, unable to maintain speed. Commodore was Vice Admiral Sir Malcolm Goldsmith, KBE, DSO. No losses. Sailed Loch Ewe 17 January 1943. Arrived Kola 27 January 1943. *Kent, Glasgow* and *Bermuda* were the cruiser force. *Anson* was deep cover. No real problems, only small air attacks.

JW-53: Twenty-eight ships. Six returned with weather damage. No losses. Commodore was Rear Admiral E. W. Leir, DSO. Sailed Loch Ewe 15 February 1943. Arrived Kola 27 February 1943, White Sea 2 March 1943. Two other merchant ships were not ready to sail on time.

The Russians sailed two merchantmen independently from Iceland to Archangel. Both arrived safely on 20 February 1943.

Convoys to North Russia were again suspended from mid-March until November 1943 for operational reasons.

Two operations took place during October 1943. The first was the passage of the destroyers HMS *Onslaught* and HMCS *Huron* and *Iroquois*, covered by the cruiser *London* and destroyer *Impulsive*. They took supplies for the escorts that had remained in Russia throughout the summer. Later in the month more escorts were sent to Russia to bring back merchant ships that had been in Russia since the spring. The destroyers HMS *Mahratta, Matchless, Milne, Musketeer, Saumarez, Savage, Scourge, Scorpion* and *Westcott* together with the corvette *Eglantine* and the fleet minesweepers *Harrier* and *Seagull* were dispatched. They were covered by the cruisers HMS *London* and USS *Augusta* and the destroyer HMS *Middleton*. Some small naval vessels for delivery to the USSR accompanied this force.

JW-54A: Eighteen ships. No losses. Commodore was Captain B. B. Grant, RD, RNR. Sailed Loch Ewe 15 November 1943. Arrived Kola 24 November 1943, White Sea 28 November 1943.

JW-54B: Fourteen ships. No losses. Commodore was Captain E. C. Denison, MVO, RN, Rtd. Sailed Loch Ewe 22 November 1943. Arrived Kola 2 December 1943, White Sea 4 December 1943.

JW-55A: Nineteen ships. No losses. Commodore was Captain W. J. Mills, RD, RNR. Sailed Loch Ewe 12 December 1943. Arrived Kola 20 December 1943, White Sea 22 December 1943.

JW-55B: Nineteen ships. No losses. Commodore was Rear Admiral M. W. S. Boucher, DSO. *Scharhorst* sunk. Sailed Loch Ewe 20 December 1943. Arrived Kola 29 December 1943, White Sea 31 December 1943.

JW-56A: Twenty ships. Five returned with weather damage. Commodore was Captain I. W. Whitehorn, RN, Rtd. HMS *Hardy* sunk. Sailed Loch Ewe 12 January 1944. Arrived Kola 28 January 1944. Three ships sunk.

JW-56B: Sixteen ships. No losses. HMS *Hardy* sunk ? (see previous convoy). Commodore was Captain M. J. D. Mayall, RD, RNR. Sailed Loch Ewe 22 January 1944. Arrived Kola 1 February 1944.

JW-57: Forty-two ships. No losses. Commodore was Captain R. D. Binks, OBE, RD, RNR. HMS *Mahrata* sunk. Sailed Loch Ewe 20 February 1944. Arrived Kola 28 February 1944.

JW-53: Forty-nine ships. One returned with ice damage. Commodore was Captain J. O. Dunn, RD, RNR. No losses. Sailed Loch Ewe 27 March 1944. Arrived Kola 5 April 1944. Twenty destroyers, five sloops, four corvettes.

A large escort force was sailed to North Russia during April 1944 in an effort to bring back the U.S. crew of the cruiser USS *Milwaukee*, handed over to the USSR. It was supposed to bring back hundreds of Russian crew to man warships that were in the UK to be transferred to the USSR. Unfortunately the transport ship had to return to harbor but the escort force went through. They were, *Diadem*, *Activity*, *Fencer*, *Beagle*, *Boadicea*, *Inconstant*, *Keppel*, *Marne*, *Matchless*, *Meteor*, *Milne*, *Musketeer*, *Ulysees*, *Verulam*, *Virago*, *Walker*, *Wescott*, *Whitehall*, and *Wrestler*. The Canadian *Cape Breton*, *Grou*, *Outremont* and *Waskesiu* went also. They arrived at Kola on 23 April.

JW-59: Thirty-three ships. No losses. HMS *Kite* sunk. Commodore was Captain G. H. Creswell, CB, DSO, DSC, RN, Rtd. Sailed Loch Ewe 15 August 1944. Arrived Kola 25 August 1944, White Sea 27 August 1944.

JW-60: Thirty ships. No losses. Commodore was Captain J. Smith, RD, RNR. Sailed Loch Ewe 15 September 1944. Arrived Kola 23 September 1944, White Sea 25 September 1944.

JW-61: Twenty-nine ships. No losses. Commodore was Rear Admiral M. W. S. Boucher, DSO. Sailed Loch Ewe 20 October 1944. Arrived Kola 28 October 1944, White Sea 30 October 1944.

JW-61A: Two fast transports, taking 11,000 Russians home. Heavy escort. Sailed from Liverpool on 31 October 1944 and arrived in Murmansk on 6 November 1944. The two transports were *Empress of Australia* and *Scythia*.

JW-62: Thirty ships. No losses. Commodore was Captain E. Ullring, Royal Norwegian Navy. Sailed Loch Ewe 29 November 1944. Arrived Kola 7 December 1944, White Sea 9 December 1944.

JW-63: Thirty-five ships. No losses. Commodore was Rear Admiral M. W. S. Boucher, DSO. Sailed Loch Ewe 30 December 1944. Arrived Kola 8 January 1945, White Sea 9 January 1945.

JW-64: Twenty-six ships. No losses. Commodore was Captain E. Ullring, Royal Norwegian Navy. Sailed Clyde 3 February 1945. Arrived Kola 13 February 1945, White Sea 15 February 1945.

JW-65: Twenty-four ships. Commodore was Captain W. C. Meek, RD, RNR. HMS *Lapwing* sunk. Sailed Clyde 11 March 1945. Arrived Kola 21 March 1945. Two ships lost.

During April 1945 British warships, with the approval of the Russians, laid an extensive anti–U-boat minefield off Kola. They sailed from the UK, refueled in north Russia, laid the mines and then returned to the UK.

JW-66: Twenty-two ships. No losses. Commodore was Captain Sir Roy K. Gill, KBE, RD, RNR. Sailed Clyde 16 April 1945. Arrived Kola 25 April 1945, White Sea 28 April 1945.

JW-67: Twenty-three ships. No losses. Commodore was Captain G. E. Sutcliffe, RN, Rtd. Sailed Clyde 12 May 1945. Arrived Kola 20 May 1945, White Sea 22 May 1945.

RUSSIAN CONVOYS (NORTH RUSSIA TO UK)

QP-1: Fourteen ships. No losses. Commodore was Captain J. C. K. Dowding, DSO, RD, RNR. Sailed Archangel 28 September 1941. Arrived Scapa Flow 9 October 1941.

QP-2: Twelve ships. No losses. Commodore unknown. Sailed Archangel 2 November 1941. Arrived Kirkwall 17 November 1941.

QP-3: Ten ships. Two returned due to weather. No losses. Commodore unknown. Sailed Archangel 27 November 1941. Arrived Seydisfjord, Iceland, 7 December 1941.

QP-4: Thirteen ships. Two returned (to Murmansk). No losses. Commodore unknown. Sailed Archangel 20 December 1941. Arrived Seydisfjord, Iceland, 16 January 1942.

QP-5: Four ships. No losses. Commodore unknown. Sailed Murmansk 13 January 1942. Arrived Reykjavik 24 January 1942.

QP-6: Six ships. No losses. Commodore was Captain Davitt. Sailed Murmansk 24 January 1942. Arrived Clyde 2 February 1942.

QP-7: Eight Ships. No losses. Commodore unknown. Sailed Murmansk 12 February 1942. Arrived Seydisfjord, Iceland, 22 February 1942.

QP-8: Fifteen ships. Commodore unknown. Sailed Murmansk 1 March 1942. Arrived Reykjavik 11 March 1942. One ship lost.

QP-9: Nineteen ships. No losses. Commodore was Captain H. T. Hudson, RD, RNR. Sailed Murmansk 21 March 1942. Arrived Reykjavik 3 April 1942. No serious problems on passage.

QP-10: Sixteen ships. One returned. Commodore was Captain D. A. Casey, CBE, DSO, DSC, RD, RNR. Sailed Murmansk 10 April 1942. Arrived Reykjavik 21 April 1942. Four ships lost.

QP-11: Thirteen ships. Commodore was Captain W. H. Lawrence. Sailed Murmansk 28 April 1942. Arrived Reykjavik 7 May 1942. This convoy was attacked by German destroyers and one merchant ship was sunk. HMS *Edinburgh* sunk.

QP-12: Fifteen ships. One returned to Murmansk. No losses. Commodore unknown. Sailed Murmansk 21 May 1942. Arrived Reykjavik 29 May 1942. Relatively quiet passage. It was a Russian ship that returned to Murmansk.

QP-13: Thirty-five ships (twelve from Archangel, twenty-three from Murmansk). Commodore was Captain N. H. Gale, DSO, RD, RNR. Sailed Archangel 26 June 1942, Murmansk 27 June 1942. Arrived Reykjavik (fourteen ships) 7 July 1942, Loch Ewe (sixteen ships) 7 July 1942. HMS *Niger* sunk. This convoy ran into a British minefield off North Cape, Iceland. Uneventful passage until North Cape minefield. One escort and five merchantmen lost.

QP-14: Fifteen ships. Commodore was Captain J. C. K. Dowding, DSO, RD, RNR. Sailed Archangel 13 September 1942. Arrived Loch Ewe 26 September 1942. HMS *Somali* and *Leda* sunk. Four ships lost.

QP-15: Twenty-eight ships. Commodore was Captain W. C. Meek, RD, RNR. Sailed Archangel 17 November 1942. Arrived Loch Ewe 30 November to 3 December 1942. The convoy had been scattered by heavy gales. Two ships lost. Anti-aircraft ship *Ulster Queen*, five minesweepers and four corvettes plus one oiler were with this convoy. There were also two Russian destroyers, *Baku* and *Sokrushitelney*; the former lost her bridge and the latter broke in half and sank due to weather damage.

Russian Convoys (North Russia to UK)

RA-51: Fourteen ships. No losses. Commodore was Rear Admiral C. E. Turle, DSO. Sailed Kola 30 December 1942. Arrived Loch Ewe 11 January 1943.

During January 1943 HMS *Obdurate* and *Obedient* brought home to the UK the seriously wounded men from the Barents Sea action with *Scharnhorst*. During this month, too, the Russians sailed four merchant ships independently to Iceland. Two were lost, two arrived safely.

RA-52: Eleven ships. Commodore was Captain R. A. Melhuish, RIN, Rtd. Sailed Kola 29 January 1943. Arrived Loch Ewe 8 February 1943. One ship lost.

RA-53: Thirty ships. Commodore was Vice Admiral Sir M. L. Goldsmith, KBE, DSO. Sailed Kola 1 March 1943. Arrived Loch Ewe 14 March 1943. Three ships lost, one foundered and another towed to safety.
RA-54A: Thirteen ships. No losses. Commodore was Captain W. L. P. Cox, RNR. Sailed Archangel 1 November 1943. Arrived Loch Ewe 14 November 1943.

RA-54B: Nine ships. No losses. Commodore unknown. Sailed Archangel 26 November 1943. Arrived Loch Ewe 9 December 1943.

RA-55A: Twenty-two ships. One returned to Kola. No losses. Commodore was Captain B. B. Grant, RD, RNR. Sailed Kola 23 December 1943. Arrived Loch Ewe 1 January 1944. *Scharnhorst* sunk 26 December 1943.

RA-55B: Eight Ships. No losses. Commodore was Captain E. C. Denison, MVO, RN, Rtd. Sailed Kola 31 December 1943. Arrived Loch Ewe 8 January 1944.

RA-56: Thirty-seven ships. No losses. Commodore was Rear Admiral M. W. S. Boucher, DSO. Sailed Kola 3 February 1944. Arrived Loch Ewe 11 February 1944.

RA-57: Thirty-one ships. Commodore was Captain M. J. D. Mayall, RD, RNR. Sailed Kola 2 March 1944. Arrived Loch Ewe 10 March 1944. One ship lost.

RA-58: Thirty-six ships. No losses. Commodore was Captain R. D. Binks, OBE, RD, RNR. Sailed Kola 7 April 1944. Arrived Loch Ewe 14 April 1944.

RA-59: Forty-five ships. Commodore was Captain J. O. Dunn, RD, RNR. Sailed Kola 28 April 1944. Arrived Loch Ewe 6 May 1944. No losses.

RA-60: Thirty ships. Commodore was Captain G. H. Greswell, CB, DSO, DSC, RN, Rtd. Sailed Kola 28 September 1944. Arrived Loch Ewe 5 October 1944. One ship lost.

RA-61: Thirty-three ships. No losses. Commodore was Rear Admiral M. W. S. Boucher, DSO. Sailed White Sea 30 October 1944, Kola 2 November 1944. Arrived Loch Ewe 9 November 1944, Clyde 10 November 1944.

RA-61A: Return of the two fast transports to UK. Same escort as outward.

RA-62: Twenty-eight ships. No losses. Commodore was Captain E. Ullring, Royal Norwegian Navy. Sailed Kola 10 December 1944. Arrived Loch Ewe 19 December 1944, Clyde 20 December 1944.

RA-63: Thirty ships. No losses. Commodore was Rear Admiral M. W. S. Boucher, DSO. Sailed Kola 11 January 1945. Arrived Loch Ewe 21 January 1945, Clyde 23 January 1945.

RA-64: One report says thirty-six ships, another says thirty-four ships. One returned to Kola. Commodore Captain E. Ullring, Royal Norwegian Navy. Sailed Kola 17 February 1945. Arrived Loch Ewe 28 February 1945, Clyde 1 March 1945. HMS *Bluebell* Sunk. Four ships lost (two just before joining convoy).

RA-65: Twenty-five ships. No losses. Commodore was Captain W. C. Meek, RD, RNR. Sailed Kola 23 March 1945. Arrived Kirkwall 31 March 1945, Clyde and Belfast 1 April 1945.

RA-66: Twenty-four ships. No losses. Commodore was Captain Sir Roy K. Gill, KBE, RD, RNR. Sailed Kola 29 April 1945. Arrived Clyde 8 May 1945. HMS *Goodall* sunk.

RA-67: Twenty-three ships. No losses. Commodore was Captain G. E. Sutcliffe, RN, Rtd. Sailed Kola 23 May 1945. Arrived Clyde 31 May 1945.

Appendix 10

Allied Escorts/Covering Forces on the North Russian Run, 1941-45

This list is not necessarily complete but there cannot be very many omissions. Any additional information would be welcomed.

Ship	Type	Captain
Acanthus	Corvette	Lt.Cdr. Bruun
Achates	Destroyer	Lt.Cdr. A. H. T. Johns
Active	Destroyer	Lt.Cdr. P. G. Merriman
Activity	Escort carrier	Capt. G. Willoughby
Adventure	Cruiser	Capt. Bowes-Lyon
Airedale	Destroyer	—
Aldersdale	RFA	—
Algonquin	Destroyer	Lt.Cdr. D. W. Piers, RCN
Allington Castle	Frigate	—
Alnwick Castle	Corvette	Lt.Cdr. H. A. Stonehouse, RNR
Alynbank	Anti-aircraft ship	Capt. H. F. Nash
Amazon	Destroyer	Lt.Cdr. Lord Teynham
Ambuscade	Destroyer	—
Angle	Trawler	—
Anguila	Frigate	—
Anson	Battleship	Capt. H. R. G. Kinahan, CBE
Antelope	Destroyer	—
Anthony	Destroyer	—
Apollo	Minelayer	—
Arab	Trawler	Lt. F. M. Proctor, RNVR
Argus	Carrier	—
Ashanti	Destroyer	Cdr. R. G. Onslow Lt.Cdr. J. R. Barnes
Athabaskan	Destroyer	Lt.Cdr. J. H. Stubbs, DSO, RCN
Aurora	Cruiser	—
Avenger	Escort carrier	Cdr. A. P. Colthurst
Ayrshire	Trawler	Lt. L. J. A. Gradwell, RNVR
Badsworth	Destroyer	Lt. G. T. S. Gray
Bahamas	Frigate	—
Baku	Destroyer	—
Bamborough Castle	Corvette	Lt. M. S. Work, DSC, RNR
Bazeley	Frigate	Lt.Cdr. J. W. Cooper, DSC, RNR

Ship	Type	Captain
Beagle	Destroyer	Cdr. R. C. Medley Lt.Cdr. N. R. Murch
Bedouin	Destroyer	Cdr. B. G. Surfield, CBE, AM
Belfast	Cruiser	—
Bellona	Anti-aircraft cruiser	Capt. G. S. Tuck, DSO
Belvoir	Destroyer	—
Bentinck	Frigate	Lt. P. R. G. Worth
Bergamot	Corvette	Lt. R. T. Horan, RNR
Bermuda	Cruiser	—
Berry	Frigate	—
Berwick	Cruiser	—
Beverley	Destroyer	Lt. R. A. Price
Blackfly	Trawler	Lt. A. P. Hughes, RNR
Black Prince	Anti-aircraft cruiser	Capt. D. M. Lees, DSO
Black Ranger	RFA Tkr	Master L. J. Mack
Blankney	Destroyer	Lt.Cdr. P. F. Powlett, DSO, DSC
Bluebell	Corvette	Lt. H. G. Walker, DSC
Blue Ranger	RFA Tkr	Master H. F. Colbourne
Blyskawica	Destroyer	—
Boadicea	Destroyer	Lt.Cdr. F. C. Brodrick
Borage	Corvette	—
Bramble	Minesweeper	Capt. J. H. F. Crombie, DSO Cdr. H. T. Rust, DSO
Bramham	Destroyer	Lt. E. F. Baines
Brissenden	Destroyer	—
Britomart	Minesweeper	Lt.Cdr. S. S. Stamwitz
Broke	Destroyer	Lt.Cdr. A. F. C. Layard
Bryony	Corvette	Lt.Cdr. J. P. Stewart, DCS, RNR
Bulldog	Destroyer	Cdr. M. Richmond, DSO, OBE
Burdock	Corvette	—
Burza	Destroyer	Lt.Cdr. Franciszek Pitulko
Bute	Trawler	—
Byard	Frigate	Lt.Cdr. J. I. Jones, DSO, DSC, RNR
Byron	Frigate	Lt. J. B. Burfield, DSC
Caesar	Destroyer	—
Cambrian	Destroyer	—
Camellia	Corvette	Lt. F. R. J. Marberley, RNVR
Campania	Escort carrier	Capt. K. A. Short
Campanula	Corvette	Lt.Cdr. B. A. Rodgers, RNR
Campbell	Destroyer	Cdr. E. C.Coats, DSO, DSC
Cape Argona	Trawler	Lt. E. R. Pate, RNR
Cape Breton	Frigate	Lt.Cdr. A. M. McLarnon, RCNR
Cape Mariato	Trawler	Lt. H. T. S. Clouston, RNVR
Cape Palliser	Trawler	—
Caprice	Destroyer	—

Ship	Type	Captain
Capps	Destroyer	Lt.Cdr. B. E. S. Trippensee
Cassandra	Destroyer	Lt. G. L. Leslie
Cavalier	Destroyer	Lt.Cdr. D. T. McBarnett, DSC
Celia	Trawler	—
Chamois	Sloop	—
Chance	Sloop	—
Charlock	Corvette	—
Chaser	Escort carrier	Capt. H. V. P. McLintock, DSO
Chiddingfold	Destroyer	—
Chiltern	Trawler	Skpr.Lt. Drake, RNR
Cockatrice	Sloop	
Conn	Frigate	Lt. P. Brett, RNR
Cooke	Frigate	Lt.Cdr. L. C. Hill, OBE, RNR
Corry	Destroyer	Lt.Cdr. E. C. Burchett
Cotton	Frigate	Lt.Cdr. I. W. T. Beloe
Cowdray	Destroyer	Lt.Cdr. C. W. North
Cumberland	Cruiser	Capt. A. H. Maxwell-Hyslop, AM
Cygnet	Sloop	Cdr. A. H. Thorald
Daneman	Trawler	Lt. G. O. T. Henderson, RNVR
Dasher	Escort carrier	Capt. C. N. Lentaigne, DSO
Deane	Frigate	Lt. E. L. Cooke
Denbigh Castle	Corvette	Lt.Cdr. G. Butcher, DSC, RNR
Devonshire	Cruiser	—
Diadem	Anti-aircraft cruiser	Capt. E. G. A. Clifford
Dianella	Corvette	Lt. J. G. Rankin, RNR / Lt. J. F. Tognola, RNR
Dido	Cruiser	—
Dommett	Frigate	Lt.Cdr. S. Gordon, RNVR
Douglas	Destroyer	Lt.Cdr. R. B. S. Tennant
Drury	Frigate	Lt.Cdr. N. J. Parker
Duckworth	Frigate	Cdr. R. G. Mills, DSO, DSC / Lt. D. Jermain, DSC
Duke of York	Battleship	Capt. G. E. Creasy, DSO, MV
Duncton	Trawler	Lt. J. P. Kilbee, RNR
Echo	Destroyer	Lt.Cdr. N. Lanyon
Eclipse	Destroyer	Lt.Cdr. E. Mack
Edinburgh	Cruiser	—
Eglantine	Corvette	Lt.Cdr. Voltersvik
Electra	Destroyer	Cdr. C. W. May
Emmons	Destroyer	Lt.Cdr. T. C. Ragan
Emperor	Escort carrier	—
Escapade	Destroyer	Cdr. E. N. V. Currey, DSC / Lt.Cdr. E. C. Peake
Eskdale	Destroyer	Lt. M. J. W. Pausey
Eskimo	Destroyer	Cdr. E. G. LeGeyt
Essington	Frigate	Lt.Cdr. W. Lambert, RNVR

Ship	Type	Captain
Farndale	Destroyer	Cdr. D. P. Trentham
Farnham Castle	Corvette	—
Faulknor	Destroyer	Capt. A. K. Scott-Moncrieff
Fencer	Escort carrier	Capt. W. W. R. Bentinck
Fitch	Destroyer	Lt.Cdr. H. Crommelin
Fitzroy	Sloop	Lt. J. Duggan
Foresight	Destroyer	Cdr. J. S. Salter
Forester	Destroyer	Lt.Cdr. G. P. Huddert Lt.Cdr. J. H. Burnett, DSC
Forrest	Destroyer	—
Formidable	Carrier	—
Foxtrot	Trawler	Lt. J. Bald, RNVR
Furious	Aircraft carrier	—
Fury	Destroyer	Lt.Cdr. C. H. Campbell, DSC
Garland	Destroyer	—
Glasgow	Cruiser	
Gleaner	Minesweeper	Lt.Cdr. F. J. G. Hewitt, DSC
Goodall	Frigate	Lt.Cdr. J. V. Fulton, RNVR
Gossamer	Minesweeper	Lt. T. C. Crease
Gremyashi	Destroyer	
Grey Ranger	RFATkr	Master H. D. Gausden
Gromki	Destroyer	
Gronzi	Destroyer	
Grou	Frigate	Lt.Cdr. H. G. Dupont, RCNR
Grove	Destroyer	Lt.Cdr. J. W. Rylands
Haida	Destroyer	Cdr. H. G. DeWolfe, RCN
Halcyon	Minesweeper	Lt.Cdr. C. H. Corbett-Singleton
Hamlet	Trawler	
Hardy	Destroyer	Capt. W. G. A. Robson, DSO, DSC
Harrier	Minesweeper	Cdr. A. D. H. Jay, DSO
Hav	Trawler	
Hazard	Minesweeper	Lt.Cdr. J. R. A. Seymour
Heather	Corvette	Lt. W. L. Turner, RNR
Hebe	Minesweeper	Lt. A. J. Gulvin
Hobson	Destroyer	Lt.Cdr. K. Loveland Lt.Cdr. R. N. McFarlane
Honeysuckle	Corvette	Lt. H. H. D. McKillican, DSC, RNR
Hound	Sloop	
Howe	Battleship	
Hugh Walpole	Trawler	Lt. J. Mackenzie, RNR
Huron	Destroyer	Lt.Cdr. H. S. Rayner, DSC, RCN
Hursley	Destroyer	Lt. W. J. P. Church, DSC
Hussar	Minesweeper	Lt. R. C. Biggs, DSO, DSC
Hyderabad	Corvette	Lt. S. C. B. Hickman, RNR
Hydra	Sloop	

Ship	Type	Captain
Icarus	Destroyer	Lt.Cdr. C. D. Maud, DSC Lt. E. M. Walmsley, DSC
Impulsive	Destroyer	Lt.Cdr. E. G. Roper, DSC Lt.Cdr. P. Bekenn
Inconstant	Destroyer	Lt.Cdr. W. S. Clouston Lt.Cdr. J. H. Eadon, DSC
Inglefield	Destroyer	Cdr. A. G. West
Inglis	Frigate	
Intrepid	Destroyer	Cdr. J. H. Lewis Cdr. C. A. DeW Kitcat
Iroquois	Destroyer	Cdr. J. C. Hibbard, DSC, RCN
Jamaica	Cruiser	Capt. J. L. Storey
Jason	Minesweeper	Cdr. H. G. A. Lewis
Javelin	Destroyer	Cdr. G. E. Fardell
Jeloy	Trawler	
Junon	Submarine	
Karmoy	Trawler	
Kent	Cruiser	Capt. C. Graham
Kenya	Cruiser	
Keppel	Destroyer	Cdr. J. E. Broome
King George V	Battleship	
King Sol	Trawler	Lt. P. A. Read
Kite	Sloop	Lt.Cdr. A. N. G. Campbell
Kuibishev	Destroyer	
Lady Madeleine	Trawler	Lt. W. G. Ogden, RNVR
La Malouine	Corvette	Lt. V. D. D. Bidwell, RNR
Lamerton	Destroyer	Lt.Cdr. C. R. Purse, DSC
Lancaster	Destroyer	Cdr. N. H. Whatley
Lancaster Castle	Corvette	
Lapwing	Sloop	Cdr. E. C. Hutton
Lark	Sloop	Cdr. H. Lambton
Lawson	Frigate	
Leamington	Destroyer	Lt. B. M. D. l'Anson
Leda	Minesweeper	Cdr. A. H. Wynne-Edwards
Ledbury	Destroyer	Lt.Cdr. R. P. Hill
Liverpool	Cruiser	
Loch Alvie	Frigate	Lt.Cdr. E. G. Old, RCNR
Loch Dunvegan	Frigate	Cdr. E. Wheeler, RNR
Loch Insch	Frigate	Lt.Cdr. E. W. G. Dempster, RNVR
Loch Shin	Frigate	Lt.Cdr. C. W. Leadbetter, RNR
London	Cruiser	Capt. R. M. Servaes, CBE
Lookout	Destroyer	Lt.Cdr. C. P. F. Brown, DSC
Lord Austin	Trawler	Lt. O. B. Egjar
Lord Middleton	Trawler	Lt. R. H. Jameson, RNR
Loring	Frigate	
Lotus	Corvette	Lt. H. J. Hall, RNR
Louis	Frigate	Cdr. L. B. A. Majendie
Loyalty	Minesweeper	Lt.Cdr. J. E. Maltby, RNR
Macbeth	Trawler	

Ship	Type	Captain
Mackay	Destroyer	Lt. J. E. Majoribanks
Madison	Destroyer	Lt.Cdr. T. E. Boyce Cdr. W. B. Ammon Cdr. D. A. Stuart
Magpie	Sloop	Lt.Cdr. R. S. Abram Lt. J. B. Butchard
Mahratta	Destroyer	Lt.Cdr. E. A. F. Drought, DSC
Malcolm	Destroyer	Cdr. A. B. Russell
Marne	Destroyer	Lt.Cdr. H. N. A. Richardson, DSC
Martin	Destroyer	Cdr. C. R. P. Thompson, DSO
Matabele	Destroyer	Cdr. A. C. Stanford, DSC
Matane	Frigate	Lt. J. J. Coates
Matchless	Destroyer	Lt.Cdr. I. Mowlam, DSO Lt.Cdr. W. S. Shaw
Mayrant	Destroyer	Cdr. E. A. Taylor
Mermaid	Frigate	Lt.Cdr. J. P. Mosse
Meteor	Destroyer	Lt.Cdr. W. J. B. Jewett
Meynell	Destroyer	Lt. B. M. D. l'Anson
Middleton	Destroyer	Lt.Cdr. D. C. Kinloch Lt.Cdr. C. S. Battersby
Milne	Destroyer	Capt. I. M. R. Campbell, DSO Capt. M. Richmond, DSO
Milwaukee	Cruiser	
MMS-90	Minesweeper	Lt. J. Dinwoodie, RNR
MMS-203	Minesweeper	Lt. J. H. Petherbridge, DSC, RNR
MMS-212	Minesweeper	Lt. W. J. Walker, RNR
Montrose	Destroyer	Cdr. W. J. Phipps
Morrow	Frigate	Cdr. E. G. Skinner, DSC, RD, RCNR
Mounsey	Frigate	Lt. F. A. J. Andrew
Musketeer	Destroyer	Cdr. E. N. V. Currey, DSC Cdr. R. L. Fisher, DSO, OBE
Myngs	Destroyer	Capt. P. G. L. Cazalet, DSC
Nabob	Escort Carrier	Capt. H. N. Lay, RCN
Nairana	Escort Carrier	Capt. H. N. Surtees, DSO
Narbrough	Frigate	
Nene	Frigate	Lt.Cdr. E. R. Shaw, RCNR
Niger	Minesweeper	Cdr. A. J. Cubison, DSC
Nigeria	Cruiser	
Norfolk	Cruiser	Capt. E. G. Bellars
Northern Gem	Trawler	Sk.Lt. H. C. Aisthorpe, RNR
Northern Pride	Trawler	Lt. A. L. F. Bell, RNR
Northern Spray	Trawler	Lt. G. T. Gilbert, RNR
Northern Wave	Trawler	Lt. W. G. Pardoe-Mathews, RNR
Notts County	Trawler	Lt. R. W. Hampton

Ship	Type	Captain
Oakley	Destroyer	Lt.Cdr. R. C. V. Thomson Lt.Cdr. T. A. Pack-Beresford
Obdurate	Destroyer	Lt.Cdr. C. E. L. Sclater, DSC Lt.Cdr. R. D. Franks, DSO, OBE
Obedient	Destroyer	Lt.Cdr. D. C. Kinloch
Offa	Destroyer	Lt.Cdr. R. A. Ewing
Oligarch	RFATkr	Master A. V. Barton
Onslought	Destroyer	Cdr. W. H. Selby, DSC Cdr. Hon. H. A. Pleydell-Bouverie
Onslow	Destroyer	Capt. H. T. Armstrong, DSC Capt. J. A. McCoy, DSO Capt. R. St. V. Sherbrooke, DSO Capt. H. W. S. Browning, OBE
Onyx	Destroyer	
Ophelia	Trawler	
Opportune	Destroyer	Cdr. M. L. Power, OBE Cdr. R. E. D. Ryder, VC Cdr. J. Lee-Barber, DSO
Orestes	Minesweeper	
Oribi	Destroyer	Cdr. J. E. H. McBeath, DSO, DSC
Orkan	Destroyer	
Orwell	Destroyer	Lt.Cdr. N. H. G. Austen, DSO Lt.Cdr. J. M. Hodges, DSO Lt.Cdr. J. R. Gower, DSC
Outremont	Frigate	Cdr. H. Freeland, RCNR, DSO
Oxlip	Corvette	Lt. C. W. Leadbetter, RNR
O-15	Submarine	
P-43	Submarine	
P-216	Submarine	
P-312	Submarine	
P-551	Submarine	
P-614	Submarine	Lt. D. J. Beckley
P-615	Submarine	Lt. P. E. Newstead
Pasley	Frigate	Lt. P. R. G. Mitchell
Paynter	Trawler	Lt. R. H. Nossiter, DSC, RANVR
Peacock	Frigate	Lt.Cdr. R. B. Stannard, VC
Piorun	Destroyer	Cdr. E. Plowski
Plunkett	Destroyer	Cdr. E. J. Burke
Polomares	Anti-aircraft Ship	Capt. J. H. Jauncey
Poppy	Corvette	Lt. N. K. Boyd, RNR Lt. D. R. O. Onslow, RNR
Port Colborne	Frigate	Lt.Cdr. C. J. Angus, RCNR
Pozarica	Anti-aircraft Ship	Capt. E. D. W. Lawford

Ship	Type	Captain
Premier	Escort Carrier	Capt. A. J. Gardiner
Punjabi	Destroyer	Cdr. Hon. J. M. Waldegrave, DSO
Pursuer	Escort Carrier	
Pytchley	Destroyer	Lt.Cdr. H. Unwin
Quadrant	Destroyer	Lt.Cdr. W. H. Farrington
Queen	Escort Carrier	Capt. K. J. D'Arcy, DSO
Queensborough	Destroyer	Cdr. E. P. Hinton, DSO, MVO
Raider	Destroyer	Lt.Cdr. K. W. Michell
Rattlesnake	Sloop	
Razumy	Destroyer	
Razyarenni	Destroyer	
Ready	Destroyer	
Redmill	Frigate	Lt. J. R. A. Denne
Renown	Battleship	
Retriever	Trawler	Lt.Cdr. G. E. K. Greeve, RNR
Rhind	Destroyer	Lt.Cdr. H. T. Read
Rhododendron	Corvette	Lt. L. A. Sayers, RNR Lt. G. L. F. Melville, RNR Lt. R. S. Mortimer, RNR
Rodman	Destroyer	Lt.Cdr. W. G. Michelet
Rodney	Battleship	
Roselys	Corvette	Lt. De V. B. Bergeret
Rowan	Destroyer	Lt.Cdr. B. R. Harrison
Rubis	Minelayer	CdeC. H. Rousselot, DSC
Rupert	Frigate	Lt. P. S. Black
Sabre	Destroyer	
Saladin	Destroyer	
Salamander	Minesweeper	Lt. W. R. Muttram
Saumarez	Destroyer	Lt.Cdr. F. W. Walmsley, DSC
Savage	Destroyer	Cdr. M. D. G. Meyrick Lt.Cdr. C. W. Malins, DSO, DSC
Saxifrage	Corvette	Lt. N. L. Knight, RNR
Scorpion	Destroyer	Lt.Cdr. W. S. Clouston Cdr. C. W. McMullen, DSC
Scourge	Destroyer	Lt.Cdr. G. I. M. Balfour
Scylla	Anti-aircraft Cruiser	Capt. I. A. P. MacIntyre, CBE
Seagull	Minesweeper	Lt. C. H. Pollock
Searcher	Escort Carrier	
Seawolf	Submarine	
Serapis	Destroyer	Lt.Cdr. E. L. Jones, DSC
Shakespeare	Submarine	Lt. R. Raikes Lt. M. F. R. Ainslie, DSC
Sharpshooter	Minesweeper	Lt.Cdr. W. L. O'Mara
Sheffield	Cruiser	Capt. A. W. Clark
Shera	Suppt.	
Shika	Trawler	
Shropshire	Cruiser	

Ship	Type	Captain
Shusa	Trawler	
Silja	Minesweeper	
Sioux	Destroyer	Lt.Cdr. E. E. G. Boak, RCN
Skate	Destroyer	
Snowflake	Corvette	Lt. H. G. Chesterman, RNR
Sokrushitelni	Destroyer	
Somali	Destroyer	Capt. J. W. Eaton, DSO, DSC Lt.Cdr. C. D. Maud, DSC
Somaliland	Frigate	
Speedwell	Minesweeper	Lt.Cdr. T. E. Williams, RNR
Speedy	Minesweeper	Lt.Cdr. J. G. Brooks
St. Albans	Destroyer	Cdr. S. V. Storheil, RNN
St. Elstan	Trawler	Lt. R. M. Roberts, RNR
St. John	Frigate	Lt.Cdr. J. H. Stubbs, RCN A/Lt.Cdr. W. R. Stacey
St. Kenan	Trawler	Lt. J. Mackay, RNR Lt. R. R. Simpson, RNR
Starling	Sloop	Capt. F. J. Walker, CB, DSO
Starwort	Corvette	Lt.Cdr. N. W. Duck, RNR
Stefa	Trawler	
Stella Capella	Trawler	Lt. W. L. Sandgrove, RANVR
Stord	Destroyer	Lt.Cdr. S. Storheil, RNN
Stormont	Frigate	Lt.Cdr. G. A. Myra, RCN
Striker	Escort Carrier	Capt. W. P. Carne
Strule	Frigate	
Sturgeon	Submarine	Lt.Cdr. M. R. G. Wingfield
Suffolk	Cruiser	Capt. R. Shelley
Sulla	Minesweeper	
Sumba	Minesweeper	
Svega	Trawler	
Sweetbriar	Corvette	Lt. J. W. Cooper, RNR
Swift	Destroyer	
Tango	Trawler	
Tartar	Destroyer	Cdr. R. T. White Cdr. Sr. J. R. J. Tyrwhit
Tavy	Frigate	
Termagant	Destroyer	
Tigris	Submarine	Lt.Cdr. G. R. Colvin
Tortola	Frigate	
Tracker	Escort Carrier	Capt. J. H. Huntley
Tribune	Submarine	Lt. M. C. R. Lumby
Trident	Submarine	
Trinidad	Cruiser	
Tromso	Trawler	
Truant	Submarine	
Trumpeter	Escort Carrier	Capt. K. S. Colquhoun
Tunsberg Castle	Corvette	
Tuscaloosa	Cruiser	Capt. N. C. Gillette
Ulster Queen	Anti-aircraft Ship	Capt. C. K. Adam
Ulysees	Cruiser	

Ship	Type	Captain
Unique	Submarine	Lt. E. R. Boddington
Unrivalled	Submarine	Lt. H. B. Turner
Unshaken	Submarine	Lt. C. E. Oxborrow, DSO
Uragan	Destroyer	
Uredd	Submarine	Lt. R. O. Roren, RNorN
Uritski	Destroyer	
Venomous	Destroyer	Cdr. H. W. Falcon-Steward
Venus	Destroyer	Cdr. J. S. M. Richardson, DSO
Verdun	Destroyer	Lt.Cdr. W. S. Donald, DSC
Verulam	Destroyer	
Victorious	Aircraft Carrier	
Vigilant	Destroyer	Lt.Cdr. L. W. L. Argles
Vindex	Escort Carrier	Capt. H. T. Bayliss Capt. J. D. L. Williams
Virago	Destroyer	Lt.Cdr. R. J. White
Vivacious	Destroyer	
Viviana	Trawler	
Vizalma	Trawler	Lt. R. J. Angleback
Volage	Destroyer	
Volunteer	Destroyer	Lt.Cdr. A. S. Pomeroy
Wainwright	Destroyer	Lt.Cdr. R. H. Gibbs
Walker	Destroyer	
Walpole	Destroyer	Lt. A. S. Pomeroy, DSC
Wallflower	Corvette	Lt.Cdr. I. Tyson
Wanderer	Destroyer	Lt.Cdr. E. C. Hulton Lt.Cdr. R. Whinney
Washington	Cruiser	
Waskesui	Frigate	Lt.Cdr. J. H. S. Macdonald, RCNR Lt.Cdr. J. P. Fraser, RCNVR Lt.Cdr. L. D. Quick, RCNVR
Wastwater	Trawler	
Watchman	Destroyer	Lt.Cdr. J. R. Clarke, DSC, RNVR
Wells	Destroyer	Lt. L. J. Pearson Lt. F. W. M. Carter Lt.Cdr. J. G. Luther
Westcott	Destroyer	Cdr. H. Lambton
Wheatland	Destroyer	Lt.Cdr. R. de l'Brooke
Whimbral	Sloop	Lt.Cdr. W. J. Moore, RNR
Whitehall	Destroyer	Lt.Cdr. P. J. Cowell, DSC
Wichita	Cruiser	
Wildgoose	Sloop	Lt.Cdr. D. E. G. Wemyss
Wilton	Destroyer	Lt. A. P. Northey, DSC
Windermere	Trawler	Skp.Lt. J. Mawer
Windsor	Destroyer	Lt.Cdr. D. H. F. Hetherington, DSC
Woolston	Destroyer	Lt.Cdr. W. K. Michell
Worcester	Destroyer	Lt.Cdr. W. A. Juniper, DSO
Wren	Sloop	Lt.Cdr. S. M. Woods, RNR
Wrestler	Destroyer	Lt. R. W. B. Lacon, DSC
Zambesi	Destroyer	Capt. J. H. Allison, DSO

Ship	Type	Captain
Zealous	Destroyer	Cdr. R. F. Jessel, DSO, DSC
Zebra	Destroyer	Lt.Cdr. E. G. Peake
Zephyr	Destroyer	
Zest	Destroyer	Lt.Cdr. R. B. N. Hicks, DSO
Zhestki	Destroyer	
Zodiac	Destroyer	

Appendix 11

Chronology of Events for Operation FB

1942

15 August (Saturday)
SS *Chulmleigh* left London for River Tyne.

17 August (Monday)
SS *Hugh Williamson* left Philadelphia. *U-435* boarded the wreck of SS *Baikal* on the west coast of Spitzbergen and removed charts.

23 August (Sunday)
SS *Hugh Williamson* left New York.

24 August (Monday)
SS *William Clark* left New York. SS *John H. B. Latrobe* left New York.

28 August (Friday)
SS *Hugh Williamson* left Boston.

30 August (Sunday)
SS *Hugh Williamson* arrived Halifax, Nova Scotia.

5 September (Saturday)
SS *Hugh Williamson* left Halifax, Nova Scotia.

10 September (Thursday)
SS *Chulmleigh* in Leith. SS *Richard H. Alvey* arrived in Loch Ewe.

17 September (Thursday)
SS *Hugh Williamson* arrived Hvalfjord, Iceland.

19 September (Saturday)
SS *William Clark* arrived Hvalfjord, Iceland.

21 September (Monday)
SS *John H. B. Latrobe* arrived Hvalfjord, Iceland. SS *John Walker* arrived Loch Ewe.

22 September (Tuesday)
SS *Empire Scott* left Clyde for Loch Ewe.

23 September (Wednesday)
SS *Empire Gilbert* left River Tyne for Loch Ewe.

27 September (Sunday)
U-212 sails from Norway.

2 October (Friday)
SS *Empire Sky* anchored Loch Ewe.

6 October 1942 (Tuesday)
SS *Empire Galliard* in Glasgow.

7 October (Wednesday)
Plans for Operation FB put to the Americans, with an invitation to take part.

9 October (Friday)
The Americans agree to take part on a one-to-one basis.

13 October (Tuesday)
U-586 sails from Norway.

14 October (Wednesday)
SS *Daldorch* arrived Loch Ewe.

18 October (Sunday)
SS *Empire Scott, John Walker, Chulmleigh, Richard H. Alvey* leave Loch Ewe in convoy for Iceland.

22 October (Thursday)
SS *Empire Scott, John Walker, Chulmleigh, Richard H. Alvey* arrive Hvalfjord.

23 October (Friday)
HM Submarine *Tuna* leaves Holy Loch for Spitzbergen. RNN Submarine *O-15* leaves Dundee for Spitzbergen. HM Trawlers *Northern Spray, Northern Pride,* and *Cape Palliser* leave the River Clyde for Reyhjavik at 1800 hours.

24 October (Tuesday)
First conference for ships Masters held at Falcon Point.

28 October (Wednesday)
Second conference for ships Masters held at Falcon Point. HM Trawlers *Northern Spray, Northern Pride,* and *Cape Palliser* arrive Reykjavik 1730.

29 October (Thursday)
SS *Richard H. Alvey* left Hvalfjord AM. SS *Empire Galliard* left Hvalfjord PM. HM Trawler *Northern Spray* left Hvalfjord 0800. SS *Mussoviet* left Kola Inlet bound for Akureyri, Iceland.

30 October (Friday)
SS *Dekabrist* left Hvalfjord AM. SS *John Walker* left Hvalfjord. SS *Empire Gilbert* left Hvalfjord PM. SS *Richard H. Alvey* saw a British Catalina aircraft.

31 October (Saturday)
SS *John H. B. Latrobe* left Hvalfjord AM. HMT *Northern Spray* attacked *U-212* in position 7012N 1418W at 1225. The trawler sustained damage and was forced to return to Iceland. Sighted a Condor FW 200 aircraft. No attack. SS *Chulmleigh* left Hvalfjord 1700 hours. SS *John H. B. Latrobe* anchored Breidibay 1700 hours. SS *Azerbaijan* left the Kola Inlet, bound Akureyri, Iceland.

Author's Note: During November 1942, the U.S. Coast Guard Cutter *Northland* (Capt. James W. Thomas), made a visit to Jan Mayen and landed 41 officers and men together with 30 tons of equipment and supplies. Their task was to set up an HF/DF station on the island. According to the U.S. Coast Guard, Jan Mayen was at this time already garrisoned by a small Norwegian party. The question must therefore be asked, why did the Master of *William Clark* decide to make for the north coast of Iceland instead of the much shorter journey to Jan Mayen? Was he unaware of the garrison there?

1 November (Sunday)
SS *John H. B. Latrobe* raised anchor and resumed voyage 0500 hours. SS *Hugh Williamson* left Hvalfjord 0730 hours. HMT *St. Elstan* left Hvalfjord 0900 hours. HM Submarine *Tuna* entered patrol zone south of Spitzbergen. SS *Empire Gilbert* detected by enemy aircraft. SS *John H. B. Latrobe* set course from North Cape, Iceland, 1615 hours. SS *Empire Sky* left Hvalfjord PM.

2 November (Monday)
SS *Empire Gilbert* torpedoed by *U-586* near Jan Mayen 0119 hours German time. At 0130 hours someone transmitted TTT on the distress frequency. SS *Hugh Williamson* passed North Cape, Iceland, 0400. SS *William Clark* left Hvalfjord AM. SS *Empire Scott* left Havlfjord PM. HMT *Cape Argona* sailed from Iokanka. SS *Richard H. Alvey* saw freighter at 2145 steaming west—*Mussoviet?* SS *Chernyshevsky* left the Kola Inlet for Akureyri, Iceland.

3 November (Tuesday)
SS *John H. B. Latrobe* passed Jan Mayen 0500. SS *Chulmleigh* in position west of Jan Mayen AM as ordered. Altered course for south Cape Spitzbergen. SS *William Clark* passed North Cape, Iceland, 0900 hours. Saw British Catalina, 0900. SS *Daldorch* left Hvalfjord. HMT *St. Elstan* sighted Greenland at 100 miles. Received signal from Admiralty but could not decode it—wrong code. SS *Hugh Williamson* saw British Catalina. SS *Richard H. Alvey* saw large freighter 1400 hours—*Azerbaijan?* SS *Empire Galliard* heard loud explosion—no explanation.

4 November (Wednesday)
SS *Briarwood* left Hvalfjord. HMT *Cape Argona* challenged a Ju 88. SS *John Walker* attacked by aircraft 1000 hours. SS *Dekabrist* attacked by aircraft near Spitzbergen, sent AAA signal. SS *Empire Scott* detected by enemy aircraft. *U-354* detcted SS *William Clark* 1000 hours. SS *William Clark* torpedoed by *U-354* 1130 hours. SS *Richard H. Alvey* sighted smoke from a steamship. Received three distress calls. SS *Chulmleigh* received distress calls from American ships. HMT *Northern Pride* off North Cape, Iceland. Received *William Clark*'s distress call, heading for position. HMT *St. Elstan* received distress call from *William Clark*, began search, 1236 hours. HM Submarine *Tuna* received distress calls from Russian ship 1040 hours and from *William Clark* 1230 hours. Heard heavy explositons to the north, all afternoon. *U-354* left the area of *William Clark* sinking 1600 hours. SS *William Clark* Chief Mates

Lifeboat saw bright white light 2300. SS *Donbass* left the Kola Inlet for Akureyri, Iceland.

5 November (Thursday)
SS *William Clark* Chief Mates lifeboat sees red flare 0300. *Hipper* leaves Altenfjord with two destroyers. SS *Chulmleigh* received Admiralty message "Pass S. Cape of Spitzbergen in full darkness." Catalina X, 330 (Norge) Sqdn., RAF, airborne to search for three lifeboats, north of Iceland. HMT *Northern Pride* searching for *William Clark* survivors. HMT *St. Elstan* searching for *William Clark* survivors. HMT *Cape Palliser* searching for *William Clark* survivors. HMT *Cape Argona* received distress from *William Clark*. Chipping ice from ship. Sighted HMT *Cape Mariato*. SS *Dekabrist* attacked again by enemy aircraft AM. SS *John H. B. Latrobe* attacked by enemy aircraft 0900. SS *Chulmleigh* detected by enemy Bv 138 flying boat 1100 hours. SS *Empire Scott* passed through heavy oil patch, nothing else seen. Found again by enemy aircraft. No attack. Catalina aircraft contacted Chief Mates lifeboat from *William Clark* 1400 hours. Messages exchanged. SS *John Walker* found by USSR aircraft. Catalina X, 330 Sqdn., sent final message about 2030 hours then disappeared, north of Iceland. SS *Dekabrist* abandoned PM. SS *Chulmleigh* ran aground 10 miles south of South Cape Spitzbergen 2330 hours. Russian submarine *S-101* received distress call from *Dekabrist* and made for position. No results despite a wide search. *U-408* sunk north of Iceland by Catalina of VP-84 Sqdn., USN. *U-212* and *U-586* returns to harbor from patrol.

6 November (Friday)
HMT *St. Elstan* saw oil patch, oil still rising from it. Saw FW 200 Condor 0915. No attack. HM Submarine *Tuna* 0045 received SOS followed by mumbo jumbo bearing 050 degrees true, Spark transmitter.)154 saw U-boat 7608N 1408E, attacked it, missed. 0300 received frther SOS from *Chulmleigh*. 0710 sighted capsized vessel in lagoon, South Cape Spitzbergen. No sign of boats or survivors. Searched up west coast. SS *Dekabrist* sunk by enemy aircraft AM after being abandoned by four lifeboats. Two lifeboats saw land and people on shore and one of these two lifeboats also reached this land safely. The other one did not, continued drifting. SS *Chulmleigh* sent final SOS at 0318 then abandoned ship. SS *Empire Scott* detected by enemy aircraft. HMT *Northern Pride* saw aircraft float (German) in the sea, forenoon. HMT *Cape Argona* received signal stating that three of the merchant ships had been recalled to Iceland. SS *Chulmleigh* bombed by enemy aircraft

soon after being abandoned. Not badly damaged. Also attacked by *U-625*, 1400 hours. SS *Daldorch* and *Briarwood* recalled to Iceland. SS *Richard H. Alvey* and *Empire Galliard* sighted off Cape Kanin by USSR aircraft. SS *John Walker* found by surface escort from North Russia. *U-625* leaves scene of *Chulmleigh* attack at 1630. *U-625* detects SS *Empire Sky*, 1830 hours. *U-625* has *Empire Sky* in sight, 1930 hours. *U-625* makes first torpedo attack on *Empire Sky*, 2014 hours, missed. SS *Hugh Williamson* and *Empire Sky* leapfrogging each other and exchange signals by lamp, approximately 2000 hours. SS *Hugh Williamson* received SOS from *Empire Sky* 2130 GMT. SS *Hugh Williamson* saw heavy explosion 2200 GMT. HM Submarine *Tuna* heard torpedo running, 2210. (*U-625* at *Empire Sky*?). SS *Empire Sky* torpedoed by *U-625*, east of the South Cape of Spitzbergen, at 2224. *U-625* receives distress call from *Empire Sky* but did not know the name of the ship. *Hipper* in position 7330N 4230E.

7 November (Saturday)
SS *Chulmleigh* lifeboats became separated, early hours. HMT *St. Elstan* sighted white light 0413 hours. Rescued Chief Mates boat from *William Clark* 0800 hours. SS *Richard H. Alvey* and *Empire Galliard* arrived Molotovsk. SS *Hugh Williamson* attacked by enemy aircraft. SS *Empire Scott* in ice to the west of Spitzbergen. HMT *Cape Argona* attacked by two Ju 88s while returning to Iokanka. HM Submarine *Tuna* left patrol area south of Spitzbergen as ordered at 1720 hours. German destroyer sank SS *Donbass*, one of westbound steamers of Operation FB, 1330 hours. SS *Mussoviet* arrived Akureyri.

8 November (Sunday)
SS *John Walker* arrived Archangel. SS *John H. B. Latrobe* anchored off Greenland until 0800. Returning to Iceland. SS *Empire Scott* still in ice west of Spitzbergen. HMT *Cape Argona* attacked again by enemy aircraft. HM Submarine *Tuna* off Soroy as ordered. HMT *St. Elstan* saw white light but could find nothing. SS *Hugh Williamson* attacked by enemy aircraft 1045 hours.

9 November (Monday)
SS *John H. B. Latrobe* off Scoresby Sound, east Greenland. Struck iceberg. SS *Chulmleigh* both lifeboats reunited AM after losing each other. SS *Hugh Williamson* found by USSR aircraft 1508 hours. SS *Empire Scott* still in ice west of Spitzbergen. German destroyer off Soroy, homeward bound. HMT *St. Elstan* still searching for other boats. Dutch submarine

O-15 left patrol area south of Spitzbergen. HMT *Cape Argona* arrived Iokanka. SS *Azerbaijan* arrived Akureyri.

10 November (Tuesday)
SS *Richard H. Alvey* ran aground Dvina Bar. SS *John H. B. Latrobe* sighted north Cape, Iceland. Struck submerged object 1800 hours. SS *Chulmleigh* (Masters lifeboat) sighted Prince Charles Foreland, west Spitzbergen PM. SS *Hugh Williamson* British surface escort arrived from north Russia. SS *Empire Scott* still searching for other lifeboats. HM Submarine *Tuna* left Soroy for home.

11 November (Wednesday)
SS *John Walker* ran aground Dvina Bar. Struck *Richard H. Alvey* in doing so. SS *John H. B. Latrobe* anchored off Ritturhuk and later in day in Isafjord. SS *Hugh Williamson* arrived Molotovsk, collided with Russian merchant ship *Volga*. SS *William Clark* (2nd Mates boat) rescued by HMT *Cape Palliser*. SS *Empire Scott* west of Spitzbergen, ordered to proceed. HMT *St. Elstan* still searching for third lifeboat, icing up. HMT *Cape Palliser* bound Akureyri with *William Clark* survivors from 2nd Mates boat. SS *Chernyshevsky* arrived Akureyri.

12 November (Thursday)
SS *John Walker* refloated. SS *John H. B. Latrobe* left Isafjord 0800 and anchored in Breidafjord later that day. SS *Chulmleigh* (Masters lifeboat) landed at Cape Linnie PM. HMT *St. Elstan* began run home to Reykjavik. HMT *Cape Argona* sailed from Iokanka.

13 November (Friday)
SS *John H. B. Latrobe* arrived Hvalfjord again.

14 November (Saturday)
SS *Dekabrist* (Masters lifeboat) landed Hope Island. SS *Empire Sky* officially posted as missing. SS *Empire Scott* obtained fix, weather bad, proceeding. HMT *Cape Argona* sighted HMT *Cape Mariato* briefly during patrol. SS *Komsomoletz* left the Kola Inlet, for Akureyri, Iceland.

17 November (Tuesday)
SS *Empire Scott* off Sem Island PM, seen by USSR aircraft. HMT *Cape Argona* iced up, bound for Iokanka. SS *Daldorch* still in Hvalfjord.

18 November (Wednesday)
SS *Empire Scott* arrived Murmansk.

19 November (Thursday)
HMT *Cape Argona* arrived Iokanka.

20 November (Friday)
Russian vessel *Shusa*, 251 grt, built 1929, foundered while on Independent passage to North Russia.

24 November (Tuesday)
SS *Dvina* left the Kola Inlet for Akureyri, Iceland. SS *Komsomoletz* arrived Akureyri.

25 November (Wednesday)
SS *Mironich* and SS *Yelina* left Kola Inlet for Akureyri, Iceland.

5 December (Saturday)
SS *Dvina, Mironich* and *Yelina* arrived Akureyri.

10 December (Thursday)
SS *Hugh Williamson* left Molotovsk, bound Murmansk.

12 December (Saturday)
SS *Hugh Williamson* arrived Murmansk.

14 December (Monday)
SS *Briarwood* returned to Loch Ewe. SS *John Walker* left Molotovsk, AM.

16 December (Wednesday)
SS *John Walker* arrived Murmansk.

26 December (Saturday)
SS *John Walker* attacked by enemy aircraft. 2nd Mate injured.

30 December (Wednesday)
SS *John Walker* left Murmansk in convoy. 2nd Mate died of injuries. SS *Hugh Williamson* left Murmansk in convoy.

1943

2 January (Saturday)
SS *Chulmleigh*'s survivors found by Norwegians.

10 January (Sunday)
SS *Hugh Williamson* arrived Loch Ewe.

1 May (Saturday)
SS *Dekabrist* survivors found by German aircraft.

10 June (Thursday)
SS *Chulmleigh* survivors board British cruisers for home.

15 June (Tuesday)
SS *Chulmleigh*'s survivors arrive in the UK.

19 July (Monday)
U-703 leaves Trondheim for patrol.

25 July (Sunday)
SS *Dekabrist* Captain Beliaev rescued by *U-703*.

3 August (Tuesday)
SS *Dekabrist* Captain Beliaev landed at Narvik.

17 August (Tuesday)
U-703 leaves Hammerfest, Norway for patrol.

7 October (Thursday)
SS *Dekabrist* remaining survivors rescued by *U-703*.

9 October (Saturday)
SS *Dekabrist* survivors landed at Narvik.

Appendix 12

Soldier — Sailor — Survivor
Doug Meadows

BOFORS gun crew member, and one of only three survivors of the SS *Empire Gilbert* sunk by U-boat *U-586* 2 November 1942 while en route to Murmansk, Russia.

In September 1942 at Southport, we were formed into a gun crew of nine men of which five of us were known to each other as we had sailed together on our previous trip to Canada. Arthur Hopkins had been previously on the *Queen Mary* and cursed his luck to be on a cargo ship. Two of the other crew were first trippers and were full of questions such as "What's it like at sea?" Once we were organized, we drew our sea going gear from storage then proceeded to South Shields. We were the last to arrive as the DEMS and the Sergeant of Marines were already aboard.

The *Empire Gilbert* was a brand new ship, loaded to the hilt with supplies for the Russians. One could hardly walk anywhere for tanks, trucks, and Spitfires in crates. Our mess deck was on the port side aft with only one entry and exit for all of us. On the starboard side, joined to our mess by a companionway, were cabins for twelve RAF pilots with all access through this companionway. Luckily, they decided not to send them with us. There was no alarm or communication system from the guns, so we rigged one up ourselves. It consisted of three empty 40 mm shell cases and a long length of light gauge cable which we scrounged from the ship's bosun. It worked a treat.

The ship was pretty well armed with a 4.7 inch QF gun, 40 mm Bofors, four Oerlikons (two each port and starboard), two Pig Troughs (one each port and starboard), sixteen .300 caliber Marlin machine guns in clusters of eight each port and starboard, three roll-off depth charges on the stern, a barrage balloon on each mast, an early model radio location set and Paravane mine sweepers.

After drawing Arctic gear from a supply ship at North Shields and storing extra ammunition and gun barrels, we were just about ready. Each article of clothing was priced and had to be paid for on our return if lost.

We proceeded to Loch Ewe without incident where a few more

ships had already arrived. A small convoy was assembled and we left very well escorted to Hvalfjord, Iceland, where quite a few ships were already assembled from Halifax and points west. Every day, we had a visit from a German reconnaissance plane which flew very high. One day, an American Airacobra fighter decided to have a go and was promptly shot down by the reconnaissance plane.

We awoke one morning to find all the escort vessels had vanished overnight and the only naval vessel remaining was HMS *Berwick*. We soon found out what was going on when a naval launch came alongside and a lot of brass came on board. We were mustered aft on the 4.7 inch gun platform and were told that we were going to Russia, as though we didn't already know. We were then told that we would be going unescorted as the escorts were needed elsewhere and we would know all about it when we returned. With regard to this, the merchant seamen had a choice but the service personnel had none—we were it.

A surgeon came with the brass to see if anyone had any medical complaints. One of our crew, Eddie Mullins, had a dicey appendix and he was replaced by a volunteer from a homeward bound ship of PQ17 convoy.

Now we came to the big dangled carrot. The brass said that maybe some of you can remember the name Potato Jones, a Welsh skipper who made a fortune by running the blockade in the Spanish Civil War. As we were about to run the gauntlet, he was donating to each man the sum of fifty pounds, cash on the spot or have it sent home, a small fortune for a serviceman. The money arrived home all right, about the same time as the official letter, "With regrets, your son is missing at sea, presumed drowned."

Before leaving the ship, the big brass had a large supply of rum loaded. We were then issued a double tot—"Splice the main brace." I saved mine and drank it just before we stopped two torpedoes. I think it might have saved my life—"God bless old Nelson's blood, up spirits, stand fast the Holy Ghost."

Another surprise to come was that there were to be thirteen ships taking part in that fatal exercise ordered by the man who smoked cigars at Whitehall. The ships left independently at twelve hour intervals at 0600 hours and 1800 hours, on staggered parallel courses approximately forty miles apart. There was to be air cover and rescue ships spaced out all the way. The only plane we saw was a German one on the mid-morning of 1 November, the day before we were scuttled.

On the night we were sunk, I was watch below when, at about 2200 hours, our home made alarm system rang out like the "Bells of St.

Mary's" and everyone came on deck very quickly. The reason for the alarm was that a U-boat was on the surface and had passed along the full length of the ship on the port side. The skipper then pulled out all stops and we zigzagged for about two hours, but to no avail. We copped two torpedoes in the port side amidships and the ship started to do a nose dive. I guess it was all over in about two to three minutes.

I was the last one to leave our gun casement as there was only one ladder and quite a drop to the deck. On starting to get on the ladder, I met Arthur Hopkins coming back up, silly bugger. He had shed his duffel coat with his pipe inside. What use was a pipe in the drink? Anyhow, he retrieved it and took it with him into captivity. Once on deck, I made for the closest raft. One rating was trying to slip the slip ring. I did it very quickly with a kick of my leather sea boot and I followed the raft overboard. I lost sight of it for awhile as I was trying to get out of my Arctic coat.

The next thing I saw was the stern of the ship, well clear of the water, with the propeller still going and the depth charges dropping off. Luckily, I think the Sergeant of Marines had pulled all the primers except for one which went off, and this was later remarked about by the U-boat commander. I think we were unique to be armed with depth charges. On finally reaching the raft, I was just about done in. There were already men on board but I don't know how many as I was pretty well frozen.

Suddenly, the U-boat surfaced very close by, about fifty feet away. They put a spotlight on us and asked for the name of the ship. No reply! Then, they edged over to us and the raft rode up on the casing of the sub. I must have been nearest because the next thing I knew was that I was being half carried toward the conning tower. I remember the commander taking my sheath knife out of my life jacket and throwing it away. Looking down, I saw this circle of light but I don't recall how I got to the bottom.

The next thing I remember I was in my birthday suit with a blanket wrapped around me. I was placed on a bunk and dried off, with a pair of socks on my feet and hands. My hands were tied to a little electric heater and two crew members rubbed my feet and body to get my circulation going. The commander held a glass of cognac and made me drink it. I promptly vomited it up. They worked on me for a long time and finally gave me a tablet to swallow.

My next recollection was one of the crew shaking me and saying, "Wake up, Tommy." I was fully dressed and in a hammock which was slung on the monorail in the forward compartment. They then told me there were two more Kameraden. It was Arthur Hopkins and Reg Urwin. We spent several days on the U-boat during which time we were well fed. All the crew members wore a badge which comprised of a bent arm with a clenched mailed fist. We were each given one when we left the U-boat. An officer would take us up in the conning tower separately for a cigarette. When we wanted to use the head, it was a fully escorted operation as the head on a submarine is very complex.

Finally, we arrived at Narvik where the subs were operating from. There were five tied up alongside the depot ship which was a British ship, *Black Prince*, captured at the Battle of Narvik earlier in the war. The subs had an insignia of a polar bear climbing out of a castle turret painted on their conning towers. They put on a great show of congratulating the crew on their sinking of our ship. They had a pennant showing 7,000 tons flying from the periscope. We were stood in the conning tower with movie cameras on us. When we turned our backs on them, we were persuaded to face the cameras with a nudge in the back from a Schmeisser machine pistol.

We were destined to spend the winter in a Russian POW camp overlooking Narvik. On arriving at the camp late at night, we were locked in a windowless hut with straw on the floor. A lump of bread was thrown in along with a dollop of jam on a piece of paper. Later in the night the door was opened and an officer joined us. He played merry hell because we ignored him, but later on he calmed down. Later we were placed in a little igloo in the corner of the camp. It was made of plywood with sods of earth on the outside and a topping of snow which got thicker with every day. We had a little wood stove in the igloo and spent the day chopping wood so we would not freeze.

Every morning we were taken for a bath. A Russian would be in the ceiling above the showers releasing hot water onto us. When the hot water finished, down came the cold water and the Russian would laugh his head off. The cold water was a shock but we livened up after it. Occasionally, a Norwegian would come to the camp on a horse drawn sleigh, and as soon as he neared, the krauts locked us in our igloo. On leaving the camp, we were told the reason for this. If the Norwegians had known that there were three Britishers in the camp, they would have had a go at getting us out and home.

We traveled to Germany on a cargo ship, *Dampher Spree Bremen*, loaded down with iron ore from Petsamo in northern Finland. We were given life jackets and locked below decks. It took the best part of a month to get to Kiel. When we passed through the Skagerrak, the ship passed right through the Swedish fishing fleet. The krauts took us on deck to have a look with a couple of fellows pointing Schmeissers at us and told not to try anything. On arriving at Kiel, we were put in a civilian jail run by the Gestapo.

We were only there for a week, thank God, when an escort of three Kriegsmarine came to escort us to Wilhelmshaven. For a change, we traveled in luxury on an express train. We had to change trains at Hamburg and whilst on the platform, a German Red Cross woman was serving ersatz coffee to the troops. I got quite a shock when she came up to me and asked, "Would you care for a cup of coffee Tommy?" I thought I was back in England—her English was perfect.

On arriving in Wilhelmshaven, we were separated and put in solitary rooms in Dulag-Nord, the interrogation center for captured naval personnel. Every morning, we were told "Promenade Tommy," and we set off at spaced intervals around the parade ground to stop communication between us. There was another prisoner dressed in a mixture of clothing. He had British battle dress trousers on so I figured he must be British. When we were eventually reunited, we found out his name was Eric Mundy and he was a Royal Engineer. He was the sole survivor of the SS *Ceramic* sunk in the South Atlantic with a contingent of Army nurses and engineer specialists on board. He had spent five months on a U-boat before he was off-loaded at St. Nazaire in France.

After one month's interrogation, we were reunited in one large room. We were receiving three cigarettes each per day until I blew it for us. The Germans gave us two books to read, *The Eight Crusade*, an anti-Jewish book, and *John L. Amery Speaks* written by an English traitor. When asked what we thought of the books, I up and said, "Schiesi propaganda!" No more cigarettes, thanks to my up and coming German vocabulary.

After Wilhelmshaven, we were escorted to Marlag und Milag Nord, the camp for naval and merchant seamen at a place called Tarmstedt, just outside Bremen. There Arthur and I parted company with Reg Urwin, he to Milag and we to Marlag. I was put in the sick bay for a while. A Canadian surgeon, Commander Fisher, tried to keep me there but the Germans thought otherwise. They purged the camp and I did not see Arthur again. He got back home okay.

I was sent to a camp near Krakow in Poland. We got out of there two steps ahead of the Russians in January 1945. We were force marched for six hundred kilometers across Germany and Czechoslovakia right down to Bavaria where we were liberated by a column of Patton's jeeps on 2 May. We then had to walk back sixty kilometers to

Regensburg where we waited for a flight to Rhiems in France, and then on to England by Lancaster bomber. I arrived back in England on 11 May.

Addendum

Jack Albert Billmeir

REFERENCES to a "Mr. Bullimore" in Albert Wray's diary (SS *Daldorch*) and of Apprentice Richard Watts of the same ship actually quoting "Mr. Bilmere" (sic) as conducting the interview on board before sailing and of promising a bonus for the crew is most interesting.

There can be very little doubt that this man was Mr. Jack Albert Billmeir, a well-known British ship owner, and founder of The Stanhope Steamship Company. He was certainly a very impressive and extrovert character. Born in London on 1 September 1900 he had plenty of experience in running independent merchant ships through blockades. Sometimes he was very successful at this, sometimes not.

His exploits during the late 1930s sending his ships to Spanish Republican ports during the civil war is well documented in British maritime history. He operated some twenty ships in this trade, charged premium freight rates to his customers and paid his crews a bonus. He also sailed ships to China after the Japanese invasion at around the same time.

His first exploits in this field during World War II were attempts to get single ships through the Axis blockade, to beleaguered Malta. This enterprise was not very successful and heavy losses in ships and men were sustained before the scheme was dropped in favor of heavily escorted convoys. I feel sure he would have been a natural choice by the Admiralty for an operation such as 'FB.' Jack Billmeir died on 22 December 1963 after a very successful business career.

Printed in Great Britain
by Amazon.co.uk, Ltd.,
Marston Gate.